Non-Governmental Actors in International Climate Change Law

Focusing on how to improve the participation of non-governmental actors in the making of international climate change laws, this book is a conversation on the relevance of a human rights-based approach to international climate change law-making.

The book considers a possible reform of the United Nations Framework Convention on Climate Change institutional arrangement, inspired by the practice and model of participation of Arctic Indigenous Peoples in the Arctic Council. Different non-State entities play a fundamental role in the development and enforcement of the climate change regime by enhancing the knowledge base of decision-making, keeping States in line with their commitments, and engaging in private initiatives aimed at mitigating the impacts of global warming. Albeit non-governmental and subnational actors increasingly work alongside States in the making of a climate change regime, the category of observers through which they participate in intergovernmental negotiations only gives them limited rights and their participation in international norm-making has at times been impaired. The relevance of a human rights-based approach consists in recognising the status of individuals and groups as rights-holders under human rights law, a paradigm that was first established by Arctic Indigenous Peoples when claiming their participatory rights in the Arctic Council, the main forum of governance of the Arctic region. This book argues that, in the absence of a globally binding treaty regulating procedural rights in intergovernmental negotiations, the emerging relationship between human rights and climate change could serve as a legal basis for the enhancement of non-governmental actors' procedural rights, establishing the right to participation as a right in itself and which can benefit the governance of climate change.

Due to the relevance of the addressed subject, the book is destined to a broad readership and will be of use to academic researchers, law practitioners, policy-makers and non-governmental organisations' representatives.

Marzia Scopelliti holds a PhD in Law from the Complutense University of Madrid (Spain). She is the author and co-editor of a number of peer-reviewed publications related to her research interests: International Environmental Law, Arctic Governance and Climate Change Law.

Routledge Research in Polar Law

Emerging Legal Orders in the Arctic
The Role of Non-Arctic Actors
Edited by Akiho Shibata, Leilei Zou, Nikolas Sellheim & Marzia Scopelliti

China's Role in the Arctic
Observing and Being Observed
Nong Hong

Philosophies of Polar Law
Edited by Dawid Bunikowsi and Alan D. Hemmings

Emerging Pathogens at the Poles
Disease and International Trade Law
Alexandra L. Carleton

Non-Governmental Actors in International Climate Change Law
The Case of Arctic Indigenous Peoples
Marzia Scopelliti

For a full list of titles in this series, please visit https://www.routledge.com/Routledge- Research-in-Polar-Law/book-series/RRPL

Non-Governmental Actors in International Climate Change Law

The Case of Arctic Indigenous Peoples

Marzia Scopelliti

Routledge
Taylor & Francis Group
LONDON AND NEW YORK

First published 2022
by Routledge
2 Park Square, Milton Park, Abingdon, Oxon OX14 4RN

and by Routledge
605 Third Avenue, New York, NY 10158

Routledge is an imprint of the Taylor & Francis Group, an informa business

British Library Cataloguing-in-Publication Data
A catalogue record for this book is available from the British Library

Library of Congress Cataloging-in-Publication Data
A catalog record has been requested for this book

ISBN: 978-0-367-64525-0 (hbk)
ISBN: 978-0-367-65200-5 (pbk)
ISBN: 978-1-003-12832-8 (ebk)

Typeset in Bembo
by Deanta Global Publishing Services, Chennai, India

To my family.

To Remo.

Contents

List of illustrations ix
Foreword x
Acknowledgements xii
List of abbreviations xiii

1 Introduction 1

PART I
Setting the context 5

2 International environmental governance and non-governmental actors 7

3 The participation of non-governmental actors in climate change law-making and governance 30

PART II
A case study on Arctic indigenous peoples 51

4 Non-governmental actors and a changing climate: Learning from Arctic indigenous peoples 53

PART III
Improving public participation in climate change law-making: International law instruments 85

5 Climate change litigation: A bottom-up approach to climate change governance 87

6 A human rights-based approach to climate change: Improving the participation of non-governmental actors in international climate change law-making 117

7 Concluding remarks: Towards a new significance for non-governmental actors in international climate change governance: a proposal for the future 147

Index 151

Illustrations

Figure

5.1 Non-U.S. Climate Change Litigation, Suits Against Governments Credit: 2020 Sabin Center for Climate Change Law U.S. Litigation Chart made in collaboration with Arnold & Porter Kaye Scholer LLP. Reproduced with permission. Retrieved from: http://climatecasechart.com/non-us-climatechange-litigation/ 89

Table

5.1 Number of Climate Change Litigation Cases by Country 88

Foreword

Citizen participation in public decision-making is an issue that is both increasingly in demand and controversial. Such participation appears as a basic requirement to make democratic legitimacy a reality and enhance the effectiveness of the political decisions adopted.

When transcendental issues such as climate change are at stake, it seems unnecessary to provide further arguments in favour of the need for decisions to be taken with due consideration of the opinion of those affected – be it the effects of global warming or the rules and policies adopted to try to mitigate or adapt to it.

However, the realisation of this demand poses many challenges. On the one hand, in international law, decisions have traditionally been adopted by State entities. However, even at this level, the determination of who holds the power to represent the State is highly regulated and measured. Indeed, the irruption on the international scene of voices alien to the typical subjects of international law – States and International Organizations – would require an unprecedented transformation of the usual rules of the game. On the other hand, even assuming that the participation of other actors could be achieved, using, for example, non-governmental organisations as representatives of citizenry and the public opinion, this option raises other problems. Is it possible to articulate a right of participation with sufficient guarantees to ensure that the procedure or model favours citizen participation and determines the distribution of responsibilities? Who responds, to what extent and to whom of a decision when it proves counterproductive?

Even where democratic rules function, the challenges derived from enabling public participation in decisions affecting people at the local level are enormous. The legal democratic procedure is based on the idea that the people express themselves through periodic elections, and through the elected representatives that express the popular will in their daily work. When we go up from the local to the State level – an easily identifiable political unit of reference – the problems to represent this social demand grows bigger, since what is called "public opinion" is not always articulated in a democratic way, and the legitimacy of its influence may be questioned. Not surprisingly, non-governmental organizations (NGOs) are only one of the facets through which civil society is organised. They do not represent a unitary subject but, rather, a conglomerate that through diverse activities – declarations, demonstrations, boycotts (in short, through the mobilisation of public opinion and its role in the media) – they try to influence, with different levels of success, intergovernmental agendas, force public action and supervise it.

In this line and as recalled in the Introduction to this book, different non-State entities play a fundamental role in the development and enforcement of the regime to address climate change by enhancing the knowledge base of decision-making, keeping States in line with their commitments, and engaging in private initiatives aimed at mitigating the impacts of global warming. But, although non-governmental and subnational actors increasingly work alongside States in the making of a climate change regime, the category of observers through which they participate in intergovernmental negotiations, only gives them limited rights, and their participation in climate change law-making has at times been impaired.

The work that I have the pleasure to introduce in these pages, boldly proposes that non-governmental actors should have better alternatives for participation in international legal decision-making. Such changes are urgent in view of climate change and its regulation. The main argument of Marzia Scopelliti's work in responding to this challenge, is that, in the absence of a universal treaty that regulates procedural rights in international negotiations, the relationship between human rights and climate change may be the ideal legal instrument to promote a procedural right from which international climate change governance can benefit.

The author's extensive training in "Arctic issues" leads her to use the case of the Arctic indigenous populations as a point of departure. Arctic Indigenous Peoples' (IPs) capacity to act in the Arctic Council (AC), as Permanent Participants (PPs), is the paradigm in which she supports her thesis for the consideration of individuals or groups as rights-holders under human rights law. The volume discusses the relevance of a human rights-based approach to international climate change law-making which concludes by considering a possible reform of the United Nations Framework Convention on Climate Change (UNFCCC) institutional arrangement, inspired by the practice and model of participation of Arctic Indigenous Peoples in the Arctic Council.

The author's research is truly innovative. It is true that there are works that have analysed the role of non-State actors in international decision-making, but only a few have referred to the question of how procedural rights can be realized in international negotiations. In addition to this, the fact of proposing options based on the model of the indigenous populations of the Arctic constitutes an undoubtedly novel contribution.

I am both proud and excited to write the first pages of the first book by Marzia Scopelliti, who has worked under my supervision for the past few years. Today she flies alone, with a refined style and a courageous proposal in an excellent and mature *opera prima*.

Madrid, October 18, 2020 (in the middle of the second wave of COVID-19)

Professor Elena Conde, Universidad Complutense de Madrid

Acknowledgements

This book is the outcome of a doctoral research in law conducted at the Complutense University of Madrid, Spain. I am very grateful to my academic supervisor, Professor Dr. Elena Conde Pérez, for her continued encouragement, and for guiding me through this research over the past four years.

I also want to thank my family for its unconditional support, and Remo for being at my side during the preparation of this book.

Abbreviations

AC	Arctic Council
AEPS	Arctic Environmental Protection Strategy
AIA	Aleut International Association
AMAP	Arctic Monitoring and Assessment Programme
ASEAN	Association of Asian Nations
A5	Arctic Five
CITES	Convention on International Trade in Endangered Species of Wild Fauna and Flora
COP	Conference of the Parties
ECOSOC	Economic and Social Council
ECOWAS	Economic Community of West African States
ECHR	European Convention on Human Rights
ECtHR	European Court of Human Rights
ESR	Effort Sharing Regulation
ETS	Emission Trading System
EU	European Union
GAP	Gender Action Plan
GCI	Gwich'in Council International
GHGs	Green House Gases
IACHR	Inter-American Commission on Human Rights
ICC	Inuit Circumpolar Council
ICCPR	International Covenant on Civil and Political Rights
ICESCR	International Covenant on Economic, Social and Cultural Rights
ICJ	International Court of Justice
ICRC	International Committee of the Red Cross
IGOS	International Governmental Organisations
IIPFCC	International Indigenous Peoples' Forum on Climate Change
ILA	International Law Association
ILC	International Law Commission
ILO	International Labour Organisation
IOs	International Organisations
IPCC	Intergovernmental Panel on Climate Change

IPs	Indigenous Peoples
IPOs	Indigenous Peoples Organisations
IWGIA	International Work Group for Indigenous Affairs
LAC	Latin American and Caribbean
LCIPs	Local Communities and Indigenous Peoples
LPAA	Lima-Paris Action Agenda
LULUCF	Land Use, Land Use Change and Forestry
MEAs	Multilateral Environmental Agreements
NAZCA	Non-State Actor Zone for Climate Action
NDCs	Nationally Determined Contributions
NGOs	Non-Governmental Organisations
NSAs	Non-State Actors
OAS	Organisation of American States
OHCHR	Office of the United Nations High Commissioner for Human Rights
PIL	Public Interest Litigation
POPs	Persistent Organic Pollutants
PPs	Permanent Participants
RAIPON	Russian Association of Indigenous Peoples of the North
REDD+	Reducing Emissions from Deforestation and Forest Degradation
SBI	Subsidiary Body for Implementation
SBSTA	Subsidiary Body for Scientific and Technological Advice
SIDS	Small Island Developing States
TFEU	Treaty on the Functioning of the European Union
UN	United Nations
UNCED	United Nations Conference on Environment and Development
UNDRIP	United Nations Declaration on the Rights of Indigenous Peoples
UNECE	United Nations Economic Commission for Europe
UNEP	United Nations Environmental Programme
UNFCCC	United Nations Framework Convention on Climate Change
UNGA	United Nations General Assembly
UNPFII	United Nations Permanent Forum on Indigenous Issues
USA	United States of America
WGP	Working Group of the Parties

1 Introduction

1.1 Background

The right to public participation emerged in the field of international environmental law to ensure access to information, participation in decision-making processes and access to justice in environmental matters to every person.[1] Considered today as an expression of environmental democracy, it was first established in 1992 by Principle 10 of the United Nations Rio Declaration on Environment and Development and was subsequently incorporated in regional conventions[2] and established by international and European case law. To date, the Aarhus Convention is the regional treaty that has contributed the most to the application and respect of procedural rights in both their domestic and international dimension. Twenty years after the adoption of this convention, and coinciding with the adoption of the Escazú Agreement in Latin America and the Caribbean States, a number of academic works have assessed the status of its implementation across its contracting States. On the contrary, just a handful of publications have explored the significance of the Aarhus Convention for participation in international environmental processes and whether procedural rights, particularly the right to participation in environmental decision-making, have been consistently secured in international fora.[3]

1 The focus of attention of this work will be the second pillar of the right to public participation: participation in (international) environmental decision-making.

2 Since the adoption of the Rio Declaration on Environment and Development in 1992, public participation has been repeatedly recognised in successive UN conferences on sustainable development and implemented by the UNECE Convention on Access to Information, Public Participation in Decision-making and Access to Justice in Environmental Matters (Aarhus Convention, 1998). In March 2018, the Ninth Meeting of the Negotiating Committee of the Regional Agreement on Principle 10 adopted the Escazú Regional Agreement for Latin American and the Caribbean States. The agreement will remain open for signature from September 2018 to September 2020.

3 See, J. EBBESSON, "Principle 10: Public Participation", in J. E. VIÑUALES (ed.) *The Rio Declaration on Environment and Development*. Oxford: Oxford University Press, 2015, pp. 288–309; S. DUYCK, "Promoting the Principles of the Aarhus Convention in International Forums: The Case of the UN Climate Change Regime", *Review of European Community & International Environmental Law*, Vol. 22, No. 4, 2015, pp. 123–137.

In the absence of a globally binding treaty regulating procedural rights in international environmental decision-making process, the participation of the public has been channelled in most multilateral environmental agreements (MEAs) through institutional arrangements in which non-governmental actors participate as observers. Under this category, non-governmental organisations usually take part in intergovernmental negotiations with no voting rights and with rather limited possibilities for intervention but have nonetheless provided vital insights to discussions on highly complex environmental problems.

In the context of climate change, the contribution of non-governmental entities has been acknowledged as fundamental for the development and implementation of an international climate change regime.[4] As recalled in the UNFCCC Guidelines for the participation of NGO-representatives: "[NGO] involvement allows vital experience, expertise, information and perspectives from civil society to be brought into the process to generate new insights and approaches."[5] Over the years, the UNFCCC system has worked – and continues to work – towards the incorporation of non-governmental actors in the creation of a climate change regime but their participation in the law-making process has at times been impaired, based on the assumption that international law-making remains a prerogative of sovereign nation states.[6] In other words, States remain the gatekeepers of the international climate change law-making process and there is no coherent and systematic approach to the exercise of procedural rights by non-governmental actors.

1.2 Objectives

Against this background, this book studies how to improve the participation of non-governmental actors in the context of international climate change norm-making in order to remedy a situation in which – although private and subnational actors increasingly work alongside States in the making of international climate regime – they are not fully recognised in this normative capacity. Albeit timely and interesting, a comprehensive assessment of procedural

4 As detailed in Chapter 3, the UNFCCC recognises as observers nine main constituencies. The latter are the reference groups of this research when it relates to NGOs and civil society organisations.

5 UNFCCC, Guidelines for the participation of representatives of non-governmental organisations at meetings of the bodies of the United Nations Framework Convention on Climate Change, Bonn, 2017. Available at: https://unfccc.int/files/parties_and_observers/ngo/application/pdf/guidelines_for_the_participation_of_ngos.pdf (Last access, 05 October 2018).

6 Several authors have reported on the exclusion of accredited observers from critical phases of climate negotiations, particularly during the Conference of the Parties (COP) 15 Copenhagen, but also in Paris at COP21. See, e.g., M. DOELLE, "The Paris Agreement: Historic Breakthrough or High Stakes Experiment?", *Climate Law*, Vol. 6, 2016, pp. 1–20 and W. J. WILSON, "Legal Foundations for NGO Participation in Climate Treaty Negotiations", *Sustainable Development Law and Policy*, Vol. 10, No. 2, 2010, p. 54.

rights in international climate change law-making would exceed the scope of this publication. Therefore, even if access to information is often a prerequisite for meaningful participation and access to justice serves the restoration of States' obligations, this book will only focus on participation in environmental decision-making processes. Looking at how this right articulates and has been secured to date in intergovernmental negotiations on climate change, the volume will consider whether and how the emerging human rights-climate change nexus could be used as a legal basis for the enhancement of non-governmental actors' participation in climate change law-making. The possibility to strike a better balance between the vital contribution that non-governmental actors provide to climate change governance and their actual law-making capacity, may be built on rights-based claims since a human rights language has been introduced for the first time in the Paris Agreement of 2015. To this end, the book builds a case study on Arctic Indigenous Peoples (IPs) and proposes to use their practice and rights-based advocacy as a relevant model for improving the participation of those non-governmental actors that already participate as observers to international climate change law-making.

1.3 Structure of the book

The book opens with **Part I**, which sets the context of the study by looking at how the right to public participation have emerged and consolidated in international environmental law. Following this introduction, **Chapter 2** traces back the inception of the principle of public participation in international environmental governance and considers why the participation of non-governmental actors is relevant to this process. Notwithstanding its widespread recognition and implementation through regional conventions, human rights instruments and jurisprudence, this chapter concludes that the application of such a principle at the international level is non-uniform and ambiguous, and the international law-making process is still formally dominated by nation states. The author also discusses here the legitimacy of non-governmental actors and how they contribute to redressing the democratic deficit inherent to international (environmental) law-making. **Chapter 3** looks at how the second pillar of the principle of public participation – participation in decision-making – has been incorporated in the regime that governs climate change. The analysis of the construction of the climate change regime presented in this section shows that, although the UNFCCC system has progressively incorporated several non-governmental entities, their participation lacks adequate systematisation and remains subject to States' interests.

In making a case for the enhancement of non-governmental actors' participatory rights in climate governance, **Part II** outlines a case study on Arctic indigenous peoples. Their practice is analysed in **Chapter 4** from three main perspectives. First, from an institutional point of view, the formal recognition and integration of Arctic IPs within the most relevant intergovernmental regional forum – the Arctic Council – provides an example of inclusive governance regimes. Second, the recognition of Arctic IPs as Permanent Participants in the Arctic Council has allowed them to perform an important epistemic function, contributing with their traditional knowledge and experience to international environmental law-making. This, in turn, have proved critical to the initiation, negotiation and adoption of several MEAs. Third, a rights-based perspective is introduced to explore how the indigenous peoples of the Arctic, through the NGOs representing them at different scales but also within the wider international indigenous climate movement, have been able to promote a human rights agenda in the context of climate change, drawing upon advocacy and litigation.

The Inuit Petition to the Inter-American Commission on Human Rights (IACHR) has translated the human rights dimension of climate change into a legal argument.[7] The petition is analysed along with other climate change litigation cases in **Chapter 5.** The latter introduces climate litigation as a transnational and bottom-up approach to climate change governance, thus as an argument in support of a more open climate decision-making process or, alternatively, as an instrument to uphold procedural rights.

Towards the end of the book, **Chapter 6** traces back the emergence of a human rights-based approach to climate change, particularly looking at the work of the different United Nations (UN) bodies on the subject, as well as providing a hermeneutical analysis of the Paris Agreement, where a reference to States' human rights obligations in the context of climate change was introduced for the first time. Finally, considering the possible affirmation of a human right to a healthy environment, this chapter exposes the advantages and limits of the interplay between human rights and international climate change law for the promotion of public participation.

The concluding remarks provide a practical proposal for the improvements of non-governmental participation in international climate change law-making.

Bibliography

Doelle, M. "The Paris Agreement: Historic Breakthrough or High Stakes Experiment?", *Climate Law*, Vol. 6, 2016, pp. 1–20.

Duyck, S. "Promoting the Principles of the Aarhus Convention in International Forums: The Case of the UN Climate Change Regime", *Review of European Community & International Environmental Law*, Vol. 22, No. 4, 2015, pp. 123–137.

Ebbesson, J. "Principle 10. Public Participation", in J. E. Viñuales (ed.) *The Rio Declaration on Environment and Development*. Oxford: Oxford University Press, 2015, pp. 288–309.

Wilson, W. J. "Legal Foundations for NGO Participation in Climate Treaty Negotiations", *Sustainable Development Law and Policy*, Vol. 10, No. 2, 2010, 54, 69.

7 There are at least two ways in which climate change is related to human rights. First, rising temperatures are likely to impede the enjoyment of basic human rights, the right to health and life, among others. Second, the implementation of mitigation and adaptation projects has the potential to further impinge on human rights.

Part I

Setting the context

2 International environmental governance and non-governmental actors

2.1 The principle of public participation in international environmental governance: evolution and application in international contexts

Public participation is today widely recognised as a core feature of environmental governance and sustainable development.[1] The principle of public participation was first enunciated during the United Nations Conference on Environment and Development (UNCED) of 1992, which established the premises for the participation of the public in environmental issues and the so-called 'environmental democracy'.[2]

In its Principle 10, the Declaration reads:

> environmental issues are best handled with participation of all concerned citizens, at the relevant level. At the national level, each individual shall have appropriate access to information concerning the environment that is held by public authorities, including information on hazardous materials and activities in their communities, and the opportunity to participate in decision-making processes. States shall facilitate and encourage public awareness and participation by making information widely available. Effective access to judicial and administrative proceedings, including redress and remedy, shall be provided.[3]

On this basis, the right to public participation emerged building upon three main pillars – access to information, participation in decision-making, and access to justice in environmental matters – aimed at promoting transparent

1 Chapter 23 of Agenda 21 recognises public participation as a "fundamental prerequisite for the achievement of sustainable development". See Report of the UN Conference on Environment and Development. UN Doc. A/CONF.151/26 of 14 June 1992.

2 While, in general terms, international norms are directed at states, this principle conceivably enables non-governmental entities to have a voice in the elaboration and implementation of these norms, thus making the decision-making process more open and transparent.

3 *Rio Declaration on Environment and Development*, "Principle 10", UN Doc. A/CONF.151/26 (Vol.1).

and inclusive environmental governance. Notwithstanding the reluctance of the International Court of Justice (ICJ) to accept Principle 10 as a general principle of international law,[4] its content has evolved into a full-fledged right to public participation, which is applied at the national level by a considerable number of States[5] and ensured in those multilateral environmental agreements that include provisions on public participation.

A right to public participation has also been acknowledged and promoted in the field of human rights law and a number of publications have considered whether case law has contributed to the affirmation of public participation as customary law.[6] While two of the constitutive elements of this principle – access to information and access to justice – reflect rights enshrined in international human rights treaties (e.g. political participation and the right to a fair trial), the United Nations Human Rights Committee has established that the right to participate in the formulation and implementation of policies at the international level falls under the scope of article 25 of the International Covenant on Civil and Political Rights (ICCPR).[7] This is important since the Rio Declaration has no binding value and failed to clarify how public participation should be carried out in international decision-making. In regional human rights systems, different regional courts have established a link between the right to participate and political and civil rights[8] and the jurisprudence of the European Court of Human Rights (ECtHR) has ascertained that procedural rights are to be protected as an emanation of the right to private and family life.[9] More recently, successive international environmental summits have reiterated the importance of Principle 10 and public participation for intergovernmental decision-making. Notably, in both the Johannesburg World Summit on Sustainable Development of 2002 and the Rio+20 Summit of 2012, States have reaffirmed their commitment to enhancing the "participation

4 See, L. DUVIC-PAOLI, "The Status of the Right to Public Participation in International Environmental Law: An Analysis of the Jurisprudence", *Yearbook of International Environmental Law*, Vol. 23, No. 1, 2012, pp. 80–115.

5 For example, and in relation with the purposes of this research, Mexico has included an explicit reference to the participation of the public in its recent law on climate change. *Ley General de Cambio Climático*, art. 7o(XII), Diario Oficial de 6 de junio de 2012. Available at: http://www.diputados.gob.mx/LeyesBiblio/ref/lgcc/LGCC_orig_06jun12.pdf (Last access, 14 May, 2018).

6 See, J. VAN BEKHOVEN, "Public Participation as a General Principle in International Environmental Law: Its Current Status and Real Impact", *National Taiwan University Law Review*, Vol. 11, No. 2, 2016, pp. 219–260; L. DUVIC-PAOLI, *supra* note 4.

7 HUMAN RIGHTS COMMITTEE, *General Comment No. 25: The Right to Participate in Public Affairs, Voting Rights and the Right of Equal Access to Public Service (Art. 25)*, (CCPR/C/21/REV.1/Add.7, General Comment No. 25, 1996).

8 See, S. JODOIN, S. DUYCK and K. LOFTS, "Public Participation and Climate Governance: An Introduction", *Review of European Community & International Environmental Law*, Vol. 24, No. 2, 2015, pp. 117–122.

9 ECtHR, *López-Ostra v. Spain*, Application no. 16798/90, Judgement of 9 December 1994; ECtHR, *Guerra and Others v. Italy*, Application no. 14967/89, Judgement of 19 February 1998; and ECtHR, *Di Sarno and Others v. Italy*, Application no. 30765/08, Judgement of 10 January 2012.

and effective engagement of civil society and other relevant stakeholders in the relevant international forums".[10]

Notwithstanding this widespread recognition, Ebbesson has argued that it is due to the recent origins of international environmental law and the close relationship between public participation in decision-making and state sovereignty that it has been difficult to agree on a global scale on the promotion of binding legal norms regarding participation.[11] Although the International Law Commission (ILC) has made efforts regarding its codification,[12] he concludes, the rules applying public participation go rarely beyond regional application.

2.1.1 *The Aarhus Convention and the implementation of Principle 10 in the international context*

The codification of Principle 10 in its domestic and international dimensions has particularly occurred at the regional level. After almost ten years from its enunciation, Principle 10 was enshrined in the *Convention on Access to Information, Public Participation in Decision-making and Access to Justice in Environmental Matters* (Aarhus Convention, 1998),[13] a regional environmental treaty adopted under the auspices of the UN Economic Commission for Europe (UNECE), which secures the three main pillars sustaining procedural rights in environmental governance.

The relevance of the Aarhus Convention for environmental democracy has been recognised by different scholars, who often underline how its content extends beyond international environmental law, to address human rights-related issues. Alan Boyle has directly equated the Convention to a human rights treaty, underlining three main relevant aspects.[14] First of all, the Convention builds on the established human rights of access to justice and on procedural elements aimed at securing the rights to life, health and family life. Second, it confers rights directly on individuals. Interestingly in this sense,

10 UNITED NATIONS, *The Future We Want. Outcome Document of the United Nations Conference on Sustainable Development*. Brazil, 2012. Available at: https://sustainabledevelopment.un.org/content/documents/733FutureWeWant.pdf (Last access, 29 May 2018).

11 See, J. EBBESSON, "Public Participation", in D. BODANSKY, J. BRUNNÉ and E. HEY (eds.) *The Oxford Handbook of International Environmental Law*. Oxford: Oxford University Press, 2007, pp. 681–703.

12 In its 2001 *Articles on Prevention of Transboundary Harm from Hazardous Activities* (ILC Articles), the International Law Commission noted that states shall provide the public that is likely to be affected by hazardous activities with information on the activity, on the risks involved and the potential harm deriving from it. Moreover, the views of the public shall be ascertained. ILC Articles, article 13.

13 UNITED NATIONS ECONOMIC COMMISSION FOR EUROPE, *Convention on Access to Information, Public Participation in Decision-Making and Access to Justice in Environmental Matters* of 25 June 1998 (2161 UNTS 447).

14 See, A. BOYLE, "Human Rights and the Environment: Where Next?", *European Journal of International Law*, Vol. 23, N. 3, 2012, pp. 613–642, at 623.

Article 15 of the Convention provides the possibility for the Meetings of the Parties to establish mechanisms for the review of compliance with its provisions and allows members of the public or NGOs to bring complaints before a non-compliance committee. Third, as already pointed out above, all essential aspects of the Convention have been integrated into European human rights law through the jurisprudence of the ECtHR, as well as by other human rights bodies. Again, Ebbsson has highlighted the rights-based approach to public participation adopted by the Aarhus Convention. This unique feature stands out when the Convention is compared with other regional arrangements that include only minimum standards for public participation, or when weighed against the references to this principle as included in international environmental agreements, which just generally endorse public participation.[15]

Despite its relevance as almost the only environmental agreement that comprehensively addresses public participation, the potential of the Convention seems undermined by its rather limited endorsement. At the moment of writing only 46 countries and the European Union (EU) have ratified it. It is nevertheless important to underline that the Convention aspires to become an international treaty since it remains open to accession by non-UNECE countries and has, as such, the potential to expand into a treaty on public participation of global application. This would fully realise what is prescribed in Article 3.7 of the Convention,[16] a provision requiring all Parties to the Agreement to promote the principles contained in the Convention in international forums. For this purpose, the *Almaty Guidelines on Promoting the Application of the Principles of the Aarhus Convention in International Forums* was adopted in 2005. This is a non-legally binding document that complements the normative content of the Aarhus Convention, providing interpretation and guidance on the application of its principles in international fora.[17] In relation to this, a Task Force on public participation in international fora was also established in 2005. Until 2011, when a Working Group of the Parties (WGP) finally substituted the Task Force, the body has maintained a double mandate. It focused on promoting the guidelines in international forums on the one hand and addressed the role of the Parties to the Convention in applying Article 3.7, on the other. To this

15 See, J. EBBESSON, "Principle 10. Public Participation", in J. E. VIÑUALES (ed.) *The Rio Declaration on Environment and Development*. Oxford: Oxford University Press, 2015, pp. 288–309.

16 It has to be noted that this provision is formulated in binding terms: "Each Party *shall* (emphasis added) promote the application of the principles of this Convention in international environmental decision-making processes and within the framework of international organisations in matters relating to the environment".

17 As laid out in paragraph 4 of the Guidelines, the term international forum includes: (1) the negotiation and implementation at the international level of multilateral environmental agreements, including decisions and actions taken under their auspices; (2) the negotiation and implementation at the international level of other relevant agreements; (3) intergovernmental conferences focusing on the environment or having a strong environmental component, and their respective preparatory and follow-up processes at the international level. ECE/MP. PP/2005/2/Add.5, June 2005.

end, the Task Force has prepared a compendium of best practices, organised different workshops for the exchange of experiences among the Parties[18] and finally contributed to the improvement of the reporting obligations established under Article 10.2 of the Convention. With the dismantlement of the Task Force, the consideration of public participation in international fora continues under thematic sessions organised within the WGP, which more broadly serves to oversee the implementation of the work programme under the treaty and to propose amendments and reviews of the Convention.

Notwithstanding the significance and potential impact of Article 3.7 for the extension of public participation to international decision-making, until 2018 the Aarhus Convention has remained the only legally binding instrument putting Principle 10 into practice. Only more recently, the Ninth Meeting of the Negotiating Committee of the Regional Agreement on Principle 10 has adopted a regional agreement for Latin American and the Caribbean (LAC) States, the *Regional Agreement on Access to Information, Public Participation and Justice in Environmental Matters in Latin America and the Caribbean* (Escazú Agreement, 2018).[19] The agreement, that will remain open to signatures from September 2018 to September 2020, was promoted during the Rio+20 summit, in which 12 Latin American and Caribbean States expressed commitment towards the adoption of a regional instrument with content similar to that in the UNECE Convention. The adoption of a new regional convention that applies to a vast majority of Latin American countries undoubtedly represents a further step towards the implementation of procedural rights worldwide. A first analysis of the document, suggests that emphasis has been given to the international dimension of procedural rights, which are expressively mentioned in Article 7.12 of the text.[20] Moreover, Article 11.4 obliges all signatories to create partnerships with States from other regions, intergovernmental and non-governmental organisations in implementing the Agreement. Nonetheless, up to the moment of writing it is not possible to assess the implications that this will have in clarifying the content of Principle 10 in intergovernmental decision-making. Moreover, the adoption of a twin convention for the Latin American continent poses the question over the uniform application

18 With regard to climate change, two relevant workshops were held. The first in 2010 on a case study on "Promoting the principles of the Aarhus Convention in the lead up to, during and after the United Nations Climate Change Conference 2009" and the second in 2011 on the theme "Making Aarhus work in international forums". See: https://unfccc.int/resource/docs/2010/smsn/igo/088.pdf (Last access, 20 May 2018).

19 *Regional Agreement on Access to Information, Public Participation and Justice in Environmental Matters in Latin America and the Caribbean* of 4 March 2018. The agreement is currently open for signature.

20 The article reads: "Each Party shall promote, where appropriate and in accordance with domestic legislation, public participation in international forums and negotiations on environmental matters or with an environmental impact, in accordance with the procedural rules on participation of each forum".

of public participation and of why, although praised internationally, the Aarhus Convention is still far from enjoying global adherence.

2.2 Non-governmental actors and international (environmental) law

The appearance of NGOs in international affairs is mainly linked to the inception of globalisation.[21] As the world became increasingly interconnected with the integration of national markets into a global economy during the 1990s, societal and political interdependence grew beyond nation states. This gave rise to concerns different from states' security, namely global commons or public goods, and favoured the affiliation of groups and individuals transnationally. As recognised by the Commission on Global Governance, especially people(s)' concerns for human rights, democracy, and environmental protection produced the emergence of a multitude of new actors that today contribute to global decision- and law-making.[22]

Traces of non-governmental influence can be found in very different fields of international law, for instance international humanitarian law, international criminal law or labour law, but it is particularly in the environmental realm and the domain of human rights where different non-State actors (NSAs), and specifically NGOs, have come up more prominently. In other words, where the limited capacity of single nation states to cope with transnational environmental problems or massive violations of human rights became evident, NGOs' contribution to the creation, implementation and fulfilment of international obligations has turned into a precondition to effective governance, along with – but also alternatively to – increased intergovernmental cooperation. As a result of a broader environmental movement that emerged already in the 1960s due to large-scale environmental problems with human rights implications (e.g., transboundary pollution, ozone layer depletion and climate change), the first UN Conference on Human Environment was held in 1972 in Stockholm,

21 In the context of this work, globalisation refers to the process of intensification of economic, political and social relations across international boundaries, what implies the overcoming of national frontiers by goods, services and people as well as the establishment of closer contacts among societies. Since public international law is primarily concerned with the existence of States and the regulation of their relations, the challenges that globalisation poses to the role of States internationally by redistributing attributes of power among different actors, are likely to impact the evolution of international law too.

22 COMMISSION ON GLOBAL GOVERNANCE, *Our Global Neighbourhood. The Report of the Commission on Global Governance*. Oxford: Oxford University Press, 1995. The Commission was established in 1992 with the scope of furthering an international agenda on global security, understood in a broad manner. With this mandate it also explored the question of universal democracy and proposed a reform of the United Nations system aimed at redressing the undemocratic character of the Security Council and the General Assembly. In this context, it promoted the establishment of an International Assembly of People and a Forum of Civil Society having direct access to the UN.

with the participation of 170 NGOs. Already in 1992, NGOs were given the possibility for directly participating in the preparatory committees of the UN Conference on Environment and Development. Finally, because of Principle 10 of the Rio Declaration, the participation of entities other than States to the law-making process has become a constant of most environmental law institutional arrangements.[23]

2.2.1 NGOs and international norm-making

In article 38 (1) of the Statute of the ICJ, the idea that States are to be considered the exclusive actors of international law-making is taken for granted. Indeed, no indication of the role and functions of actors other than States is found in this article and exclusive sources of law are (a). international conventions, general or particular, establishing rules expressively recognised by contesting states; (b). international custom, as evidence of a general practice accepted as law; and (c). the general principles of law recognised by civilised nations.[24] Finally, judicial decisions and the writings of the most qualified publicists are also listed by the Statute as subsidiary means for the determination of the rules of law.

The state-driven nature of international law-making is not disputed in this work. The democratically elected nature of most states explains why they are primarily entitled to the conduct of international relations and why their consent is central to the process of law-making internationally.[25] Nonetheless, it is to be recognised that the international system has also evolved towards the incorporation of actors other than states along the entire norm creation process.

Historically, the first acknowledgement of a role to be played by NGOs in international law-making occurred in 1945, with the adoption of the United Nations Charter. Article 71 of the UN Charter expressively prescribes that the UN Economic and Social Council (ECOSOC)

> may make suitable arrangements for consultation with non-governmental organisations which are concerned with matters within its competence. Such arrangements may be made with international organisations and, where appropriate, with national organizations after consultation with the Member of the United Nations concerned.[26]

23 See, e.g., M. BETSILL and E. CORELL, *NGO Diplomacy. The Influence of Nongovernment Organizations in International Environmental Negotiations*. Cambridge, MA: The MIT Press, 2008.

24 *Statute of the International Court of Justice* of 18 April 1946, art. 38 (1).

25 See, on the notion of State consent and its relevance to international law-making, S. BESSON, "State Consent and Disagreement in International Law-Making. Dissolving the Paradox", *Leiden Journal of International Law*, Vol. 29, 2016, pp. 289–316.

26 *Charter of the United Nations* of 26 October 1945 (1 UNTS XVI), article 71.

Certainly, this arrangement introduced a novel form of cooperation between this major state-based entity and one of the most influential categories of NSAs.[27] Nowadays, the ECOSOC Resolution 1996/31 on Consultative relationship between the United Nations and NGOs governs the consultative arrangement initially outlined by article 71.[28] The consultative status accorded to NGOs whose mandates are in conformity with the UN Charter is further divided into three main categories:

(1) *General consultative status*, through which NGOs get the right to attend the meeting of the ECOSOC and its subsidiary bodies, as well as the possibility for speaking, circulating statements and making proposals for provisional agendas;
(2) *Special consultative status*, which is close to the general one but reserved to NGOs with smaller scope of activities, although these are not allowed to speak at ECOSOC meetings; and finally
(3) *Roster*, which can only attend meetings within their field of competence and if consultation with them is requested by ECOSOC or its subsidiary bodies. The practice concerning the adjudication of the status is usually based on the ability of the NGO to contribute to the work of the ECOSOC and thus advance the objectives of the UN.

As a result of this acknowledgement, diverse NGOs have gained access to the UN system and can now participate in international decision-making processes, including some treaty-based regimes as the ones on global climate change. It is, in fact, this consultative status that allows NGOs qualified in a relevant field to become observers to multilateral intergovernmental conferences or summits held under the auspices of the UN. Alternatively, a request for accreditation can be directly sent to the UN Secretariat, the organ in charge of adjudicating applications for participation in UN processes. Either way, clearer rules for the participation of observers are provided in the rules of procedure established by single organisations or treaty-based systems. In institutional terms, there are at least five main categories under which the inclusion of NGOs in the international treaty-making system may be realised:

- The first, and arguably the more advanced, category is the participation with voting rights. Probably due to the state-centric nature of international law, this category is not very widespread. The exceptional tripartite consultative status created in the International Labour Organisation (ILO) has likely been influenced by the way in which labour law is created

27 Although criticism has also been moved by different authors. See, e.g., M. ABAD CASTELOS, *¿Una alternativa solidaria frente a la barbarie? Las ONG en la nueva sociedad global.* Madrid: CIDEAL, 2004, p. 221.

28 United Nations, Economic and Social Council, *Resolution on Consultative Relationship between the United Nations and Nongovernmental Organizations*, 1996 (Resolution 1996/31).

nationally, where trade unions and employers largely bargain on contracts and employment standards.

- Participation without voting rights is the second category in point and, arguably, the most widespread in both treaty-based systems and international organisations. This so called 'observer status' may entail the exercise of very different 'rights',[29] from the possibility of exclusively attending multilateral conferences, to direct engagement and lobbying *via* participation in a state delegation. This category, as applied in the climate change regime, will be largely detailed in the following chapter of this work.
- A third possible mode of participation is that of concertation, which entails the need to consult with different NGOs before a decision is taken. This model seems very suitable for decision-making based on consensus and largely deliberative systems.
- Finally, the least advanced model would be consultation, through which NGOs are merely required to provide information and their points of view on the issue under discussion.

Therefore, even if NGOs are not formal subjects of international law, what Boyle and Chinkin noted already in 2007 is all the more true today: "The international legal system has moved far beyond the categorisations of the sources of international law of the Statute of the ICJ".[30] Increasingly, by looking at the practice of international law-making, the ICJ assumption of an exclusively state-based law-making system seems to be in contrast with the evidence of different non-governmental actors contributing to the success of multilateral negotiations, as well as to their failure.[31] An often-cited example of the latter is the Multilateral Agreement on Investment, largely criticised and finally exhausted by civil society NGOs. The negotiations of the treaty, initiated in 1995, raised criticism when the draft agreement was leaked in 1997. Particularly, the lack of transparency in the intergovernmental process and concerns that the treaty would disproportionately favour the interests of financial corporations to the detriment of human and labour rights as well as of environmental standards caused NGOs' strong reactions. After a global campaign lead by global NGOs and paired with the opposition of some developing states, the negotiations

29 In this sense, it is important to remember that there is no general right to observer status granted to NGOs. Rather, this is established on a case-by-case basis.

30 A. BOYLE and C. CHINKIN, *The Making of International Law*. Oxford: Oxford University Press, 2007, p. 36.

31 For a detailed account of this topic, see the International Law Association (ILA) Report on Non-State Actors of 2012: INTERNATIONAL LAW ASSOCIATION COMMITTEE ON NON-STATE ACTORS, Second Report of the Committee. *Non-State Actors in International Law: Law-making and participation rights*. ILA Conference in Sofia, 2012. Available at: http://www.ila-hq.org/index.php/committees (Last access, 11 July 2018); as well as the case studies provided in A. BOYLE and C. CHINKIN, *supra* note 30, at 67.

were suspended in 1998, with the decision not to resume them.[32] Conversely, in the fields of human rights law, NGOs took initiative for intergovernmental law-making contributing to the drafting of the *International Covenant on Civil and Political Rights*,[33] as well as the *International Covenant on Economic, Social and Cultural Rights*[34] (ICESCR). The role of the International Committee of the Red Cross (ICRC) in the formation and implementation of international humanitarian law is also largely recognised.[35] By the same token, environmental and human rights NGOs were determinant to the negotiation, adoption and implementation of several multilateral environmental treaties, including the *Convention on International Trade in Endangered Species of Wild Fauna and Flora*[36] (CITES) and, most recently, the *Paris Agreement* of 2015.[37] Concerning the latter, Jacobs has recalled how a global coalition of NGOs and the civil society have put pressure on governments in the aftermath of the failure of COP15 in Copenhagen, through the mobilisation of public opinion and advocacy, but also working towards the definition of acceptable emissions levels to be agreed upon in Paris, thus bringing expert advice and scientific evidence to the negotiation table. The celebration of the 2014 Climate Summit organised by the UN Secretary General Ban Ki-Moon, in which leaders from business, NGOs and city majors were brought together along with governments, also prepared the ground for effective ambitious intergovernmental negotiations, since commitments to climate action were made by private entities for the first time.[38] While in all the above mentioned cases it is difficult to exactly trace NGOs' influence on the law-making process, a clear example in which non-governmental entities amount to co-creators of international law is the case of the ILO in which, as mentioned above, the participation of workers' and

32 See, on the proposed agreement: https://www.oecd.org/investment/internationalinvestmentagreements/multilateralagreementoninvestment.htm (Last access, 29 April 2019).

33 UNITED NATIONS GENERAL ASSEMBLY, *International Covenant on Civil and Political Rights* of 16 December 1996 (999 UNTS 171).

34 UNITED NATIONS GENERAL ASSEMBLY, *International Covenant on Economic, Social and Cultural Rights* of 16 December 1966 (993 UNTS 3).

35 Extensive account of the ICRC role in the promotion of International Humanitarian Law is found in M. HARROFF-TAVEL, "The International Committee of the Red Cross and the Promotion of International Humanitarian Law: Looking Back, Looking Forward", *International Review of the Red Cross*, Vol. 96, 2014, pp. 817–857.

36 UNITED NATIONS, *Convention on International Trade in Endangered Species of Wild Fauna and Flora* of 3 March 1973 (993 UNTS 243). The wildlife monitoring network TRAFFIC, a partnership between the World Wildlife Fund for Nature and the World Conservation Union, plays a key role in implementing the provisions of the CITES Convention but also provides essential evidence aimed at catalysing actions by governments and business concerning the trade of wild species. See: https://www.traffic.org/about-us/our-mission/ (Last access 29 April 2019).

37 UNITED NATIONS, *Paris Agreement to the United Nations Framework Convention on Climate Change* of 12 December 2015 (UN Doc. FCCC/CP/2015/10/Add, 1).

38 See, M. JACOBS, "High Pressure for Low Emissions: How Civil Society Created the Paris Climate Agreement", *Juncture*, Vol. 2, No. 4, 2016, pp. 314–323.

employers' representatives is completely institutionalised through the conferral of voting rights.

Apart from this example, NGOs' influence on treaty-making usually follows a rather common pattern and may be tracked down to diverse advocacy techniques, for example, strategies of 'inside' or 'outside' advocacy, as labelled in the literature.[39] In the first case, NGOs directly take part in international diplomacy by attending and influencing intergovernmental negotiations, thus having direct access to decision-makers in an area of concern to the general public. On the contrary, when a topic still does not ride high on the social agenda, strategies of outside advocacy can be used to introduce a subject of concern into the domestic or global public opinion debate, so that different national governments will be pressured to accommodate it in their political agenda. As a result of this work, NGOs may be able to introduce an issue in the international arena and become very active advocates, even lobbyists, in intergovernmental negotiations, where fundamentally states will, at least formally, control the law-making stage. It is in fact important to stress that, while not recognised with a formal norm-making mandate, NGOs perform different and relevant functions and immensely contribute to the law-making process. From the supply of information and expertise, to the work done on bracketed texts, NGOs aim at keeping high the ambitions of government delegates on the issue they have raised. Then again, the possibility for NGOs to directly impact the making of international legal norms varies very much from subject to subject, and from one institutional setting to the other, as reflected in the examples provided above.

Overall, this section has tried to understand how NGOs relate to the practice of international law-making. A conventional consideration of what constitutes a source of law primarily suggests that law-making is a state-centred practice, although this definition neglects the role that actors other than states may play for the emergence of customary law and treaty-law internationally. Indeed, the consideration of the practice of international law-making suggests that this process has evolved towards accommodating actors different from states and that, even under an institutional perspective, law-making is a more plural and horizontal legal practice, which comprises the contributions of entities that are not states and do not enjoy a full legal personality. This is, for instance, the case of many NGOs that, to different extents, have been able to influence the adoption of multilateral treaties. As a result, while the normative – or quasi-normative – functions displayed by different non-governmental actors do not point to the emergence of new sources of international law, inasmuch as soft law is considered binding only in political terms, there is little doubt that different non-governmental entities have contributed and still

39 See, on this topic, C. BETZOLD, "Business Insiders and Environmental Outsider? Advocacy Strategies in International Climate Change Negotiations", *Interest Groups & Advocacy*, Vol. 2, No. 3, 2013, pp. 302–322.

contribute to the emergence and development of international law, particularly environmental law.

2.2.2 *The relevance of public participation in international environmental governance*

The participation of the public in international environmental arrangements through NGOs serves a set of different functions and occurs at very different stages. Spiro provides a rather intuitive classification.[40] By considering law-making as a linear succession of decision-making phases in which NGOs are able to intervene, he argues, NGOs usually take part in the *before* (agenda setting and events that bring an issue into policy-makers attention), the *during* (negotiations on a specific issue), and the *after* (both the implementation and enforcement phases) of such a process. As a result, traces of public participation may be found across the whole spectrum of international environmental law-making and enforcement. The degree of non-governmental influence over one or another stage of this process may change based on specific institutional settings established to enable participation and NGOs' size and resources, as well as governmental responsiveness.[41] All the same, scholars largely concur on the idea that public participation is relevant to the deliberative process inasmuch as it contributes transparency, along with public opinion acceptance for intergovernmental decisions. By fostering public awareness, NGOs can trigger great support for intergovernmental decisions or, conversely, urge advocacy against one or another policy or the maintenance of the status quo.

Especially in the context of highly complex and transnational environmental problems, support for public participation stems from the perception that if environmental laws and policies must be effective, they require the contribution and involvement of a broad range of actors, representing diverse views, expertise and concerns. It goes without saying that, when a determined lobbying strategy is meant to advance a specific and non-altruistic interest over public good, a distortion of the primary essence of public participation occurs. This can be the case with NGOs working on a hidden agenda, as well as with government-organised NGOs.[42] Also in this regard, although they are not formally democratic, NGOs' participation may be relevant in enhancing the knowledge base of decision-making, in giving voice to the voiceless or in bringing the concerns of those distant from the *loci* of decision-making[43] to the

40 See, P. SPIRO, "Non-Governmental Organizations and Civil Society", in D. BODANSKY, J. BRUNNÉ and E. HEY (eds.) *The Oxford Handbook of International Environmental Law*. Oxford: Oxford University Press, 2007, pp. 770–790.

41 See, C. BETZOLD, "Responsiveness or Influence? Whom to Lobby in International Climate Change Negotiations", *International Negotiations*, Vol. 19, 2014, pp. 35–61.

42 K. MARTENS, "Examining the (Non-) Status of NGOs in International Law", *Indiana Journal of Global Legal Studies*, Vol. 10, No. 2, 2003, pp. 1–24, at 9.

43 This is what Sconfienza has addressed as thick participation. The engagement with non-governmental instances is able to provide information to help the design of more equitable policies, as

intergovernmental process. Accordingly, public participation can provide relevant information and knowledge[44] on highly complex environmental issues, improve the legitimacy of intergovernmental negotiations and overall foster good governance and inclusive decision-making.[45]

In general terms, therefore, the participation of the public in environmental contexts is believed to contribute democracy, transparency and expertise to law-making, improving the overall effectiveness of decision-making. Especially in global contexts, participation can create a sense of ownership with proposed solutions, helping to reconcile global expectations and local demands. In conclusion, and although not exhaustive, the account of private activities provided in this section reveals that public participation is relevant to environmental governance, although it requires further consideration in terms of how it should be conducted, by whom and on the basis of which representative mandate.

2.3 NGOs and international norm-making: redressing a democratic deficit?

The creation of legal norms at the international level happens through the negotiation of multilateral treaties conducted by States' representatives. States' officials are vested with the authority to negotiate international treaties on behalf of their citizens, based on the mandate obtained at the national level. While State consent is aimed at representing the will expressed by citizens through democratic legitimisation, the creation of norms at the international level makes the 'delegation of powers' secured by national elections less straightforward. As a result, although States remain central to the process of international law-making, a so-called 'democratic deficit' is rooted in the creation of international law. Clearly, this deficit is further hampered in non-democratic countries, in which the claims and interests of citizens are simply left unrepresented. Moreover, since the divide between national and international law is thinner today, and international law increasingly affects the lives of individuals more directly, a problem with the way in which legal norms are created internationally is undeniable. Therefore, a question of legitimacy

well as the ability to bring new perspectives to the decision-making table. See, U. SCONFIENZA, "The Narrative of Public Participation in Environmental Governance and its Normative Presuppositions", *Review of European Community & International Environmental Law*, Vol. 24, No. 2, 2015, pp. 139–151.

44 In both the conservation of biological diversity and the tackling of climate change, scientific knowledge has been progressively complemented by the traditional ecologic knowledge of Indigenous Peoples. Accordingly, both regimes expressively make reference to these different sources of knowledge. This is why the author uses the word "knowledge" in a plural form here.

45 T. BERNAUER and C. BETZOLD, "Civil Society in Global Environmental Governance", *The Journal of Environment & Development*, Vol. 21, No. 1, 2012, pp. 62–66.

affects states and NGOs alike when they intervene in the creation of international norms.

In this context, proposals for the improvement of the international law-making process can be found across the literature developed around the rise of non-governmental actors. The academic debate usually points to the need of making the creation of norms at the international level more plural and open to the participation of the civil society, assuming that the legitimacy of international law-making would be enhanced by according a more prominent role to civil society representatives throughout institutional processes. On the contrary, those opposing an unconditioned opening of international law-making to those entities usually claim that, from a democratic perspective, non-governmental actors are not elected entities and cannot therefore legitimately claim to represent a specific group of citizens, interests or constituencies. Accordingly, a review of the literature developed around this topic highlights a divide between authors that oppose and criticise a more traditional positivist paradigm of international law and those who are, instead, in favour of a more complementary model of law-making, in which State and non-State entities of different kinds are comprised. In the latter case, it is sustained that non-governmental actors cannot replace states in their normative functions but that these entities should be integrated into the law-making process because of their expertise and ability to inject democracy into the overall procedure.

In relation to this, the Commission on Global Governance proposed already in 1995 the institution of an International Assembly of People and a Forum of Civil Society, which would have direct access to the UN system. Following on the perceived need to reform the UN, and as part of a broader set of reforms, in 2000 the former UN Secretary General Kofi Annan invited over 1400 civil society representatives to expose their views at the NGO Millennium Forum, held in parallel to the Millennium Assembly. As a final proposal, the forum agreed on the establishment of a permanent assembly of civil society representatives to meet every two years before the celebration of the United Nations General Assembly (UNGA) annual session. At the moment of writing, this proposal has yet to materialise. However, the idea of a global parliament has been recovered and refined by Falk and Strauss.[46] The authors have proposed the creation of a popularly elected Global People Assembly constituted of global citizenry, in which elected delegates would represent individuals – and not states – and vote independently from the latter. Such a system, which should not necessarily be constituted on the basis of a formal treaty, would redress the ad hoc nature of civil society access to global decision-making and institutionalise civil society participation in intergovernmental processes. Without directly advocating for the creation of a global assembly but strictly referring to the environmental realm, Biermann has also criticised multilateral institutions for being centred

46 R. FALK and A. STRAUSS, "Toward Global Parliament", *Foreign Affairs*, Vol. 80, No. 1, 2001, pp. 212–220.

on governmental representatives.[47] In his *Earth System Governance*, the author advocates for the creation of a World Environment Organisation. According to his proposal, this could be realised through an upgrade of the United Nations Environmental Programme (UNEP) into a UN specialised agency, to be conceived as the focal point among the different and independent organisations operating on an environmental mandate (FAO, WMO, etc.). In detailing the characteristics of this institutional reform, Biermann also argues in favour of a stronger role for civil society organisations in such institutions. By advocating that their primary role should be to serve as 'institutionalised watchdogs,' he recalls the theories of liberal institutionalism or cosmopolitanism where the creation of civil society chambers, parliamentary or deliberative assemblies as consultative organs of international institutions are advanced. Global constitutionalism, on the contrary, has more broadly focused on researching the constitutional features of the international legal system, examining the role that the State, individuals, and NGOs play in it.[48] Under this perspective, the rights and obligations held by NGOs should be suited to their functions, in order to "reconcile the conflicting objectives of inclusiveness and transparency with the preservation of the authority and ultimate responsibility of States".[49] The authors adhering to this view ultimately propose to grant a voice but not a vote to NGOs in the law-making process, and to introduce a uniformed procedure for their participation.

Although not exhaustive, this brief account demonstrates that several proposals to overcome the shortcomings of a state-centric model of international law-making have been made from exponents of different international law theories. Yet, it is sustained here, all proposals are also problematic to some extent. First, any suggestion is usually made in very abstract terms, not providing a clear indication of how the creation of a global assembly should be operationalised, and the election of its representatives carried out. Also, the idea of civil society is very general, debatable and undefined. Any concrete proposal should be able to define or constrain this concept and its content, at least to a minimum. Moreover, when the proposal to grant a voice but not a vote to NGOs is made – as in the context of global constitutionalism – it seems fair to say that the model of participation recommended by this approach is often already in place, at least in environmental contexts. Finally, a problem common to most of these approaches is that they usually justify the claim for more direct participation of civil society on a social understanding of legitimacy instead of a normative one, sustaining that public participation injects transparency and democracy to the decision-making, and should, therefore, be

47 F. BIERMANN, *Earth System Governance. World Politics in the Anthropocene*. Cambridge, MA: The MIT Press, 2014, p. 127.

48 See, e.g., J. KLABBERS, A. PETERS and G. ULFSTEIN, *The Constitutionalization of International Law*. Oxford: Oxford University Press, 2009.

49 *Ibid*, at 225.

justified. Although this might be true in principle, the introduction of criteria for assessing the accountability of different NSAs could help legitimising them while maintaining their primary role of contestation.

As a result, what is sustained in this work is a non-hierarchical[50] halfway position, in which the deficiencies of a primarily dogmatic statist model are complemented by the normatively relevant functions unfolded by non-governmental actors, at least for as much as the climate change law-making process is concerned. This requires further considering the legitimacy of NGOs.

2.3.1 Defining legitimacy

Boyle and Chinkin have defined legitimacy as the normative belief that a rule or institution ought to be obeyed.[51] While such a definition may seem unproblematic at a first glance, the strict relation that the concept of legitimacy holds with the ideas of morality, legality, authority, and power makes whatever definition object of further scrutiny. Indeed, what one is to consider moral, legal or just may be strictly subjective and irreducible to objective categories, as well as it is perfectly possible for powerful and authoritative institutions to be illegitimate. Another problem that entails the definition of *what* or *who* is to be considered legitimate, is the difficulty to ascertain this term in its sociological dimension – namely *what* or *who* people perceive to be legitimate – and its normative one – *who* in fact is entitled to legitimacy.[52] The difficulty of agreeing on a unique definition has brought the theorisation of this concept under four main broad categories,[53] which have been differently used to better detail the multidimensional nature of this concept and applied to assess the authority of States and non-State actors in international law-making.

50 As it will be made clear in subsequent sections and chapters of this work, the voluntary or involuntary hierarchy perpetrated by the present international law-making system is, in the view of the author, not sufficiently reflective of the importance of the individual in international law as primer subject and ultimate recipient of the norms constituting the international legal system.

51 A. BOYLE and C. CHINKIN, *supra* note 30, at 24.

52 See, for a legal perspective on legitimacy, R. WOLFRUM and V. RÖBEN (eds.) *Legitimacy in International Law*. Heidelberg: Springer, 2008. While, on the distinction between justice and legitimacy and on the legitimacy of the sources of international law more broadly, see J. L. MARTÍ, "Sources and the Legitimate Authority of International Law: Democratic Legitimacy and the Sources of International Law", in S. BESSON and J. D'ASPREMONT (eds.) *The Oxford Handbook on the Sources of International Law*. Oxford: Oxford University Press, 2017, pp. 724–745.

53 For a detailed account on the concept of legitimacy and related theorisation, see D. BODANSKY, "Legitimacy", in D. BODANSKY, J. BRUNNÉ and E. HEY (eds.) *The Oxford Handbook of International Environmental Law*. Oxford: Oxford University Press, 2007, pp. 705–721; A. BUCHANAN, "The Legitimacy of International Law", in S. BESSON and J. TASIOULAS (eds.) *The Philosophy of International Law*. Oxford: Oxford University Press, 2010, pp. 79–96. On a democratic conception of legitimacy, see T. CHRISTIANO, "Democratic Legitimacy and International Institutions" in *ibid*, pp. 119–137.

Often related with a normative understanding of legitimacy are the categories of *substantive* and *procedural legitimacy*. The authority of an international norm, so the argument goes, will be legitimised by its substance or by the procedure or sources through which it has come into being. This idea is often paired with a legal positivist view, due to the legitimising role played by State consent, understood as representing the peoples that constitute it, and thus conflated with an idea of legality.[54] Two other conceptualisations point instead to the functioning of the institutions where decision- and law-making are carried out. *Input legitimacy* refers to the transparency and representativeness of a certain institutional arrangement, including how its members are selected, and the procedures followed to take decisions. In the context of climate change, for instance, input legitimacy has been questioned after the adoption of the Copenhagen Accord of 2009, mainly concluded by the representatives of only 28 States acting as Friends of the Chair group and with the exclusion of other actors, States and non-States alike.[55] Finally, perhaps the most intuitive categorisation is the one of *output legitimacy*, stemming from the idea that an institution will gain legitimacy for the success and results of its own work. This is, for example, the case of the International Committee of the Red Cross or, in an environmental context, of the UN Environment Programme. Conversely, the output legitimacy of the United Nations Framework Convention on Climate Change[56] has been perceived as very much constrained until the conclusion of the Paris Agreement in 2015, especially due to the non-adherence of major political actors, such as China and the United States of America (USA) to the Framework Convention.[57]

As a result, the authority of international norms and processes, as well as of the actors participating therein, may be the result of a variable combination of the above-mentioned understandings of legitimacy, including the possibility that, for instance, a high degree of input legitimacy compensates for the more limited results obtained by a certain institution and vice versa. This may be better illustrated by the case of the ILO in which, although input legitimacy ranges very high for the inclusion of non-governmental entities with a high

54 R. WOLFRUM, "Legitimacy of International Law from a Legal Perspective: Some Introductory Considerations", in R. WOLFRUM and V. RÖBEN (eds.) *Legitimacy in International Law*. Heidelberg: Springer, 2008, pp. 1–24.

55 K. BÄCKSTRAND, J., W. KUYPER, B. LINNÉR and others, "Non-State Actors in Global Climate Governance: From Copenhagen to Paris and Beyond", *Environmental Politics*, Vol. 24, No. 4, 2017, pp. 561–579.

56 UNITED NATIONS, *United Nations Framework Convention on Climate Change* of 09 May 1992 (1771 UNTS 107).

57 Interestingly in this regard, when dealing with the concept of legitimacy, Boyle and Chinkin also explored the idea of 'system legitimacy'. By using this term, they aim at referring to the US practice of often resorting to unilateralism and rejecting of multilateralism in international law-making what, in turn, may have the effect to weaken the legitimacy of the overall international legal system. See, A. BOYLE and C. CHINKIN, *supra* note 30, at 28.

degree of representation, the overall output legitimacy of this system is to some extent undermined by the relatively slow path at which decisions are taken.

At this point, and in relation to the creation of international legal norms, one is to wonder on which of the following or other criteria the legitimacy of States and non-governmental actors should be ultimately evaluated.

2.3.2 The legitimacy of NGOs

As already said regarding State entities, legitimacy is, in intergovernmental rule-making, based on the accountability[58] of governments representatives to their voters. While, as Besson and Martí have rightly pointed,[59] States' democratic legitimisation is not exempt from potential improvement, non-governmental actors certainly raise more problems. As recalled above, arguments in support of the participation of NGOs in international law-making invariably range from the opinion that they inject transparency and democracy into the decision-making, to the conviction that their knowledge and expertise confers them authority.

Wheatley, for example, has underlined the epistemic authority of non-governmental actors.[60] Recalling Haas' definition of epistemic communities, the author puts forward an instrumental argument to justify why NGOs and NSAs should be able to influence international law-making: non-State entities will be able to exercise political authority only if they demonstrate their normative legitimacy, which is given by evidence of their competence and epistemic authority. It could be safely said that this is the kind of authority appreciated today by the Intergovernmental Panel on Climate Change (IPCC), which has been able to build its profile by virtue of the knowledge of its members and its knowledge production on climate change dynamics and impacts. Outside knowledge-based communities, Spiro has considered the legitimacy and accountability of NGOs.[61] While the author expressively recognises that NGOs may not necessarily act in the interest of the public, he also sustains that the putative lack of accountability and legitimacy of such entities is mediated in different ways. Although not formally democratic, NGOs are subject

58 In this context, the author borrows the definition of accountability given by Biermann, understood as the willingness to accept responsibility and to account for one's action. In this sense, accountability is comprised of four elements: (1) a normative element, a defined standard of behaviour; (2) a relational element, which links those who are held accountable to those that have the right to hold them accountable; (3) a decision element, the judgment of those able to held other accountable about whether the expected standard of behaviour has been met; (4) behavioural element, which allows the governing actor to punish deviant behaviours. See, F. BIERMANN, *supra* note 47, at 122.

59 S. BESSON and J. L. MARTÍ, "Legitimate Actors of International Law-Making: Towards a Theory of International Democratic Representation", *Jurisprudence*, 2018, pp. 1–38.

60 S. WHEATLEY, "Democratic Governance beyond the State: The Legitimacy of Non-State Actors", in A. PETERS, L. KOECHLIN, T. FÖRSTER and G. FENNER ZINKERNAGEL (eds.) *Non-State Actors as Standards Setters*. Cambridge: Cambridge University Press, 2009, pp. 215–240.

61 P. SPIRO, *supra* note 40.

to both internal and external accountability mechanisms. Besides the informal oversight exercised by the members of an NGO over their directorates, reputational considerations are likely to influence their work. The competition with other NGOs may positively influence their behaviour too. From an external standpoint then, NGOs become part of an institutional context in which States and international institutions mediate their work. In this context, the need to achieve their objective will constrain their capacity to opt out of any institutional set, subsequently obliging them to perform as socialised actors.

Drawing on democratic theories of representation, Besson and Martí have tackled this question more thoroughly,[62] and proposed what they have named a 'multiple representation model', based on the consideration and fulfilment of the democratic principles of ultimate and effective popular control; political equality; deliberative contestability and the protection of human rights, on which the legitimisation of both States and non-State entities should be constantly evaluated. In this sense, their view is somehow in line with that of other authors. Moravcsik, for instance, claims that any requirement of democratic legitimacy imposed on NSAs should not be stricter than those existing for States.[63]

While not advocating for the legitimisation of NGOs *tout court* and referring to the legitimacy of the overall legal system, Abad Castelos has more broadly spoken of the existence of a gap between the theory and practice related to how NGOs participate in the international system. The author points out that international law has been deficient in regulating the legal status of NGOs if one is to compare the actual relevance and weight that these NSAs have gained on decision-and law-making, and their normative status.[64] She recalls Cutler when criticising the legal structures inherited from a positivist legal order, arguing that this gap may in turn trigger a crisis of legitimacy of the overall international legal system.[65]

In fact, the current situation of international law is one in which non-dem ocratically elected NGOs are rather socialised with the institutions they aim at influencing and are thus able to intervene in the law-making process. In this sense, the fact that they do not enjoy (in most cases) formal democratic election and legitimisation has not precluded them from being decisive to the success or failure of international law-making.

Against this backdrop, any sound proposal for improving the legitimacy of international law-making and of the NGOs intervening in it, would need to

62 S. BESSON and J. L. MARTÍ, *supra* note 59.

63 A. MORAVCSIK, "Is there a 'Democratic Deficit' in World Politics? A Framework for Analysis", *Government and Opposition*,Vol. 39, No. 2, 2004, pp. 336–363.

64 It is here important to underline, as Abad Castelos does in her analysis, that not only States should be blamed for the lack of recognition of an international legal status for NGOs. In this regard, the author is critical towards the conduct of different NGOs that, she sustains, prefer to carry on their work in this context of legal uncertainty. See, M. ABAD CASTELOS, *supra* note 27, at 257.

65 *Ibid.*

balance all the considerations and concerns exposed so far. Ideally, the possibility to directly elect NGOs' representatives would secure the establishment of a democratic link between the citizens of a globalised world and those claiming to represent their interests internationally. The question of representation is fundamental if one is to avoid the perpetuation of a state-centred view, in which the appreciation of NSAs as legitimate actors requires their recognition by States. In other words, the source of authority (and thus legitimacy) of NGOs must be found outside States. In this sense, no further obstacle would be placed on NGOs than to conduct global elections for their representatives. Realising one of the suggestions made by Besson and Martí, this could be done through the organisation of electronic elections secured by block chain or the opening of consultations over NSA's actions. In all such cases, particular attention should be paid to the geographical representation of NGOs, as well as to the fact that major organisations should not overrun smaller ones.[66]

Until such a proposal is made possible, a second-best option rests in the possibility to foresee incremental models of participation and representation in which, the more NGOs are allowed to influence the international law-making process, the more their legitimisation should be made explicit. It follows that, if voting rights were to be granted to a specific constituency acting on the same foot as states, the NGO in question should at least enjoy the same legitimisation of states, establishing, therefore, a direct and democratic link with the constituency it aims at representing. On the other hand, if NGOs were to be admitted in the decision-making process as participants but without voting rights, the criteria for assessing their legitimisation and accountability could be less demanding. In any case, participation should be institutionalised and secured at any stage of decision-making, in order to avoid recreating existing model of participation in which states remain the gatekeepers of procedural rights. In this regard, the model of participation of Arctic Indigenous Peoples in the Arctic Council, which will be exposed in the fourth chapter of this work, may offer an interesting insight.

2.4 Concluding remarks

The participation of non-governmental actors in international environmental governance and law-making has dramatically increased since the affirmation of Principle 10 of the Rio Declaration of 1992. While the content of such a principle is non-binding under international law, it has been institutionalised as part of most multilateral environmental agreements, interpreted by human rights courts and further implemented with the adoption of regional agreements. In this regard, the Aarhus Convention is the regional treaty that has

66 In the context of climate-change governance, these complexities have been exposed in H. STEVENSON and J. S. DRYZEK, *Democratizing Global Climate Governance*. Cambridge: Cambridge University Press, 2014.

contributed the most to the application and respect of procedural rights in both their domestic and international dimension.

As limited subjects of international law, the possibility for NGOs of being entitled with a normative function remains uncertain. Yet, the analysis of the practice of international law-making has also underlined that different NGOs are often determinant to the success or failure of the creation of international legal norms internationally. A brief analysis of the contributions that civil and non-governmental representatives are able to make to international environmental law, has shown the importance of public participation to intergovernmental processes. This further highlights an underlining contradiction between the theory and practice of international law-making and somehow hampers the perceived legitimacy of the overall legal system, already concerned with the democratic deficit of intergovernmental international law-making and the contested authority of the subjects intervening in it. Particularly, the realms of international human rights law and environmental law are where the influence of non-governmental actors has shown more prominently. Encompassing the latter area, the next chapter of this work aims at exploring the international legal framework that authorises the participation of non-state entities in international climate change law-making.

Bibliography

Abad Castelos, M. *¿Una alternativa solidaria frente a la barbarie? Las ONG en la nueva sociedad global.* Madrid: CIDEAL, 2004.

Bäckstrand, K., Kuyper, J. W., Linnér, B. and Others. "Non-State Actors in Global Climate Governance: From Copenhagen to Paris and Beyond", *Environmental Politics*, Vol. 24, No. 4, 2017, pp. 561–579.

Bernauer, T. and C. Betzold. "Civil Society in Global Environmental Governance", *The Journal of Environment & Development*, Vol. 21, No. 1, 2012, pp. 62–66.

Besson, S. "State Consent and Disagreement in International Law-Making. Dissolving the Paradox", *Leiden Journal of International Law*, Vol. 29, 2016, pp. 289–316.

Besson, S. and J. L. Martí. "Legitimate Actors of International Law-Making: Towards a Theory of International Democratic Representation", *Jurisprudence*, Vol. 9, No. 3, 2018, pp. 504–540.

Betsill, M. and E. Corell. *NGO Diplomacy. The Influence of Nongovernment Organizations in International Environmental Negotiations.* Cambridge, MA: MIT Press, 2008.

Betzold, C. "Business Insiders and Environmental Outsider? Advocacy Strategies in International Climate Change Negotiations", *Interest Groups & Advocacy*, Vol. 2, No. 3, 2013, pp. 302–322.

Betzold, C. "Responsiveness or Influence? Whom to Lobby in International Climate Change Negotiations", *International Negotiations*, Vol. 19, 2014, pp. 35–61.

Biermann, F. *Earth System Governance. World Politics in the Anthropocene.* Cambridge, MA: MIT Press, 2014.

Bodansky, D. "Legitimacy", in D. Bodansky, J. Brunné and E. Hey (eds.) *The Oxford Handbook of International Environmental Law.* Oxford: Oxford University Press, 2007, pp. 705–721.

Boyle, A. "Human Rights and the Environment: Where Next?" *European Journal of International Law*, Vol. 23, No. 3, 2012, pp. 613–642.

Boyle, A. and C. Chinkin. *The Making of International Law*. Oxford: Oxford University Press, 2007.

Buchanan, A. "The Legitimacy of International Law", in S. Besson and J. Tasioulas (eds.) *The Philosophy of International Law*. Oxford: Oxford University Press, 2010, pp. 79–96.

COMMISSION ON GLOBAL GOVERNANCE. *Our Global Neighbourhood. The Report of the Commission on Global Governance*. Oxford: Oxford University Press, 1995.

Duvic-Paoli, L. "The Status of the Right to Public Participation in International Environmental Law: An Analysis of the Jurisprudence", *Yearbook of International Environmental Law*, Vo. 23, No. 1, 2012, pp. 80–115.

Ebbesson, J. "Public Participation", in D. Bodansky, J. Brunné and E. Hey (eds.) *The Oxford Handbook of International Environmental Law*. Oxford: Oxford University Press, 2007, pp. 681–703.

Ebbesson, J. "Principle 10. Public Participation", in J. E. Viñuales (ed.) *The Rio Declaration on Environment and Development*. Oxford: Oxford University Press, 2015, pp. 288–309.

Falk, R. and A. Strauss. "Toward Global Parliament", *Foreign Affairs*, Vol. 80, No. 1, 2001, pp. 212–220.

Harroff-Tavel, M. "The International Committee of the Red Cross and the Promotion of International Humanitarian Law: Looking Back, Looking Forward", *International Review of the Red Cross*, Vol. 96, 2014, pp. 817–857.

HUMAN RIGHTS COMMITTEE. *General Comment No. 25: The Right to Participate in Public Affairs, Voting Rights and the Right of Equal Access to Public Service (Art. 25)*, (CCPR/C/21/REV.1/Add.7, General Comment No. 25, 1996).

INTERNATIONAL LAW ASSOCIATION COMMITTEE ON NON-STATE ACTORS. *Second Report of the Committee. Non-State Actors in International Law: Law-making and Participation Rights*. ILA Conference in Sofia, 2012. Available at: http://www.ila-hq.org/index.php/committees.

Jacobs, M. "High Pressure for Low Emissions. How Civil Society Created the Paris Climate Agreement", *Juncture*, Vol. 2, No. 4, 2016, pp. 314–323.

Jodoin, S., Duyck, S. and K. Lofts. "Public Participation and Climate Governance: An Introduction", *Review of European Community & International Environmental Law*, Vol. 24, No. 2, 2015, pp. 117–122.

Klabbers, J., Peters, A. and G. Ulfstein. *The Constitutionalization of International Law*. Oxford: Oxford University Press, 2009.

Martens, K. "Examining the (Non-) Status of NGOs in International Law", *Indiana Journal of Global Legal Studies*, Vol. 10, No. 2, 2003, pp. 1–24.

Martí, J. L. "Sources and the Legitimate Authority of International Law: Democratic Legitimacy and the Sources of International Law", in S. Besson and J. D'aspremont (eds.) *The Oxford Handbook on the Sources of International Law*. Oxford: Oxford University Press, 2017, pp. 724–745.

Moravcsik, A. "Is There a "Democratic Deficit" in World Politics? A Framework for Analysis", *Government and Opposition*, Vol. 39, No. 2, 2004, pp. 336–363.

Sconfienza, U. "The Narrative of Public Participation in Environmental Governance and its Normative Presuppositions", *Review of European Community & International Environmental Law*, Vol. 24, No. 2, 2015, pp. 139–151.

Spiro, P. "Non-Governmental Organizations and Civil Society", in D. Bodansky, J. Brunné and E. Hey (eds.) *The Oxford Handbook of International Environmental Law*. Oxford: Oxford University Press, 2007, pp. 770–790.

Stevenson, H. and J. S. Dryzek. *Democratizing Global Climate Governance*. Cambridge: Cambridge University Press, 2014.

UNITED NATIONS. *Convention on International Trade in Endangered Species of Wild Fauna and Flora of 3 March 1973* (993 UNTS 243).

UNITED NATIONS. *United Nations Framework Convention on Climate Change of 09 May 1992* (1771 UNTS 107).

UNITED NATIONS. *The Future We Want. Outcome Document of the United Nations Conference on Sustainable Development*. Brazil, 2012. Available at: https://sustainabledevelopment.un.org/content/documents/733FutureWeWant.pdf.

UNITED NATIONS. *Paris Agreement to the United Nations Framework Convention on Climate Change of 12 December 2015* (UN Doc. FCCC/CP/2015/10/Add, 1).

UNITED NATIONS ECONOMIC COMMISSION FOR EUROPE. *Convention on Access to Information, Public Participation in Decision-Making and Access to Justice in Environmental Matters of 25 June 1998* (2161 UNTS 447).

UNITED NATIONS GENERAL ASSEMBLY. *International Covenant on Economic, Social and Cultural Rights of 16 December 1966* (993 UNTS 3).

UNITED NATIONS GENERAL ASSEMBLY. *International Covenant on Civil and Political Rights of 16 December 1996* (999 UNTS 171).

Van Bekhoven, J. "Public Participation as a General Principle in International Environmental Law: Its Current Status and Real Impact", *National Taiwan University Law Review*, Vol. 11, No. 2, 2016, pp. 219–260.

Wheatley, S. "Democratic Governance Beyond the State: The Legitimacy of Non-State Actors", in A. Peters, L. Koechlin, T. Förster and G. Fenner Zinkernagel (eds.) *Non-State Actors as Standards Setters*. Cambridge: Cambridge University Press, 2009, pp. 215–240.

Wolfrum, R. "Legitimacy of International Law from a Legal Perspective: Some Introductory Considerations", in R. Wolfrum and V. Röben (eds.) *Legitimacy in International Law*. Heidelberg: Springer, 2008, pp. 1–24.

Wolfrum, R. and V. Röben (eds.) *Legitimacy in International Law*. Heidelberg: Springer, 2008.

3 The participation of non-governmental actors in climate change law-making and governance

3.1 Introduction

When the Paris Agreement was adopted in 2015, the treaty was presented to the media as a major achievement, a turning point in climate talks. Indeed, the text represents the capstone of previously disappointing climate conferences,[1] during which States' delegations seemed no longer able to agree on how to face *the defining challenge of our age*.[2] For the first time in decades, the treaty is bringing together all nations of the world in tackling global warming, including major emitters of greenhouse gases (GHGs) such as the USA and China. According to some commentators,[3] part of this success was due to the multilevel structure and a rather hybrid legal form of the agreement.

The main goal of the treaty is to keep global temperature rise below 2 degrees Celsius above pre-industrial levels; it also aims to further limit the temperature increase to 1.5 degrees Celsius. For that, it builds on a rather unusual combination of hard and soft-law provisions,[4] to be implemented through national pledges and reviewed by a mechanism of international stocktaking. This notwithstanding, and although it carefully considers and builds on different national circumstances,[5] under the provisions of the Vienna Convention on the Law of Treaties, the Paris Agreement is a legally binding instrument.

1 Even if primarily referring to the role of the European Union, an account of the most recent climate talks is provided by X. RUIZ, "El Papel de la Unión Europea en las Negociaciones sobre el Cambio Climático", *UNISCI Journal*, Vol. 39, 2015, pp. 105–126.

2 As defined by the former UN Secretary General Ban Ki-Moon during the Bali climate change conference of 2007. Available at: https://www.theguardian.com/environment/2007/dec/12/bali.climatechange1 (Last access, 12 May 2018).

3 See, e.g., L. RAJAMANI, "The 2015 Paris Agreement: Interplay Between Hard, Soft and Non-Obligations", *Journal of Environmental Law*, Vol. 28, No. 2, 2016, pp. 337–358; A. SAVARESI, "The Paris Agreement: A New Beginning?", *Journal of Energy & Natural Resources Law*, Vol. 34, No. 1, 2016, pp. 16–26.

4 L. RAJAMANI, *Ibid.*

5 The agreement mainly relies on Nationally Determined Contributions (NDCs), these are the pledges and climate actions that all Parties are willing to pursue at the domestic level to achieve the objective of the Paris Agreement.

Adopted by the Conference of the Parties' decision 1/CP.21, the text consists of a 16 lines long Preamble and 29 articles regulating mitigation and adaptation ambitions, as well as issues related to finance, technology development and transfer, transparency, capacity-building and loss and damage.[6] In its final provisions, the agreement includes specific clauses for ratification, entry into force, dispute settlement and States' withdrawal.

This last provision was first triggered after the election of Donald Trump to the US Presidency, when the newly elected President announced the American pull-out from the Agreement in 2017.[7] Although the withdrawal, as regulated under article 28 of the treaty, was not effective before November 2020, it raised great international concern and opposition at the national level. Betsill has given an account of the reactions that followed Trump's announcement.[8] Different public statements voiced opposition to the US decision, and legal proceedings have been launched by US citizens due to federal inaction.[9] Especially remarkable is the number of domestic coalition of governors, mayors, business leaders and universities that declared their reiterated support to the Paris Agreement. For instance, the city of New York has already released a plan listing action that the municipality will apply to accelerate the reduction of GHGs, the first of its kind from any city in the world.[10] A study by Chan and others has reported that cities account for 70 per cent of global greenhouse gas emissions.[11] Echoing a 2014 United Nations Environmental Programme report that clearly assessed that collective national pledges would fall short in meeting the goals set in the Paris Agreement,[12] the authors have stressed the importance of NSAs' action at a different level to achieve, even improve, effective mitigation and adaptation objectives under the Agreement. This was also recognised in 2017 by the President of the COP23 in Bonn, at the start of the First Open Dialogue between Parties and Non-Party stakeholders.[13]

6 See, D. BODANSKY, J. BRUNNÉE and L. RAJAMANI, *International Climate Change Law*. Oxford: Oxford University Press, 2017, pp. 209–250.

7 The US State Department sent a formal communication to the United Nations on its withdrawal on the 4th of August 2017.

8 M. BETSILL, "Trump's Paris Withdrawal and the Reconfiguration of Global Climate Change Governance", *Chinese Journal of Populations Resources and Environment*, Vol. 15, No 3, 2017, pp. 189–191.

9 Juliana v. U.S. – Climate Lawsuit. The details of the case are available at: https://www.ourchildrenstrust.org/us/federal-lawsuit/ (Last access, 16 May 2018).

10 The plan is available at: http://www1.nyc.gov/office-of-the-mayor/news/634-17/nyc-delivers-first-ever-city-plan-meet-goals-the-paris-climate-agreement (Last access, 12 May 2018).

11 S. CHAN, H. VAN ASSELT, T. HALE and others, "Reinvigorating International Climate Policy: A Comprehensive Framework for Effective Nonstate Action", *Global Policy*, Vol. 6, No. 4, 2015, pp. 466–473.

12 UNITED NATIONS ENVIRONMENT PROGRAMME, *Climate Commitments of Subnational Actors and Business. A Quantitative Assessment of Their Emission Reduction Impact*. Nairobi: UNEP, 2015.

13 Open Dialogue Between the Parties and Non-Party Stakeholders. *Fijian Presidency's Report*, p. 2. Available at: https://cop23.com.fj/cop23-presidency-hosts-first-ever-open-dialogue-government-parties-non-state-actors/ (Last access, 16 May 2018).

In this context, the American example serves as an evidence of two phenomena. On the one hand, as it will be argued in the third section of this chapter, non-governmental entities or, as more broadly defined by decision 1/CP.21 "non-Party stakeholders", can effectively contribute to the achievement of the treaty goals. Especially in light of the structure of the Paris Agreement that, in contrast with the top-down logic of the Kyoto Protocol, is based on nationally determined contributions and favours a bottom-up approach to climate change, entities other than States are key to the achievement of the agreements' objective. On the other hand, and contradictorily, although the participation of these entities in climate governance is widely acknowledged and instrumental to the fulfilment of the climate regime, their participation in the law-making process is inconsistent, lacks systematisation and it is often subject to States' interests.[14] As the review of the UNFCCC system will show, several attempts have been made to enhance procedural rights in the climate context but often without contesting the state-driven nature of the intergovernmental process.[15]

3.2 Public participation in the climate change regime

From the outset, public participation has been recognised as paramount for climate change intergovernmental negotiations. Already during the negotiation of the UNFCCC, more than 100 NGOs participated as observers and this number has grown exponentially in recent years, with over 2000 accredited NGOs attending COP21. The same Guidelines for the participation of NGOs' representatives at meetings of the bodies of the UNFCCC read in the introductory section: "[NGOs] involvement allows vital experience, expertise, information and perspectives from civil society to be brought into the process to generate new insights and approaches".[16]

14 Several authors have reported on the exclusion of accredited observers from critical phases of climate negotiations, particularly during the COP15 of Copenhagen, but also in Paris at COP21. See, *supra* note 6 in Introduction. It should also be noted that in none of these occasions the non-compliance procedure established under the Aarhus Convention have been triggered, although both COPs have been held under European presidencies.

15 A report from the Secretariat of the Aarhus Convention on "Good practice and challenges for public participation in international forums" (2011) quotes the UNFCCC procedures as example of best practices in terms of public participation. However, it also notes pending challenges concerning the volume of participants, their capacity-building or limitations regarding the rights of freedom of expression and peaceful assembly of participants.

16 UNITED NATIONS FRAMEWORK CONVENTION ON CLIMATE CHANGE, *Guidelines for the Participation of Representatives of Non-Governmental Organizations at Meetings of the Bodies of the United Nations Framework Convention on Climate Change*. Bonn: UNFCCC, 2017. Available at: https://unfccc.int/files/parties_and_observers/ngo/application/pdf/guidelines_for_the_participation_of_ngos.pdf (Last access, 05 October 2018).

Indeed, the engagement with the public has helped establish new international standards, bringing distinct values and topics to the decision-making table. More recently, this has been the case with environmental NGOs and Indigenous Peoples' representatives who advanced a human rights agenda prior to and during the negotiation of the Paris Agreement. Or, again, when these same constituencies vindicated the imbalances created by market-based mechanisms such as the Reduce Emissions from Deforestation and from Forest Degradation (REDD+) programme.[17] Moreover, while the participation of the public in the climate change regime has manifested in all the forms that have been considered in the previous chapter of this work (inside and outside advocacy, knowledge sharing, etc.), different NGOs, civil society organisations and subnational actors have also gone a step further by directly taking initiatives to address this environmental problem.

In his work on authority in global climate governance, Thomas Hickmann has given an account of the growing importance of sub- and non-governmental actors[18] in governance arrangements that exceed the international climate regime. While the scholarly debate referred by the author varies in the understanding of hierarchical relationships existing between the different actors and institutions involved in this process, they all point to the fact that NSAs and NGOs are an integral and progressively more authoritative component of the institutional set(s)[19] developed to address climate change. As explained below, the same regime developed to tackle global warming has progressively moved towards including both public and private initiatives. While the core obligations of the UNFCCC, the Kyoto Protocol and the Paris Agreement inevitably fall on the nation states that have consented to them, the reach of climate change – which touches upon the regulation and management of a range of public and private activities as broad as energy, security and transportation – requires the partnership with stakeholders originating from different sectors and levels of government.

17 See, generally, S. DUYCK, S. JODOIN and A. JOHL (eds.) *Routledge Handbook of Human Rights and Climate Governance*. New York: Routledge, 2018.

18 T. HICKMANN, *Rethinking Authority in Global Governance: How Transnational Climate Initiatives Relate to the International Climate Regime*. Oxon: Routledge, 2016, p. 20.

19 Distinct approaches to climate change governance have been proposed by different authors, as a result of the complexity characterising and emerging from climate change. Keohane and Victor, for example, has coined the idea of "regime complexes", as a loosely coupled system of institutions aimed at governing climate change as opposed to a comprehensive and integrated regime. The idea of "policentricity" has been introduced by Ostrom in 2010 to identify a polycentric system of governance, in which different units and authorities have considerable independence in making norms within a specific domain. The more classical idea of multilevel governance has also been applied to this environmental problem. Finally, Savaresi has written on the issue of fragmentation of international law in relation to climate change, as a consequence of multiple international regimes conflicting or overlapping while addressing the same legal question.

Evidence of that is, *inter alia*, the private certification schemes developed under the Kyoto Protocol, the manifold and transnational initiatives created by private entities to meet the objective of the Paris Agreement (e.g. city networks and majors' coalitions), as well as the adaptation projects elaborated and implemented at the subnational level, which overall improve States' ability to tackle climate change. Finally, since the primary channel of influence for most NGOs is the realm of domestic politics, the bottom-up approach to climate change designed in the Paris Agreement assumes relevance since non-governmental influence may prove persuasive in keeping States' commitment in line with the objectives included in their NDCs and, more broadly, with the goal of the agreement.[20]

Under a more strictly normative perspective, subnational entities have also begun to fill important normative gaps. This is, for example, the case of many autonomous communities in Spain which, based on their regional competence on the environment[21] and on the principle of subsidiarity, have filled the regulatory gap left by the central government until 2017, when the Spanish State eventually developed a national Law on Climate Change and Energy Transition.[22] Most likely, similar developments will occur in the United States after the complete withdrawal of the USA from the Paris Agreement. If the elected nature of these subnational entities allows them to exercise a certain regulatory power, interesting and arguably more controversial is the recent practice of NGOs that have resorted to climate litigation to press legislators to promote regulatory actions or advocated for the promotion of more ambitious policy-and law-making against climate change. This is, as it will be detailed in Chapter 6, the case of the *Urgenda Foundation case.*

As a result, although it is not always easy to assess in concrete terms its influence, public participation undoubtedly is relevant to the creation, implementation and oversight of the climate change regime. In the light of its complex, global, cross-sectoral and intergenerational nature, the development, implementation and fulfilment of climate change law heavily relies on the contributions of the private sector, non-State inputs and subnational initiatives alike.

20 See, H. VAN ASSELT, "The Role of Non-State Actors in Reviewing Ambition, Implementation, and Compliance under the Paris Agreement", *Climate Law*, Vol. 6, 2016, pp. 91–108.

21 Article 148.1.9° of the Spanish Constitution allows the Autonomous Regions to assume statutory powers in the area of environmental protection. Based on this provision, the regions of Andalusia, Catalonia and the Valencian Community have adopted different strategies aimed at responding to the impacts of climate change in their territories. A compilation of the latter is available at the AdapteCCa.es platform, established to favour the exchange on climate change adaptation in Spain. Available at: http://www.adaptecca.es/administracion-autonomica-local/comunidades-autonomas (Last access, 9 May 2018).

22 For information on the law, see L. LÁZARO TOUZA, "Cambio climático en 2018: de la gobernanza climática global post Trump a España", *ARI 22*, 2018, pp. 1–7, at 5.

3.3 Progresses and setbacks in the application of the principle of public participation in International Climate Change Law-Making: from the UNFCCC to the Paris Agreement

3.3.1 The international climate change regime: An introduction

In his "Climate Change and State Consent", Christiano refers to the climate change regime creation as a universal treaty-making method.[23] This is the creation of a nearly universal treaty in the form of a framework convention where only aspirations, general principles and procedures are set and the development of more ambitious commitments is let to the negotiation of future implementing agreements. Such a broad context is likely to favour and result in a more inclusive decision-making process since Parties will only progressively deepen their ambitions. This is the idea that, since 1992, underpins the present climate change regime, which today consists of a UNFCCC and two subsequent implementing treaties, the Kyoto Protocol of 1997 and the Paris Agreement of 2015.

The architecture of the UNFCCC as a framework convention sharply reflects the political, scientific and economic complexity of dealing with climate change, as it just provides the structure for the development of the international climate change law, setting the foundations of this regime. The core of the text is composed of definitions, principles and objectives that States are required to follow in order to solve the climate change urgency (articles 1–6). The main objective of the UNFCCC is to stabilize the concentration of greenhouse gas emissions at a safe level (article 2) but neither a determined emissions level nor a clear time frame is set. The first articles of the convention include the general principles by which parties should be guided in taking effective actions against global warming. Among the most relevant ones are intergenerational equity, the precautionary principle and the principle of common but differentiated responsibilities. Particularly, the latter has represented an important and innovative achievement in the consideration of environmental matters.[24] Taking into account the different level of economic development among the contracting parties and thereby the divergent and historical responsibility that States hold in the production of greenhouse gases emissions,[25] all developed

23 T. CHRISTIANO, "Climate Change and State Consent", in J. MOSS (ed.) *Climate Change and Justice*. Cambridge: Cambridge University Press, 2015, pp. 17–38.

24 See, generally, P. BIRNE, A. BOYLE and C. REDGWELL, *International Law and the Environment*. Oxford: Oxford University Press, 2009.

25 Based on an implicit differentiation between developed and developing countries, a list of developed states and economies in transition is included into Annex I and Annex II of the Convention. In Annex I parties are generally called for assisting developing countries (non-Annex I parties) with technology transfer and funding and have more specific commitments regarding mitigation and reporting. In general terms, article 4 includes a series of possible actions that states may undertake to address the objective of the Convention (e. g. national and regional programmes, promotion and

countries are given a leading role in tackling climate change. Having been a guiding criterion in the implementation of the Kyoto Protocol, its relevance has been to some extent lessened with the adoption of the Paris Agreement that, in search for global ratification and homogeneous climate action, builds on the more realistic approach of NDCs.

Significantly, already during the first COP of Berlin in 1995, the provisions included in the UNFCCC were considered insufficient and needed to be further specified on the basis of the last report of the Intergovernmental Panel on Climate Change.[26] Therefore, building on article 17 of the Convention, the result of the COP 1 was the so-called *Berlin Mandate*, which exhorted the negotiation of more rigorous obligations and originated the Kyoto Protocol, adopted in 1997. Several new aspects were included in this Protocol. Primarily, the specific definition of the quantitative restrictions on emission for industrialised countries – included in Annex B of the Protocol – as well as the introduction of supplemental market-based mechanisms for emission reduction,[27] whereby the partnership with the private sector obtained a prominent role. A first commitment period (2008–2012) for all Parties was also defined, after which the Protocol has been revised and extended until 2020 through the Doha Amendment to the Kyoto Protocol (1997), although the latter has yet to enter into force.[28] Parallel to the renegotiation of the Protocol, a dialogue for the conclusion of a new legal agreement started among the UNFCCC Parties, which resulted in the conclusion of the Paris Agreement on the 12th of December 2015.[29]

Opinions differ on the effectiveness of the Kyoto Protocol. Despite the importance that this implementing agreement has had in converting the

---

cooperation in different research areas, exchange of relevant information, integration of climate change in national public policies, etc.) which will be then communicated and revised during the Conferences of the Parties.

26 The progressive building of a climate change regime is based on the best available scientific knowledge provided by the IPCC. Established in 1988, it provides assessments of climate change, its impacts and options for mitigation and adaptation.

27 Essentially three new *Flexibility Mechanisms* were elaborated: the Clean Development Mechanism (CDM), the Joint Implementation (JI) and the International Emission Trading Mechanism (IET) that have been at the centre of climate action as conceived until the Paris Conference.

28 As reported by the UNFCCC website, in March 2018 111 Parties have ratified the Amendment to the Kyoto Protocol against the 144 instruments of acceptance required for its entry into force. Available at: https://unfccc.int/process/the-kyoto-protocol/the-doha-amendment (Last access, 9 May 2018).

29 The Paris Agreement was adopted on the 12th of December 2015 as an outcome of the COP21 held in Paris, France, and entered into force on the 4th of November 2016. It consists of 29 articles and a Preamble that gives guidance in interpreting its objectives and provisions. Annexed to it is a decision adopted by the COP, which formally adopts the agreement and develops some technical aspects of the treaty. An Ad Hoc Working Group on the Paris Agreement has also been established to specify the rules, modalities and the content of the treaty which, in many cases, includes only very general provisions. As a result, the COP22 of Marrakech, Morocco, and the COP23 of Bonn, Germany, has been held to date among its Parties.

stabilisation targets included in the UNFCCC into quantitative emission reduction objectives for developed countries, a feeling of failure was triggered by the impossibility to count on the cooperation of key international actors. Not only China – a major world polluter – fell under the category of developing countries, thus not bound to particular reduction targets, but the USA withdrew from the Protocol shortly after its entry into force. After 2012, New Zealand, the Russian Federation, and Japan did not set new reduction targets and Canada eventually withdrew from the Protocol too. To avoid replication of such a situation, the preparation phase for COP21 marked the fundamental stages for the success of a new agreement, especially promoting a new bottom-up approach, completely alien to the previous Protocol. Since the COP19 of Warsaw in 2013, Parties were tasked with the preparation and submission of their "intended nationally determined contributions", forerunners of the NDCs that are today at the core of the Agreement reached in Paris. These are voluntary pledges related to mitigation and adaptation actions that all Parties intend to achieve over a determined amount of time.

This stressed how, as opposed to the Kyoto system – which imposed reduction commitments on developed countries – the Paris Agreement aimed at reaching a virtually universal acceptance, while adopting a broader approach to reduction commitments and establishing effective mechanisms for their review and progression.[30] Bodansky and others have detailed the hybrid architecture of the Agreement, "[...] in which bottom-up substance to promote participation is combined with a top-down process to promote ambition and accountability".[31]

Clearly, such a mechanism leaves a great deal of autonomy to each State – perhaps one of the reasons for its swift adoption – but Parties are nevertheless obliged to prepare, communicate and maintain their NDCs (article 4.2), and are as well subject to three different review mechanisms. In light of the agreement's transparency framework (article13), States are required to submit periodical reports on their emissions reduction and removal, together with information on the support they provide in terms of technology, finance and capacity-building measures to developing countries. An initial mechanism for implementation and compliance review is then set in article 15. Finally, the effectiveness of the overall agreement is to be reviewed every five years as part of a global stocktake, in which the collective progress made by all Parties towards the achievement of the treaty goal will be assessed. At the moment of writing, technical negotiations for establishing the rules that will govern the implementation of the Agreement (for example how to implement the transparency framework and the compliance review) are still ongoing. The

30 In this regard, no express reference is made to the principle of common but differentiated responsibilities. Rather, the agreement more often refers to the "different national circumstances" of its signatories.

31 D. BODANSKY, J. BRUNNÉE and L. RAJAMANI, *supra* note 6, at 214.

so-called Paris Rulebook was largely agreed during the COP24 of Katowice, Poland, but COP25 of Madrid has failed to conclude discussions on article 6 of the agreement, dealing with international carbon markets.

Meanwhile, the agreement institutes a series of advances: the mechanism for monitoring emissions' reductions and the compliance with national plans, the general relevance accorded to greater transparency, as well as the establishment of a principle of non-regression underscoring the reduction of greenhouse gases emissions of each Party. These are all aspects that, in a perspective of future implementation, leave ample room of manoeuvre to the Parties, but also open possibilities for non-governmental entities and other non-State actors to contribute to the effective review of the pledges made by States at the national and international level.

3.3.2 Public Participation in the Climate Change Regime: Institutional Arrangements

As a framework convention, the UNFCCC set the basic regulation for the participation of the public in climate change law-making. It is not surprising that, having been negotiated in parallel with the UN Conference on Environment and Development, the Convention welcomes and acknowledges the participation of representatives of the civil society through different procedural mechanisms.[32]

Primarily article 4(i), which makes explicit reference to the widest participation of the public, including that of non-governmental organisations, provides the legal basis for the application of Principle 10 in climate change law-making. This is a general commitment that applies to all the Parties. Whereas article 6(a) also relates to education, training and public awareness, its scope is confined to the national level and, as appropriate, to the sub-regional and regional levels. As a matter of fact, only article 7.6 further specifies how non-Parties stakeholders can engage in the intergovernmental process. The article established that any agency or body willing to be represented at the COP as an observer has to fulfil the following criteria:

(1) to be qualified in the matters covered by the Convention; and
(2) to have informed the Secretariat of its wish to be represented as an observer.

Finally, it states that any observer will be admitted unless at least one-third of the Parties present will object to its application, and more broadly indicate that the admission and participation of observers are subject to the Rules of Procedures to be adopted by the Conference of the Parties.

32 Already during the negotiation process for the Convention in 1991 different NGOs were accredited as observers.

This Rules of Procedure was negotiated in the first Conference of the Parties of 1995 but was eventually never adopted due to a controversial provision on majority voting. Nevertheless, this "Draft Rules" informs us on a range of different procedural aspects, including the participation of observers and the UNFCCC currently operates under them. In paragraph V, dedicated to observers, Draft Rules 6, 7 and 8 add little to what is already stated in the Convention. While article 7.1 directly mirrors article 7.6 of the Convention, the other provisions add that observers *may be represented at sessions of the Conference of the Parties as observers* (Rule 6.1) and that such observers may, *upon invitation of the President, participate without the right to vote in the proceedings of any session* (Rule 6.2) or *in the proceedings of any session in matters of direct concern to the body or agency they represent, unless at least one third of the Parties present at the session object* (Rule 7.2). Based on these dispositions, the Secretariat of the Convention has developed procedures for the admission of intergovernmental organisations (IGOs) and NGOs as observes. To be considered eligible, applicants are required to provide a statement of competence in the convention matter, a confirmation of independent juridical personality and confirmation of their non-profit status. More recently, the possibility for non-admitted observers to participate in side events and exhibition has also been established.

As the UNFCCC website summarises, there are three categories of participants at the UNFCCC meetings and conferences: representatives of Parties to the convention and observer States, members of the press and media and representatives of observer organisations. These are further divided into three categories: (1) the UN System and its Specialized Agencies; (2) Intergovernmental Organisations; and, most relevant for this research, (3) non-governmental organisations. Due to the rise in the number of observers' NGOs – there are currently more than 2000 admitted observers' NGOs – they have formed themselves into loose groups that are recognised under the convention as constituencies that mirror the nine major groups established in Agenda 21[33]: Business and industry NGOs; Environmental NGOs; Farmers and agricultural NGOs; Indigenous Peoples Organisations (IPOs); Local Government and municipal authorities; Research and independent NGOs; Trade union NGOs; Women and gender constituency and Youth NGOs.[34] Each of them has a Focal Point serving as a contact point for the UNFCCC Secretariat. Nasiritousi, Hjerpe, and Linnér have assessed the influence of single NGOs and specific constituencies in the UNFCCC process.[35]

33 Since 2016, the UNFCCC Secretariat has recognised three informal NGO groups: Faith Based Organisations (FBOs); Education and Capacity Building and Outreach NGOs (ECONGO) and Parliamentarians, although they do not enjoy the same privileges of an official constituency.

34 These constituencies are the reference groups of this research when it refers to NGOs and civil society organisations participating in international climate change governance.

35 N. NASIRITOUSI, M. HJERPE and L. B., LINNÉR, "The Roles on Non-State Actors in Climate Change Governance: Understanding Agency through Governance Profiles", *International Environmental Agreements: Politics, Law and Economics*, Vol. 16, No. 1, 2016, pp. 109–126.

Until the adoption of the Paris Agreement, the main channels for participation of NGOs consisted of the following actions:[36]

(1) Access to the conference venue, which allows observers' participation in public sessions and, at times, access to open-ended contact groups;
(2) Oral intervention during debates. With the growing number of admitted observers, the possibility to make joint constituencies' statements during plenary meetings has also been provided;
(3) Holding of bilateral meetings with government delegates and face to face lobbying, which is generally considered the most powerful way to influence law-making and inform delegations and deliberations;
(4) Development of position papers in response to call for information by negotiating bodies in between sessions. After a call for improved transparency and record from observers, most submissions presented by the constituencies are accessible on the UNFCCC website;
(5) The organisation of press conferences, side events and exhibition, which recently have been allocated increasing space and attention;
(6) The preparation of briefings with presiding officers and the Executive Secretary;
(7) The inclusion of NGOs' representatives into a national delegation, which provides more direct access to negotiators and the possibility to attend closed meetings. This is an often-applied practice with regard to Indigenous Peoples because of their specific conditions of *peoples* within a nation state.

It is nevertheless to be noted that neither the Draft Rules of Procedures nor the Guidelines for participation formalise or clearly establish how participation is to be carried out in climate conferences. As Oberthür has noted, formal rules define NGOs' participation in terms of what they are not allowed to do, namely voting, as opposed to what they can do.[37] As a consequence, not much clarity has been added to the content of the Framework Convention which, by definition, merely aims to give guidance on the issue.

On this, authors have expressed divergent views. Konrad has critically assessed the implementation of Principle 10 as regulated under the UNFCCC. The author notes that both the Draft Rules of Procedures and the Guidelines for representatives of non-governmental organisations are by far not as ambitious or comprehensive as those of the Aarhus Convention and the Almaty Guidelines, and proposes the revision of these Guidelines as a first step to avoid

36 Oberthür and others provide a detailed analysis of observers' participation in the climate change regime. See, S. OBERTHÜR, M. BUCK, S. MÜLLER and others (eds.) *Participation of Non-Governmental Organisations in International Environmental Governance: Legal Basis and Practical Experience*. Berlin: Ecologic-Institute for International and European Environmental Policy, 2003, at 128–135.

37 *Ibid*, at 128.

UNFCCC bodies discretion over the participation of the public.[38] In 2017, notwithstanding the adoption of revised Guidelines, their primarily administrative character has remained unchanged, which makes them something closer to a code of conduct. This notwithstanding, Riedel and Bodle have sustained in a recent publication on the Local Communities and Indigenous Peoples (LCIPs) Platform,[39] that the rather limited guidance provided in the Draft Rules of Procedures and the Guidelines, may be understood in the light of the need to provide flexibility to this process and find new format and modes of participation for non-Party stakeholders over time. While it is not the aim of this work to provide an answer to this debate, a half-way perspective is sustained by the author of this work. Certainly, from an institutional point of view, a great deal of procedures has been developed in order to accommodate the increasing number of non-Party stakeholders that have expressed an interest in participating in the climate change regime formation. While their content has added little clarity as to the question of who should legitimately participate and how participation should be exercised in the formation of a climate regime, informality has favoured flexibility and adjustments of the institutional architecture of the UNFCCC system. On the other hand, as will be exposed below, informality can also be counterproductive and hinder participation and therefore represent a critical aspect to be addressed when dealing with NGOs' participation in climate change law-making. Another characteristic that the UNFCCC practice reveals, is the largely remedial character with which the issue of participation has been considered. A piecemeal approach to participation has prevailed over a more ambitious reconsideration of the issue. As a result, informality has coexisted with periodical efforts by the Subsidiary Body for Implementation (SBI) and the Subsidiary Body for Scientific and Technological Advice (SBSTA) to structure NGOs' participation,[40] particularly after the dramatic rise of applicants observers and the complaints of already admitted NGOs.[41] The mentioned UNFCCC bodies especially addressed the issue of participation after COP15 in 2009, during which thousands of duly

38 C. KONRAD, "UNFCCC and the Aarhus Convention: An Analysis of Existing Rules", *Justice and Environment*, 2011, pp. 1–9. The following section further considers this, exploring how the Aarhus Convention provisions have been promoted in the climate change regime.

39 A. RIEDEL and R. BODLE, *Local Communities and Indigenous Peoples Platform – Potential Governance Arrangements under the Paris Agreement*. Denmark: Nordic Council of Ministers, 2018, at 19. Extensive reference to the Platform will be made in following section of this chapter.

40 Already between 2010 and 2011, the SBI placed the issue of enhancing the engagement with observers on its agenda. In this context, a workshop was convened in 2011 to discuss opportunities for improved engagement with observers. On the result of the meeting, see H. STEVENSON and J. S. DRYZEK, *Democratizing Global Climate Governance*. Cambridge: Cambridge University Press, 2014, p. 125.

41 Koivurova, Duyck and Heinämäki give further information on the objections raised by observers over time. See, T. KOIVUROVA, S. DUYCK and L. HEINÄMÄKI, "Climate Change and Human Rights", in E. J. HOLLO, K. KUVOLESI and M. MEHLING (eds.) *Climate Change and the Law*. Dordrecht: Springer, 2013, pp. 287–325.

accredited observers remained excluded from the conference due to logistical challenges, clearly revealing some of the problems affecting public participation in the present climate change regime.

3.3.3 The promotion of the Aarhus Convention in the Climate Change Regime

One of the above-mentioned efforts relates to attempts made by the bureaucracies of the Aarhus Convention and the UNFCCC to promote public participation in the context of climate change governance. Sébastien Duyck has assessed the role played by the Aarhus Convention and its bodies in the realisation of public participation in the UN climate change regime.[42] In his analysis, the author takes into consideration three ways in which bridges between the two legal regimes have been created: (1) the actions triggered by different stakeholders; (2) the initiatives taken by the Aarhus parties to promote the Convention's principles in the UNFCCC system; and finally (3) the institutional role played by the Secretariats of the Aarhus and the UNFCC Conventions.

A first link between the two regimes was created by the interventions of the members of the public during both the UNFCCC sessions and the Task Force and WGP meetings dedicated to the application of art. 3.7 in international contexts, recalled in Chapter 2 of this work.[43] The importance of the principles of the Aarhus Convention with regard to enhancing stakeholders' participation has been reiterated in the UNFCCC context during the oral interventions of civil society representatives. On several occasions, NGOs have voiced concerns about the obstacles faced in obtaining access to relevant information as well as to negotiating sessions. For example, during the COP15 of 2009, public participation was severely restricted by the Danish Presidency, which turned out unable to cope with the logistical challenges posed by an unprecedented level of attendance by civil society representatives. In this regard, it is worth remembering that the Arhus Convention also established a Compliance Mechanism under its article 15, where the public is given the possibility to report a breach of the treaty by one of its Parties. It seems reasonable to observe that the Mechanism would have provided an appropriate venue for the discussion of the problems raised by civil society representatives on this occasion. Interestingly, however, the Mechanism has never been triggered or used to report a violation of article 3.7 of the Aarhus Convention. Even after

42 This section will largely rely on the analysis made in 2015 by S. Duyck since, to the author's knowledge, this is the only study specifically addressing the implementation of art. 3.7 of the Aarhus Convention in the UNFCCC framework. See, S. DUYCK, S. "Promoting the Principles of the Aarhus Convention in International Forums: The Case of the UN Climate Change Regime", *Review of European Community & International Environmental Law*,Vol. 22, No. 4, 2015, pp. 123–137.

43 Reference to the work of the WGP is also found in S. KRAVCHENKO, "Procedural Rights as a Crucial Tools to Combat Climate Change", *Georgia Journal of International and Comparative Law*,Vol. 38, No. 3, 2010, pp. 614–648, p. 637.

the restriction to public participation occurred in 2009, 50 NGOs only suggested a breach of the Convention by Denmark in a joint statement. Since the complaint did not follow the formal procedures established under article 15, the case was finally dismissed and no assessment of the state of implementation of article 3.7 has been made by the Compliance Committee to date.[44] It is the author's view to consider that the mechanism has not been formally used because it would have been difficult to demonstrate the responsibility of a specific Party of the Aarhus Convention for the breach of article 3.7, and because the problems concerning participation have been subsequently discussed within the UNFCCC Subsidiary Body for Implementation.[45]

This notwithstanding, other Aarhus Convention institutions have served for the exchange of good practices and information among its Parties. Duyck reports that three of the Aarhus meetings addressing public participation have been dedicated to discussing its implementation in the UNFCCC. Those States that are contemporarily Aarhus signatories and Parties to the UNFCCC have had the chance to report on the actions undertaken to promote public participation, which mainly pointed to the practice of including civil society representatives at the domestic decision-making phase or in national delegations at the UNFCCC sessions. Further exchanges have occurred through the reports prepared by the convention's Parties to the Aarhus Convention Secretariat under article 10.2 and via the national communications presented by UNFCCC Parties under article 12 of the framework convention.

Finally, the interactions between the Secretariats of the two conventions have provided yet another opportunity to influence the implementation of public participation in the formulation of policies and law pertaining to climate change. Once again, this has primarily occurred thanks to the participation of representatives from the UNFCCC Secretariat in the Aarhus Task Force meetings on participation. Although no direct normative development has derived from this, the UNFCCC Secretariat has nevertheless promoted awareness over the relevance of the Aarhus provisions among the Parties of the framework convention, as well as voiced concerns whenever the rights of observers to the framework convention have been restricted, as in the case of the COP15. The maintenance of a sustained dialogue between the two international bureaucracies can therefore play a crucial role in upholding public participation in the climate context.

As a result, it is undeniable that the work of the Aarhus Task Force on public participation, as well as of the WGP, has provided its Parties with an opportunity to discuss the implementation of public participation in the international climate change regime. Such an exchange has been primarily

44 Ebbesson provides a brief review of the most relevant "jurisprudence" of the Committee until 2015. See, J. EBBESSON, "Principle 10. Public Participation", in J. E. VIÑUALES (ed.) *The Rio Declaration on Environment and Development*. Oxford: Oxford University Press, 2015, pp. 288–309.

45 T. KOIVUROVA, S. DUYCK and L. HEINÄMÄKI, *supra* note 41.

initiated due to the concerns raised by the observers to the UNFCCC system and progressively endorsed by the UNFCCC Secretariat. The participation of those States that are parties to both conventions in the Task Force meetings, underlines their general commitment to the provisions of the Aarhus Convention although their reports have informed on the seldom inclusion of civil society representatives in national delegations and that, for most of the time, the engagement with the public has occurred at the domestic level. Therefore, while the continued exchange between the Parties of both conventions and their institutions is a good practice, to date this has contributed little to the promotion of the Aarhus Convention principles beyond the UNECE region, pursuant to its article 3.7. In fact, as little as 40 UNFCCC Parties are simultaneously signatories of the Aarhus Convention. This notwithstanding, the adoption of the Escazú Agreement on Public Participation is a synonym of the growing awareness towards public participation beyond the European context, which will hopefully create new momentum for reconsidering the scale, scope and exercise of public participation in international forums.

3.3.4 Public participation after the adoption of the Paris Agreement

Further to what reported above, the renegotiation of the Kyoto Protocol opened the way to new opportunities for the Parties to the UNFCCC and non-State actors to cooperate towards the development of multilateral climate action. As a result, the participation of non-Party stakeholders in this UN framework gained momentum before and during the negotiation of the Paris Agreement.

For example, in 2014 the UN climate conference in Lima launched the Non-State Actor Zone for Climate Action (NAZCA) portal, an online platform aimed at tracking and accelerating cooperative climate actions between States and non-State actors. Likewise, before the celebration of the COP21, the Peruvian and French governments initiated the Lima-Paris Action Agenda (LPAA) for scaling up multilateral climate actions, with the support of the UN Secretary General and the UNFCCC Secretariat. Although relevant because they gradually formalise the fundamental and transnational contribution made to climate governance by different NSAs and NGOs, these initiatives do not directly bear on the participation of the public in international climate change law-making. If anything, they are another evidence of the imbalanced position of non-State actors in a system that alternates the support and promotion of NSAs' actions, to their exclusion from the law-making process by virtue of their status as mere observers.

Nevertheless, other interesting developments have occurred after the conclusion of the Paris Agreement, which in article 12 expressively reads: "Parties shall cooperate in taking measures, as appropriate, to enhance climate change education, training, public awareness, public participation and public access to information, recognizing the importance of these steps with respect to enhancing actions under this Agreement".[46] For example, the decision accompanying the text adopted in Paris specifically recognised the value of indigenous peoples' knowledge in responding to climate change. A similar reference is made in both the Preamble (paragraph 11) and article 7.5 of the agreement. These acknowledgements, paired with the advocacy exercised by the International Indigenous Peoples' Forum on Climate Change (IIPFCC) – the caucus of Indigenous Peoples at the UNFCCC – and more prominently by the United Nations Permanent Forum on Indigenous Issues (UNPFII),[47] led to the establishment of the Local Communities and Indigenous Peoples Platform in 2015. The overall purpose of the Platform is to foster the exchange of experiences and best practices on mitigation and adaptation in the climate context. The operationalisation of the Platform has been carried out in subsequent COPs and has been the subject of a multi-stakeholder dialogue at SBSTA in which knowledge, climate change policies and actions, and capacity for engagement in the UNFCCC process also emerged as its functions. Up to the moment of writing, the operationalisation of the Platform is still ongoing. However, its institution has already raised important questions. During COP23, for example, the IIPFCC called for three main principles to be adopted for the participation of IPs in the Platform, among them, the full and effective participation of IPs – that expressively echoes the status held by IPOs in the Arctic Council – and an equal standing between IPs and the Parties to the UNFCCC and the Paris Agreement.

As Riedel and Bodle have pointed out, beyond the form and governance structure that the Platform will assume, its establishment touches upon a number of sensitive topics.[48] Significantly improving the participation of a specific constituency, as in the case of IPOs, could set a precedent for other non-Party stakeholders. While the development of the LCIPs Platform points to the necessary recognition of the status of IPs as rights-holders under international law,[49] and as such has been recognised by other observers,[50] undoubtedly the process represents an experience on which new arrangements for NGOs participation may be drawn, especially in the case of more marginalised groups or of those whose rights are – and will likely be – disproportionally impaired by climate change. As this book will argue, the status of civil society's members as

46 Paris Agreement, art. 12

47 A review of the advocacy exercised by indigenous peoples in the climate change context is available in B. POWLESS, "The Indigenous Rights Framework and Climate Change", in S. DUYCK, S. JODOIN and A. JOHL, *supra* note 17, at 213–221.

48 A. RIEDEL and R. BODLE, *supra* note 39, at 36.

49 In the light, for example, of the United Nations Declaration on the Rights of Indigenous Peoples.

50 The UNFCCC Constituencies Joint submission on the Local Communities and Indigenous Peoples Platform of May 2017 reads in paragraph 9: "Given the unique rights and position of Indigenous Peoples, we call for the establishment of a platform that promotes indigenous knowledge and the participation of Indigenous Peoples in the UNFCCC process in a manner that is specific only to this constituency". Available at: http://unfccc.int/files/parties_observers/submissions_from_observers/application/pdf/887.pdf (Last access, 9 May 2018).

rights-holders under international law, could also be at the basis of improved procedural rights for NSAs and NGOs, provided that the latter are legitimately standing for the individuals and interests that they claim to represent.

Another positive improvement has occurred in relation to women, whose rights are recalled in the Preamble of the Paris Agreement, as well as in article 7.5 and 11.2 of the treaty. The UN Climate Gender Action Plan (GAP) has been approved, in order to integrate a gender perspective into national climate policies and, notably, "to achieve and sustain the full, equal and meaningful participation of women in the UNFCCC process".[51] Although the terms of its implementation are still unclear, actions under the Plan should include, *inter alia*, increased access for women to international climate negotiations and specific training programmes.

About other non-Parties stakeholders and their engagement at the intergovernmental level, the negotiation of the Paris Agreement has put back on the agenda the issue of public participation. Similar to what occurred in 2009, several negotiating sessions remained closed to observers at a very early stage and limited opportunities to follow the negotiations were provided for civil society representatives.[52] In response to the concerns raised by observers, and as encouraged by the SBI at its forty-sixth session, the Parties agreed to address the issue considering possibilities to enhance their participation. On this premise, the First Open Dialogue between Party and Non-Party stakeholders was held in 2017 during COP23. In the application of the Talanoa tradition,[53] nearly 50 Parties and a broad cross-section of non-Parties stakeholder members to all constituencies gathered to discuss two main topics: (1) the enhancement and implementation of NDCs, with the aim to create greater collaboration between Parties and Non-Parties stakeholders at the national level; and (2) the enhancement of observers' access to and participation in formal meetings.

Already proposed in a report of the SBI to enhance the participation of the public in the climate process, the dialogue is expected to continue in future COPs. Despite this important development, it is also fundamental to note that the decision of the SBI mandating the dialogue expressively reasserts the state-driven nature of the UNFCCC process.[54] In other words, although the

51 A thorough analysis of the role of women in the climate change regime and of the steps that brought to the establishment of the GAP is provided in T. PRIOR and L. HEINÄMÄKI, "The Rights and Role of Indigenous Women in The Climate Change Regime", *Arctic Review on Law and Politics*, Vol. 8, 2017, pp. 193–221.

52 M. DOELLE, "The Paris Agreement: Historic Breakthrough or High Stakes Experiment?", *Climate Law*, Vol. 6, 2016, pp. 1–20.

53 The Talanoa tradition has been introduced by the Fijian Presidency during the COP23 in Bonn and refers to a tradition of thoughtful, respectful and productive contributions among different parties.

54 The decision FCCC/SBI/2017/7 reads at paragraph 119: "The SBI identified opportunities to further enhance the openness, transparency and inclusiveness of the effective engagement of non-Party stakeholders. [...] Encouraging future Presidencies, subject to the availability of resources, to explore ways to enable admitted NGO constituencies to have an open dialogue with Parties,

dialogue represents an opportunity for further engaging with non-Party stakeholders, and is as such a much-welcomed improvement of the UNFCCC system, this is not aimed at opening the decision-making process to NSAs or NGOs. The decision- and law-making process may be opened to the public, but only by means that do not challenge the authority of States as final decision-makers in international law. As underlined by van Bekhoven, "[...] giving full and unconditional effect to public participation provisions may impact State sovereignty and governance and existing institutions and structures of power that States are not willing to accept".[55]

3.4 Concluding remarks

A brief analysis of the contributions that non-governmental representatives are able to make to international climate change law, has shown the importance of public participation in these intergovernmental processes. Since climate change governance entails the regulation of different sectors on a multilevel scale and the undertaking of transnational climate actions, public participation has proved relevant to effective law-making and enforcement. It follows that, in the light of the widely recognised importance attached to non-State entities and transnational actions in the climate governance context, their participatory rights and duties in intergovernmental decision-making should be clearly stated and their participation be a constant of climate negotiation. Instead, a piecemeal approach to public participation has prevailed in the climate change regime so far.

As sustained by several authors, this is meant to provide a more flexible context in which public participation can be progressively scaled up. Notwithstanding this, the lack of a coherent and systematic approach to participation has at time impaired the rights of the public to participate in climate change law-making. Undoubtedly, several improvements have occurred in recent years as a result of the dialogue initiated between those States that are contemporarily signatories of the Aarhus Convention and the UNFCCC regimes, the Conventions Secretariat and as a result of the work initiated by the SBI. Yet, NGOs are still prevented from being decision-makers in international climate change law. In light of this, the dialogue initiated on how to enhance the participation of observers, started as a result of the exclusion of NGOs from the Paris conference, is a timely opportunity to provide non-Parties stakeholders with a new role in climate change law-making.

---

whereby agenda setting as well as programming of the dialogue are conducted jointly among the admitted NGO constituencies, the Presidency, the Bureau and the secretariat as appropriate, on the understanding that any outcomes of such a dialogue should have persuasive value only, respecting the Party-driven nature of the UNFCCC process".

55 J.VAN BEKHOVEN, "Public Participation as a General Principle in International Environmental Law: Its Current Status and Real Impact", *National Taiwan University Law Review*, Vol. 11, No. 2, 2016, pp. 219–260, at 250.

Bibliography

Betsill, M. "Trump's Paris Withdrawal and the Reconfiguration of Global Climate Change Governance", *Chinese Journal of Populations Resources and Environment*, Vol. 15, No 3, 2017, pp. 189–191.

Birne, P., Boyle, A. and C. Redgwell. *International Law and the Environment*. Oxford: Oxford University Press, 2009.

Bodansky, D., Brunnée, J. and L. Rajamani. *International Climate Change Law*. Oxford: Oxford University Press, 2017, pp. 209–250.

Chan, S., Van Asselt, H., Hale, T. And Others. "Reinvigorating International Climate Policy: A Comprehensive Framework for Effective Nonstate Action", *Global Policy*, Vol. 6, No. 4, 2015, pp. 466–473.

Christiano, T. "Climate Change and State Consent", in J. Moss (ed.) *Climate Change and Justice*. Cambridge: Cambridge University Press, 2015, pp. 17–38.

Duyck, S. "Promoting the Principles of the Aarhus Convention in International Forums: The Case of the UN Climate Change Regime", *Review of European Community & International Environmental Law*, Vol. 22, No. 4, 2015, pp. 123–137.

Duyck, S., Jodoin, S. and A. Johl (eds.) *Routledge Handbook of Human Rights and Climate Governance*. New York: Routledge, 2018.

Hickmann, T. *Rethinking Authority in Global Governance. How Transnational Climate Initiatives Relate to the International Climate Regime*. Oxon, NY: Routledge, 2016.

Koivurova, T., Duyck, S. and L. Heinämäki. "Climate Change and Human Rights", in E. J. Hollo, K. Kuvolesi and M. Mehling (eds.) *Climate Change and the Law*. Dordrecht: Springer, 2013, pp. 287–325.

Konrad, C. "UNFCCC and the Aarhus Convention. An Analysis of Existing Rules", *Justice and Environment*, 2011, pp. 1–9.

Kravchenko, S. "Procedural Rights as a Crucial Tools to Combat Climate Change", *Georgia Journal of International and Comparative Law*, Vol. 38, No. 3, 2010, pp. 614–648.

Lázaro Touza, L. "Cambio climático en 2018: de la gobernanza climática global post Trump a España", *ARI*, Vol. 22, 2018, pp. 1–7.

Nasiritousi, N., Hjerpe, M. and L. B. Linnér, "The Roles on Non-State Actors in Climate Change Governance: Understanding Agency through Governance Profiles", *International Environmental Agreements: Politics, Law and Economics*, Vol. 16, No. 1, 2016, pp. 109–126.

Oberthür, S., Buck, M., Müller, S. And Others (eds.) *Participation of Non-Governmental Organisations in International Environmental Governance: Legal Basis and Practical Experience*. Berlin: Ecologic-Institute for International and European Environmental Policy, 2003.

Powless, B. "The Indigenous Rights Framework and Climate Change", in S. Duyck, S. Jodoin and A. Johl (eds.) *Routledge Handbook of Human Rights and Climate Governance*. New York: Routledge, 2018, pp. 213–221.

Prior, T. and L. Heinämäki. "The Rights and Role of Indigenous Women in The Climate Change Regime", *Arctic Review on Law and Politics*, Vol. 8, 2017, pp. 193–221.

Rajamani, L. "The 2015 Paris Agreement: Interplay Between Hard, Soft and Non-Obligations", *Journal of Environmental Law*, Vol. 28, No. 2, 2016, pp. 337–358.

Riedel, A. and R. Bodle. *Local Communities and Indigenous Peoples Platform – Potential Governance Arrangements under the Paris Agreement*. Denmark: Nordic Council of Ministers, 2018.

Ruiz, X. "El Papel de la Unión Europea en las Negociaciones sobre el Cambio Climático", *UNISCI Journal*, Vol. 39, 2015, pp. 105–126.

Savaresi, A. "The Paris Agreement: A New Beginning?", *Journal of Energy & Natural Resources Law*, Vol. 34, No. 1, 2016, pp. 16–26.

Stevenson, H. and J. S. Dryzek, *Democratizing Global Climate Governance*. Cambridge: Cambridge University Press, 2014.

UNITED NATIONS ENVIRONMENT PROGRAMME. *Climate Commitments of Subnational Actors and Business. A Quantitative Assessment of Their Emission Reduction Impact*. Nairobi: UNEP, 2015.

UNITED NATIONS FRAMEWORK CONVENTION ON CLIMATE CHANGE. *Guidelines for the Participation of Representatives of Non-Governmental Organizations at Meetings of the Bodies of the United Nations Framework Convention on Climate Change*. Bonn: UNFCCC, 2017. Available at: https://unfccc.int/files/parties_and_observers/ngo/application/pdf/guidelines_for_the_participation_of_ngos.pdf.

Van Asselt, H. "The Role of Non-State Actors in Reviewing Ambition, Implementation, and Compliance under the Paris Agreement", *Climate Law*, Vol. 6, 2016, pp. 91–108.

Van Bekhoven, J. "Public Participation as a General Principle in International Environmental Law: Its Current Status and Real Impact", *National Taiwan University Law Review*, Vol. 11, No. 2, 2016, pp. 219–260.

Part II

A case study on Arctic indigenous peoples

4 Non-governmental actors and a changing climate

Learning from Arctic indigenous peoples

4.1 Introduction

In a previous chapter, this research has detailed the characteristics of the recently established Local Communities and Indigenous Peoples Platform as a rather advanced channel for the participation of local and indigenous communities in the international climate change law-making process. Although a final judgement on its effectiveness will only be possible after its complete operationalisation, it is interesting to note that one of the main objectives it aims at achieving is the recognition of an equal standing between Indigenous Peoples and State parties in the framework of climate negotiations. This, in turn, is nothing less than a reflection of the status of Permanent Participants that Arctic indigenous peoples enjoy within the Arctic Council, the main intergovernmental forum devoted to the governance of the Arctic region.[1]

To be sure, in recent decades Arctic IPs have been at the forefront of regional and international efforts to revert global warming. Indeed, it is in the polar regions where the increase in global temperatures has been most pronounced worldwide, to the extent that the South and North poles have become the symbols and barometers of these climate alterations.[2] While major warmings of the Antarctic peninsula are capturing international headlines,[3] the

1 As detailed in the third chapter of this work, after the institution of the LCIPs Platform, the IIP-FCC called for three main principles to be adopted for the participation of IPs in the Platform. Among them is the full and effective participation of IPs, which expressively echoes the status held by Indigenous Peoples Organisations in the Arctic Council. In fact, as reported by Heinämäki, already during the Seventh Session of the PFII, the Arctic Caucus – formed by the Sámi Council and the ICC – required the creation of a reserved seat for IPs at the UNFCCC negotiations. Thus, the transposal of the Arctic model to other fora of decision-making has often been advocated by Arctic IPs. See, L. HEINÄMÄKI, *The Right to Be a Part of Nature – Indigenous Peoples and the Environment*. Rovaniemi: Lapland University Press, 2010, p. 74.

2 S. DUYCK, "Which Canary in the Coalmine? The Arctic in the International Climate Change Regime", in T. KOIVUROVA, G. ALFREDSSON and W. HASANAT (eds.) *The Yearbook of Polar Law, Volume 4*. Leiden, Boston: Brill, 2012, pp. 583–617.

3 See, e.g., M. TAYLOR, "Antarctic Ice Melting Faster Than Ever, Studies Show", *The Guardian*, 13 June 2018. Available at: https://www.theguardian.com/environment/2018/jun/13/antarctic-ice-melting-faster-than-ever-studies-show (Last access, 22 August 2019).

loss of sea ice in the Arctic is likely to have global repercussions on sea levels and precipitation patterns, but also on the likelihood of the region to be used for the exploitation and transportation of different resources.[4]

Therefore, it comes as no surprise that the inhabitants of the Arctic region[5] – whose livelihoods and identities are largely dependent on the use of ice and ice-related resources, as well as on the exercise of traditional practices – have been among the most vocal advocates in the fight against climate change regionally, transnationally and internationally. As this chapter aims to show, this has partially been the result of a generalised recognition of indigenous' rights under international law,[6] but also a consequence of their transnational organisation and empowerment within the Arctic Council, where these populations enjoy a high degree of representation and participation.

4.2 Arctic Indigenous Peoples: main features, impacts derived from climate change and transnational organisation

4.2.1 Indigenous Peoples of the Arctic, an overview

According to the second *Arctic Human Development Report* of 2014, today 4 million people live in the Arctic, among which roughly ten percent are Arctic indigenous peoples.[7] Approximately 155,000 Inuit live in Alaska,

4 See, e.g., J. WATTS, "Arctic's Strongest Sea Ice Break Up for First Time on Record", *The Guardian*, 21 August 2018. Available at: https://www.theguardian.com/world/2018/aug/21/arctics-strongest-sea-ice-breaks-up-for-first-time-on-record (Last access, 22 August 2019).

5 There are no indigenous peoples living in Antarctica, and human settlement in this region are confined to seasonal research expeditions.

6 A fundamental recognition of indigenous peoples' rights occurred in 2007 with the adoption of the United Nations Declaration on the Rights of Indigenous Peoples (UNDRIP, 2007). Although this is not a formal binding instrument under international law, most of its provisions are today endorsed by a majority of UN Member States and have been referred by national and international courts in the adjudication of cases concerning the rights of IPs, to the point that several authors have been discussing on whether its key provisions could be considered as international customary law. See, on this point, S., G. BARNABAS, "The Legal Status of the United Nations Declaration on the Rights of Indigenous Peoples (2007) in Contemporary International Human Rights Law", *International Human Rights Law Review*, Vol. 6, 2017, pp. 242–261. See also the work and conclusions of the ILA Committee on the Rights of Indigenous Peoples as reported in D. S. DOROUGH, "Our Homeland. Arctic Indigenous Peoples' Perspectives on Non-Arctic States", in A. SHIBATA, L. ZOU, N. SELLHEIM and M. SCOPELLITI (eds.) *Emerging Legal Orders in the Arctic: The Role of non-Arctic Actors.* New York: Routledge, 2019, pp. 69–90, at 84–85.

7 T. HELENIAK, "Arctic Populations and Migration", in J. NYMAND LARSEN and G. FONDAHL (eds.) *Arctic Human Development Report. Regional Processes and Global Linkages.* Copenhagen: Nordic Council of Ministers, 2014, pp. 53–103, at 53. It seems important to remember here that indigenous peoples represent about half of the total population in Canada, as well as the majority of the population in Greenland.

Canada, Greenland and Russia; 55,000 Athabaskans and Gwich'in people inhabit Alaska and Canada; 15,000 Aleut reside in different territories of Alaska and Russia, and other 250,000 members of different indigenous groups live in northern Russia.[8] Finally Sámi, who are the only native people recognised within continental Europe, live across the territories of Norway, Finland and Sweden, as well as in the Kola Peninsula of Russia.

These are rural and nomadic communities that mostly subsist on farming, fishing, reindeer herding and hunting, holding a unique knowledge and expertise in the management of natural resources and of their ancestral territories. Arctic indigenous peoples have also acquired control over different natural resources in the region[9] and are progressively developing an entrepreneurial spirit, especially in those sectors like the textile, the art or food industries, in which it is possible to promote their cultures and identities internationally.[10]

Yet, indigenous peoples of the North are not exempt from the hurdles that affect most indigenous peoples worldwide, including disputes over land and resource ownership, or the alternatively conflicting relationships with newcomers.[11] Indeed, the legacy of the colonialist era in the region is still reflected in the manifold social problems that affect large portions of these populations: violence, alcohol abuse and high rates of suicide, among others. As for other indigenous peoples of the world, since the 19th century, Arctic IPs have been assimilated to the values and customs introduced by the European colonisers, who brought to the region the ideas of sovereignty and statehood. Although justified in legal terms by the doctrine of discovery, these concepts and legal structures were completely unknown to the first Northern inhabitants.[12] Their previously autonomous ways of living were suddenly permeated with an invasive governmental structure. This, in turn, has contributed to the development of a sense of estrangement that, at least to some extent, persists today.

8 M. BYERS, *International Law and the Arctic*. Cambridge: Cambridge University Press, 2014, p. 218.

9 This is the case of Greenland, in which almost the 90% of the population is of Inuit origins. As a result of the Home rule of 1979 Greenlandic Inuit people obtained self-government which, as extended by a referendum held in 2008, entitled the population to a right to extract natural resources. See, on this, P. STEINBERG, J. TASCH, H. GERHARDT and A. KEUL, *Contesting the Arctic. Rethinking Politics in the Circumpolar North*. London: I.B.Tauris, 2015.

10 As in the case of the book *EALLU – Food, Knowledge and How We Have Thrived on the Margins*, recently awarded at the 2018 Gourmand World Cookbook Awards. K. STEPHEN, "Arctic Indigenous Cookbook Wins Gourmand World Cookbook Award", *High North News*, 30 May 2018. Available at: http://www.highnorthnews.com/arctic-indigenous-cookbook-wins-gourmand-world-cookbook-award/. (Last access, 22 August 2018).

11 See, generally, K. HUSSAIN and A. PETRÉTEI (eds.) *Understanding the Many Faces of Human Security: Perspectives of Northern Indigenous Peoples*. Leiden: Brill Nijhoff, 2016.

12 This is the doctrine aimed at justifying the occupation and acquisition of newly discovered lands under international law. To date, however, the doctrine largely converges on considering unwarrantable the acquisition of a territory in breach of the right to self-determination. See, on these topics, A. CASSESE, *Self-Determination of Peoples. A Legal Reappraisal*. Cambridge: Cambridge University Press, 1995.

Nonetheless, these indigenous peoples are also keeping the pace of a fast-changing Arctic and adapting to an increasingly globalised region, no longer perceived as *terra nullius*.[13]

Given the context of increasing globalisation, indigenous people are less and less living in a condition of isolation and their prosperity and cultural survival are closely linked to their resilience and adaptability skills. The advent of urbanisation, the competition for natural resources and the expansion of tourism in the Arctic are but a few of the challenges that indigenous peoples have to cope with if they are to maintain their identity as peoples while developing new and hybrid ones. Most of these challenges are caused or at least amplified by the dynamics of climate change, which has notoriously and negatively affected the Arctic region in recent decades.

4.2.2 Arctic Indigenous Peoples and the impacts of climate change in the Arctic

With the publication of the *Arctic Climate Impact Assessment Report* in 2004, the effects of climate change on the Arctic became known internationally. This seminal work, which also brought the Arctic region to the attention of the IPCC, assessed the impacts of warming temperatures on socio-economic conditions in the region.[14] A unique feature of the report – as it will be recalled later on – is the direct involvement and participation of Arctic IPs in its elaboration and drafting. In fact, an entire section of the document is devoted to indigenous communities.[15]

What bonds together different indigenous people around the world is the intrinsic relationship between their livelihood and nature. The lands and natural environments in which IPs live, hunt or gather sustain their culture and are essential to the maintenance and transmission of their traditions. This is no exception to the indigenous peoples living in the Arctic, who primarily depend on using the resources of Arctic lands and sea. Much to Arctic IPs' dismay, however, climate change is having dramatic impacts on the Arctic environment. Rising temperatures are first of all affecting the characteristics of permafrost and ice, making it thinner and less stable. Seasonal temperature and the quality of snow are also changing, contributing to the migration of animals as well as to the emergence of alien species. On the other hand, the possibility

13 See, on the Arctic as a globally embedded region, K. KEIL and S. KNECHT (eds.) *Governing Arctic Change: Global Perspectives*. London: Palgrave Macmillan, 2017.

14 For a broader consideration of the impacts of climate change on indigenous peoples, see, R. S. ABATE and E. A. KRONK WARNER, "Commonality Among Unique Indigenous Communities: An Introduction to Climate Change and its Impacts on Indigenous Peoples", in R., S. ABATE and E. A. KRONK WARNER (eds.) *Climate Change and Indigenous Peoples: The Search for Legal Remedies*. Cheltenham: Edward Elgar, 2013, pp. 3–18.

15 See, S. J. HASSOL, *Impacts of a Warming Arctic: Arctic Climate Impact Assessment*. Cambridge: Cambridge University Press, 2004, p. 92.

of extinction of some species is increased by the shrink of the marine habitat. As the distribution of animals is changing and travelling on ice becomes more dangerous, access to food also gets harder. This has negative effects on Arctic IPs' diet, which largely relies on plants and animals found in ice-covered areas. The emergence of new diseases, for example diabetes or poisoning, have also been reported to be increasingly widespread.[16] Similarly, skin cancer and immune system disorders are heightened by the increase in temperatures and intensity of the sun. Being traditionally coastal communities, the recession of ice has further impacted Arctic indigenous peoples' way of living. This is the case of those indigenous that have been relocated from the coasts to in lands. Unable to harvest marine mammals in remote and eroded coastal areas, these peoples are obliged to rapidly adapt to new living conditions, reinventing their social and economic practices. Yet, it has been noticed by these same populations that climate change is occurring faster than indigenous knowledge can adapt, which increases their vulnerability to its impacts. Finally, the retreat of ice and poor snow quality affects indigenous peoples in their housing conditions too.

Therefore, climate change represents for these populations a major pattern of change which, by influencing already new socio-economic dynamics and accentuating them through alterations of the natural environment, has in many cases led to their migration and displacement.[17] Faced with these challenges, the largest indigenous groups of the region have relied on their transnational organisation to reciprocally support their work on climate change and other environmental problems at the local, regional and international level.

4.2.3 The Transnational Organisation of Arctic Indigenous Peoples

With the decolonisation of the Arctic, the indigenous peoples of the region summed to the broader indigenous movement that was prising the abandonment of the paternalistic and assimilation policies that had characterised colonialism in Europe and abroad. During the 1970s, the Arctic's indigenous peoples started their journey towards the recognition of their political, social and economic rights primarily – but not exclusively – enshrined in the right to self-determination. Distant from a claim of complete independence, the latter entails the achievement of self-government within existing States, including the possibility to participate in political processes, local decision-making and the ownership over natural resources. The former UN Special Rapporteur on the Rights of Indigenous Peoples, James Anaya, has qualified the right to

16 S. TORRECUADRADA GARCÍA-LOZANO and R., M. FERNÁNDEZ EGEA, "Environmental Challenges for Arctic Peoples", in E. CONDE and S. SÁNCHEZ IGLESIAS (eds.) *Global Challenges in the Arctic Region*. London: Routledge, 2017, pp. 236–253.

17 See, on this, N. ARENA HIDALGO, "Climate Change Induced Displacement: Migration as an Adaptation Strategy also in the Arctic?" in *Ibid*, pp. 254–277.

self-determination as a foundational one, essential for the enjoyment of IPs' human rights.[18]

While the achievement of these objectives certainly requires the ability to influence national policy- and decision-making, the practice of Arctic indigenous peoples has contemporarily relied on diverse strategies, all aimed at furthering their political interests.[19] Their constitution as political actors in the region (*polities*) or their transnational organisation and participation in the AC and UNPFII (United Nations Permanent Forum on Indigenous Issues) are just two examples of how Arctic IPs have aimed at influencing the development of regional and international law which, in turn, will more likely force the advancement of laws and policies related to indigenous rights at the national level.[20] Monika Tennberg, for instance, has underlined how the establishment of the UNPFII has contributed to the reconfiguration of power relations between States and IPs internationally.[21] Likewise, but referring to the practice of Inuit peoples and to the emergence of the Inuit Circumpolar Council (ICC), Jessica Shadian has extensively written on how Arctic IPs have challenged the westphalian concept of sovereignty.[22] When compared with the possibilities and conditions of other and arguably larger indigenous populations, Arctic IPs enjoy more favourable conditions at the national level too.[23] To the exception of the Russian Federation, where Arctic IPs have faced governmental opposition for the same time,[24] it seems fair to recall here that the condition of empowerment that most Arctic IPs enjoy at the regional and international

18 United Nations Human Rights Council, *Report of the Special Rapporteur on the situation of human rights and fundamental freedoms of indigenous peoples, James Anaya*, 15 July 2009, par. 41 (UN Doc. A/HRC/12/34).

19 As made clear by Loukacheva, to which degree political rights are granted to indigenous peoples ultimately is and depends on a State decision. N. LOUKACHEVA, "Arctic Indigenous Peoples' Internationalism: In Search of a Legal Justification", *Polar Record*, Vol. 45, No. 23, 2009, pp. 51–58.

20 See T. KOIVUROVA and A. STEPIEN, "How International Law Has Influenced the National Policy and Law Related to Indigenous Peoples in the Arctic", *Waikato Law Review*, Vol. 19, No. 1, 2011, pp. 123–143. This was also expressively recognised in the Inuit Circumpolar Council's *Principle and Elements for a Comprehensive Arctic Policy* of 1992.

21 M. TENNBERG, "Indigenous Peoples as International Political Actors: A Summary", *Polar Record*, Vol. 46, No. 238, 2010, pp. 264–270.

22 See, for instance, J. SHADIAN, "From States to Polities: Reconceptualizing Sovereignty through Inuit Governance", *European Journal of International Relations*, Vol. 16, No. 3, 2010, pp. 485–510 and J. SHADIAN, "Rethinking Westphalian Sovereignty: The Inuit Circumpolar Council and the Future of Arctic Governance", *Working Papers on Arctic Security*, Vol. 8, 2013, pp. 1–58.

23 See, as a general reference, the last International Work Group for Indigenous Affairs (IWGIA) report on the situation of indigenous peoples around the world. P. J. ANDERSEN (ed.) *The Indigenous World 2018*. Copenhagen: The International Work Group for Indigenous Affairs, 2018.

24 For instance, in 2012, the activities of the Russian Association of the Peoples of the North have been suspended due to the enactment of a legislation regulating the founding of NGOs and requiring that all non-profit organisations accepting foreign funding must be registered as foreign agents. This, in turn, required to comply with additional and more stringent reporting obligations and brought the Russian Federal Ministry of Justice to order in 2013 the suspension of the Association's activities, the modification of its statute and the registration of its logo.

level is also a consequence of their residing in States with relatively high living standards and fairly positive human rights' records. This is for instance the case of Inuit peoples living in the USA and Canada,[25] as well as of the Sámi residing in Scandinavia where, for instance, the negotiation of a Nordic Sámi Convention on Sámi rights and culture have been discussed since 1995 and its ratification seems now forthcoming.[26]

To this end, even the association of Arctic indigenous peoples into major non-governmental organisations has been a crucial tool for the success of their advocacy. Although it would be impossible to precisely enclose the great variety of indigenous groups living in the region into clearly recognisable groups, today six major organisations act as representatives of Arctic indigenous peoples regionally and internationally. Such organisations have formed following two main patterns: being an association that includes a single indigenous group that resides in more than one Arctic State or, conversely, including more than one Arctic indigenous peoples' group resident in a single Arctic country.[27] Either way, their grouping into transnational organisations has been possible because they share territories, harsh climate conditions and a language that is different from that of the colonising nation states, thus similar histories of colonialism, coerced relocation, land seizure and the imposition of state borders.[28] At present, the following are the non-governmental organisations representing the peoples of the Arctic, who are also acting as Permanent Participants in the Arctic Council:

- *The Sámi Council*

  The Sámi Council was created in 1956 as a non-governmental organisation for the promotion of the rights of the 70,000 Sámi people living in Norway, Sweden, Finland and Russia, both internationally and nationally. The Council

25 Especially with the inception of the Trudeau administration, indigenous rights have seen increased recognition in Canada. For instance, in 2016, Canada officially adopted the UNDRIP after years of opposition. In the same year then, Prime Minister Trudeau also announced the Government commitment to enact an Indigenous Language Act, to be co-developed with Canadian IPs. Finally, in 2017 the Inuit-Crown Partnership Committee was created with the aim of advancing the cooperation between the Canadian Government and Inuit peoples on land claims agreements, social development and reconciliation. See, M. COPPES, "Canada's Acceptance of the United Nations Declaration on the Rights of Indigenous Peoples: Implications for the Inuit", *The Arctic Institute*, 09 August 2016. Available at: https://www.thearcticinstitute.org/canadas-acceptance-declaration-rights-indigenous-peoples/ (Last access, 03 October 2018).

26 See, for a commentary on the draft for a Nordic Sámi Convention, T. KOIVUROVA, "The Draft for A Nordic Saami Convention", *European Yearbook of Minority Issues*, Vol. 6, 2006, pp. 103–136. At present, the Sámi Parliaments and the Governments of Finland, Norway and Sweden are discussing on the final wording of the Convention. Particularly challenging to the adoption of the Draft Convention is the fact that only Norway have ratified the ILO Convention 169 to date.

27 This classification has also been recalled in the Ottawa Declaration of 1996. For more details on the Declaration see section 3.2 in this chapter.

28 S. PLAUT, "Cooperation Is the Story: Best Practices of Transnational Indigenous Activism in the North", *The International Journal of Human Rights*, Vol. 16, No. 1, 2012, pp. 193–215.

deals with activities related to Arctic environment, human rights and culture, and it first developed in order to reverse the policies of linguistic and cultural assimilation imposed by the colonising states. At present its main tasks consist in the promotion of Sámi rights and interests in the countries where these populations live, in the consolidation of the relations among Sámi peoples, and the pursuing of agreements among the nation states and the Sámi Parliaments. As for the Inuit Circumpolar Council, it takes turn representing the Arctic indigenous at the UNPFII and it has received the consultative status at the UN ECOSOC (Economic and Social Council).

- *The Inuit Circumpolar Council (ICC)*

  The Inuit Circumpolar Council was established in 1977 and today it is a major international non-governmental organisation representing 150,000 Inuit in four states: Alaska, Canada, Denmark (Greenland) and Russia (Chukotka). To date, it enjoys the participation in several international fora with different degrees of engagement: it holds a consultative status at the UN ECOSOC, and it alternatively participates as indigenous representative at the United Nations Permanent Forum on Indigenous Issues. It is composed by an ICC Chair and Executive Council, but at the core of its actions there is a General Assembly, held every four years. At this meeting, all the delegates from the circumpolar regions gather in order to adopt the agenda for the coming term, developing policies and initiatives in different areas: environment and sustainable development, human rights and cultural issues. Besides these activities, the Assembly can adopt resolutions aimed at pursuing their principal goals: the reinforcement of the unity among all Inuit, the promotion of their rights and interests at the international level and the development of strategies to safeguard the Arctic environment.

- *The Russian Association of the Peoples of the North (RAIPON)*

  After the Soviet collapse, RAIPON was created in 1990 on the ruins of the *Association of Peoples of the North of the USSR,* which gathered up to twenty-six indigenous groups of the former Soviet Union. Today it counts on the participation of forty-one groups of indigenous peoples of the North, Siberia and the Far East (Chukchi, Nenets, Kets, etc.). Therefore, it is considered an umbrella organisation for the 270,000 peoples living in the region, from Murmansk to Kamchatka. Its highest body is the Congress of all Indigenous Peoples of the North, Siberia and the Far East, held every four years. The main objectives and purposes of RAIPON are the protection and defence of indigenous rights and legal interests. Moreover, it assists indigenous peoples in solving environmental, social, cultural and educational issues.

- *The Aleut International Association (AIA)*

  The Association is a not-for-profit organisation representing Alaskan natives of the Arctic. It was created in 1998 to address environmental, cultural concerns and with the aim of improving the overall well-being of Aleuts peoples living in the Arctic.

- *The Gwich'in Council International (GCI)*

  This organisation represents the Gwich'in of Canada and the USA since 1999, when it was first established. Its main aim is to secure the participation of this indigenous group into the making of circumpolar policies, especially in its priority areas, which are: environment, youth, culture and tradition, as well as economic development and education.

- *The Arctic Athabaskan Council (AAC)*

  Established in 2000 to defend the rights and further the interests of the American and Canadian Athabaskans, it comprises around 76 communities representing 45,000 peoples of Athabaskan descent.

Although the last three organisations are very recent, the collaboration among these indigenous NGOs – and particularly the Sámi Council and the ICC – began already in 1973 with the celebration of the first Arctic Peoples' Conference in collaboration with the International Work Group for Indigenous Affairs. Even if no Russian organisations participated in this meeting, the latter has had great relevance because it was celebrated within the Danish Parliament, and thus accepted by national and international authorities at a time where Greenlanders had initiated the process that would lead them to obtain the Home Rule in 1979. More broadly, it gave Arctic indigenous peoples renewed confidence and awareness of their condition, as they became familiar for the first time with the concept of 'indigeneity' and the provisions contained in the ILO Convention No. 169. As Dahl has accounted, reporting the testimony of Aqqaluk Lynge, former president of the ICC: "The Arctic Peoples' Conference was a turning point for us. We were first of all thinking of ourselves as 'Inuit' but Helge Kleivan urged us to include the Saami in our organizing efforts and he inspired us to consider ourselves as part of a broader indigenous movement".[29]

The formalisation of this cooperation arrived two years later during the First International Indigenous Conference and developed during the '80s and the '90s, solidifying the efforts and exchanges among the Sámi and the Inuit within several UN bodies. The indigenous peoples of the North became soon aware of the benefits of working together. As Plaut has rightly pointed:

> The Saami Council and the ICC seek to address multiple audiences and, without directly confronting them, demand accountability from all: the colonising nation-states, international governing bodies, and the larger world of transnational actors. It is not unusual for the ICC to publicly support initiatives promoted by the Saami Council (and vice versa).[30]

29 J. DAHL, *IWGIA: A History* Copenhagen: International Work Group on Indigenous Affairs, 2009, at 38. Helge Kleivan was a Norwegian anthropologist and the founder of the International Work Group for Indigenous Affairs.

30 S. PLAUT, 2012, *supra* note 28, at 198.

Since its inception, this cooperation primarily occurred through the membership of these organisations in the Arctic Council which, by creating a space and an institutionalised practice of participation at the regional level, has enabled Arctic IPs to gain normative weight and representation in intergovernmental negotiations, to influence the development of international (environmental) agreements and, finally, to claim their rights as peoples. In this regard, the following section will detail the participation of Arctic IPs in the AC while subsequent parts of this chapter will mostly describe the advocacy strategy of Inuit peoples as one of the most empowered indigenous communities in the Arctic and internationally.

4.3 From observers to permanent participants: Arctic Indigenous Peoples in the Arctic Council

Tracing back the origins of the Arctic Council, Shadian has pointed out that "the process leading to the establishment of the Arctic Council was based on the desire to break away from the limitations of the Cold War and focus on cooperation rather than security, in order to ensure the sustainable development of the Arctic".[31] Indeed, with the end of the confrontation between the two Cold War superpowers, an era of region-building revolved around scientific research and the protection of the Arctic environment led to the creation of a long-lasting and peaceful political cooperation in the region. This, in turn, had the direct effect of legitimising Arctic IPs as stewards of the region, prompting their inclusion in its environmental governance. As a matter of fact, the Sámi Council and the Inuit Circumpolar Council contributed since its inception to the Rovaniemi Process initiated in 1989 as they, and afterwards the predecessor of RAIPON as well, assisted to the creation of the Arctic Environmental Protection Strategy (AEPS), being invited as observers.[32] The adoption of the Rio Declaration, and particularly the reference made to indigenous rights in Principle 22, also had a great influence on the development of the AEPS, to the extent that in the Nuuk Declaration of 1993 a direct reference to this principle was made in its text.[33]

31 J. SHADIAN, *The Politics of Arctic Sovereignty: Oil, Ice and Inuit Governance*. New York: Routledge, 2014, p. 122.

32 The Rovaniemi Process started as a Finnish initiative in 1989 and was aimed at commencing a stable scientific cooperation among the different Arctic States.

33 Moreover, the declaration recites at paragraph 7: "[We] recognize the special role of the indigenous peoples in environmental management and development in the Arctic, and of the significance of their knowledge and traditional practices, and will promote their effective participation in the achievement of sustainable development in the Arctic". ARCTIC ENVIRONMENTAL PROTECTION STRATEGY, *The Nuuk Declaration on Environment and Development in the Arctic* of 16 September 1993. Available at http://arcticcircle.uconn.edu/NatResources/Policy/nuuk.html. (Last access, 6 August 2018).

Launched in 1991 with the Arctic Environmental Protection Strategy, the governance of the Arctic region today builds on its successor – the Arctic Council – an intergovernmental forum serving the representation and cooperation between the eight Arctic States and the six non-governmental organisations representing the Arctic indigenous peoples and acting as Permanent Participants.[34] Created by the Ottawa Declaration of 1996, this political forum also allows the contribution of diverse non-Arctic States, intergovernmental bodies and NGOs.[35] Though decision-making is limited to the Council Member States and PPs, non-Arctic states and organisations can be granted the right to attend its meetings as observers.[36] In the light of the status that the Council grants to Northern indigenous peoples, and considering the success of its twenty years of work,[37] the forum has not only become an interesting example of regional cooperation, but a particularly interesting case study for the participation of non-governmental entities in decision-making processes.

34 For extensive reference to the AEPS and the AC, see: D. VANDERZWAAG, R. HUEBERT and S. FERRARA, "The Arctic Environmental Protection Strategy, Arctic Council and Multilateral Environmental Initiatives: Tinkering While the Arctic Marine Environment Totters", in A. G. OUDE ELERINK and D. R. ROTHWELL (eds.) *The Law of the Sea and Polar Maritime Delimitation and Jurisdiction*. The Hague: Martinus Nijhoff, 2001, pp. 225–248; D. NORD, *The Arctic Council: Governance Within the Far North*. New York: Routledge, 2016; E., J. MOLENAAR, "Current and Prospective Roles of the Arctic Council System within the Context of the Law of the Sea", *The International Journal of Marine and Coastal Law*, Vol. 27, No. 3, 2014, pp. 553–595. It seems also important to specify here that, as recognised by all Arctic States, the Law of the Sea Convention is the major international legal instrument that governs the Arctic, being the latter an ocean surrounded by lands.

35 It should be recalled here that the Council was created as a high-level intergovernmental forum and without legal personality. Its main objective is to ensure sustainable development and environmental protection in the Arctic, excluding from its agenda any issue related to military security. The work of the Council is primarily carried out by six Working Groups (Arctic Contaminants Action Program; Arctic Monitoring and Assessment Programme; Conservation of Arctic Flora and Fauna; Emergency Prevention Preparedness and Response; Protection of Arctic Marine Environment; Sustainable Development Working Group), which are responsible for the preparation of studies and scientific reports. These Groups are flanked by other subsidiary bodies (Expert Groups and Task Forces) and the Senior Arctic Officials (SAOs), in charge of directing the daily agenda of the Council and which meets in a plenary session every two years. Today the forum enjoys the participation of 39 observers and manages more than 80 different projects related to its main objectives. More details on the Arctic Council are available at: https://arctic-council.org/index.php/en/ (Last access, 21 August 2019).

36 Observers' rights and duties are detailed in the Roles of Procedure adopted by the Council in 1998 and revised in 2013, as well as in an Observer Manual for Subsidiary Bodies adopted in 2013 and amended in 2015 and 2016. See, Arctic Council, *Arctic Council Rules of Procedure*, as adopted by the Arctic Council at the First Arctic Council Ministerial Meeting of Iqualuit, Canada, in September 1998, and revised by the Arctic Council at the Eight Arctic Council Ministerial Meeting of Kiruna, Sweden, in May 2013. Available at https://oaarchive.arctic-council.org/handle/11374/940 (Last access, 20 August 2019).

37 O. YOUNG, "The Arctic Council at Twenty: How to Remain Effective in a Rapidly Changing Environment", *UC Irvine Law Review*, Vol. 6, No. 99, 2016, pp. 99–120.

Although international law today recognises and protects the rights of indigenous peoples through different instruments,[38] the degree of representation and participation that indigenous peoples enjoy in the Arctic is rather unique. As an evolution of the system of representation established by the AEPS which, as said, granted to three Arctic IPs organisations the same observer status accorded to non-Arctic states or international NGOs, the rights of active participation and full consultation enshrined in the Ottawa Declaration[39] were fully realised through the creation of the category of Permanent Participants. Tennberg has ascribed such a development to the negotiations for the establishment of the AC, where the discussion "on whether to use the term 'people' or 'peoples' opened up the opportunity for indigenous peoples to act in the Arctic Council as permanent participants instead of as observer NGOs".[40] Anyhow, respectively in 1998 and 2000, the Aleut International Association, the Arctic Athabaskan Council and the Gwich'in Council International were included in the work of the Council under the same category. While this development highlights the positive contribution made by PPs to the work of the Council, it should also be understood in the light of the need to include more indigenous people in Arctic governance parallel to the development and greater recognition of their rights as today outlined in the United Nations Declaration on the Rights of Indigenous Peoples (UNDRIP).

At present, therefore, the six non-governmental organisations representing the indigenous peoples of the Arctic make up the core of the Council, since they are able to shape and influence the consensus-based decision-making process on which the AC operates. Despite lacking proper voting rights, PPs hold the ability to block any measure discussed by the Council. Exercising what has been defined as a *veto-kind power*, they ultimately act on an equal footing with the eight Arctic States and are able to balance the voting rights exclusively granted to States. For instance, the resistance of Arctic PPs may be determinant

38 Currently, the only binding instrument that makes explicit reference to the collective rights of indigenous peoples is the Convention Concerning Indigenous and Tribal Peoples in Independent Countries: INTERNATIONAL LABOUR ORGANISATION, *Indigenous and Tribal Peoples Convention, C 169*, of 27 June 1989 (28 ILM 1382). Although non-binding, the United Nations Declaration on the Rights of Indigenous Peoples was adopted by the UN General Assembly in 2007 and enjoys the support of UN member states. See, UNITED NATIONS GENERAL ASSEMBLY, *United Nations Declaration on the Rights of Indigenous People* of 02 October 2007 (UN Doc. A/Res/61/295). Finally, rights applicable to indigenous groups are recognized in general human rights instruments, such as the International Covenant on Civil and Political Rights. For an extensive review of the rights that apply to indigenous people, see J. ANAYA, *Indigenous Peoples in International Law*. Oxford: Oxford University Press, 2004; S. TORRECUADRADA GARCÍA-LOZANO, *Los pueblos indígenas en el orden internacional*. Madrid: Dykinson, 2001.

39 The Declaration affirms "The category of Permanent Participants is created to provide for active participation and full consultation with the Arctic indigenous representatives within the Arctic Council". See: ARCTIC COUNCIL, *Declaration on the establishment of the Arctic Council* of 19 September 1996 (35 ILM 1382).

40 M. TENNBERG, 2010, *supra* note 21, at 268.

on the decision to grant or deny the observer status to non-Arctic entities, as it may have occurred in the cases of the European Union and Greenpeace for their anti-sealing and conservationist positions, respectively.[41] Moreover, in their role as Permanent Participants, Arctic IPs can submit proposals and statements for decision, influencing the agendasetting of the Council, and actively participate in the research activities of the AC's Working Groups. In any case, and this is exceptional, the PPs hold greater influence over decision-making than any other non-Arctic state entities which, as recalled above, are only entitled to observe the work of the Council.

As a result, the indigenous peoples living in the different Arctic States now enjoy effective representation in this forum of cooperation. Furthermore, following the reform made with the adoption of the Nuuk Rules on the criteria for admission of new observers to the Council,[42] the weight of indigenous peoples has been strengthened in such a way that their position is not undermined by the large number of observers admitted after 2011. Quite the opposite, the rules establish the obligation for each new admitted observer to respect "the values, interests, culture and traditions of Arctic indigenous peoples and other Arctic inhabitants" and to support the work of the Council "including through partnership with member states and Permanent Participants bringing Arctic concerns to global decision-making bodies", making the maintenance of their status as observer conditional to these criteria.[43]

It follows that the views and interests of Arctic IP should be reflected in the negotiating positions of all Arctic States and non-Arctic observer States, whenever they negotiate any legal framework that is relevant for or directly applicable to the Arctic.[44] On this subject, the Arctic Council system has been praised by different commentators as a model for the advancement of participatory rights of non-governmental actors and minority groups.[45] In 2012, the

41 See, on this, M. SCOPELLITI and N. SELLHEIM, "Sustaining a Conservationist Agenda? NGO-Influence on Arctic Sealing, Whaling and Hydrocarbon Regimes", in A. SHIBATA, L. ZOU, N. SELLHEIM and M. SCOPELLITI (eds.) *Emerging Legal Orders in the Arctic: The Role of Non-Arctic Actors*. New York: Routledge, 2019, pp. 91–106.

42 P. GRACZYK and T. KOIVUROVA, "A New Era in the Arctic Council's External Relations? Broader Consequences of the Nuuk Observer Rules for Arctic Governance", *Polar Record*, Vol. 50, No. 254, 2014, pp. 225–236.

43 Arctic Council, *Arctic Council Rules of Procedure*, 1998, *op. cit.*, at 14.

44 This is the case in UNFCCC negotiations but also of other international and regional agreements. For instance, the negotiation process of the Agreement to prevent unregulated high seas Fisheries in the Central Arctic Ocean or of the International Code for Ships Operating in Polar Waters. On this topic, see S. DUYCK, *The Arctic Voice at the UNFCCC Negotiations. Interplay Between Arctic & Climate Governance*. LL.M. programme dissertation, 2015. A. SHIBATA, L. ZOU, N. SELLHEIM and M. SCOPELLITI (eds.) *Emerging Legal Orders in the Arctic: The Role of non-Arctic Actors*. New York: Routledge, 2019.

45 See, M. P. POTO and L. FORNABAIO, "Participation as the Essence of Good Governance: Some General Reflections and a Case Study on the Arctic Council", *Arctic Review on Law and Politics*, Vol. 8, 2017, pp. 139–159.

UNPFII also conducted a study, as example of good practice, on the participatory mechanism in the Arctic Council.[46] Yet, other critical voices still call for more commitments from Arctic and non-Arctic states towards Arctic IPs, including the possibility to upgrade the status of Permanent Participants to that of voting members.[47]

To this end, if the real possibility for these peoples to participate in the work of the Council relates to their economic capacity, these new Rules of Procedure make it mandatory for all observers to provide financial assistance to this category. In this regard, it is also worth mentioning some problems that still affect this system of cooperation which, although very advanced, is not exempt from possible improvements. For instance, the lack of economic resources is an issue that still affects the capacity of PPs, although this question has been partially addressed since 2016 with the institution of the Álgu fund, created to distribute financial resources among all the PPs and aimed at supporting their work in the Council while ensuring their independence.[48] Moreover, despite the creation of the AC Indigenous Peoples' Secretariat to support the cooperation among the different indigenous peoples of the region, the lack of human resources is a problem that has made it difficult to monitor and follow the rapid development of regional policies.[49]

4.3.1 *The Indigenous practice within the Arctic Council: regional and international implications*

Despite the non-binding nature of the AC declarations and decisions, the indigenous representation in the Council is of great relevance at the regional and international level for at least a number of reasons. The consolidated practice of indigenous participation through the Working Groups that operate within the Council – particularly the one on sustainable development – has made it possible to recognise the importance of their traditional knowledge to the science diplomacy that is so key to the governance of the Arctic region. In 2015,

46 UNPFII, "Study, as an example of good practice, of the Indigenous participatory mechanisms in the Arctic Council, the Circumpolar Inuit Declaration on Resource Development Principles in Inuit Nunaat, and the Laponia management system", 2012. E/C. 19/2012/10.

47 D. S. DOROUGH, "The Rights, Interests and Role of the Arctic Council Permanent Participants", in R. BECKMAN, T. HENRIKSEN, K. DALAKER KRAABEL and others (eds.) *Governing Arctic Shipping*. Leiden: Brill, 2017, pp. 68–103.

48 Extensive information on the establishment of the fund is provided by J. GAMBLE and J. SHADIAN, "One Arctic…But Uneven Capacity: The Arctic Council Permanent Participants", in W. LACKENBAUER, N. HEATHER and W. GRAVES (eds.) *One Arctic. The Arctic Council and Circumpolar Governance*. Ottawa: Canadian Arctic Resources Committee and Centre on Foreign Policy and Federalism, 2017, pp. 142–156.

49 The Arctic Council Indigenous Peoples' Secretariat has been established in 1994 for the support of Permanent Participants. It primarily facilitates the participation of Arctic IPs' organisations in the Arctic Council but it also disseminates information on Permanent Participants, raising international public awareness on their work and status within the Council.

the relevance of indigenous contribution to the work of the Council was fully endorsed with the adoption of the *Ottawa Traditional Knowledge Principles*,[50] thirteen principles for the practical use of indigenous peoples' expertise and know-how within the Council. By virtue of this knowledge, Arctic indigenous peoples have substantially contributed to the drafting of regional reports on the state of the Arctic environment. This is the case of the *Arctic Monitoring Assessment Programme Report: Arctic Pollution Issues* of 1997, and of the above-mentioned *Arctic Climate Impact Assessment Report* of 2004.

The process that has led to the drafting of these reports can be considered as an example of good practice because it has promoted the fruitful cooperation between indigenous peoples and the Arctic scientific community. Besides its practical relevance, such a model of exchange and complementarity between scientific and indigenous knowledge empowers the indigenous peoples of the region by giving space to their expertise in processes that are normally guided by technocratic rationality. Moreover, as it will be discussed below, their direct involvement in the drafting of these documents has on different occasions prompted international action towards the conclusion of binding international agreements of relevance to these populations and to the scientific community as a whole. In the case of climate change governance, the institution of a Local Communities and Indigenous Peoples Platform constituted for providing formal opportunities for IPs' knowledge, best practices and expertise to guide climate decisions-making at the international level, proves the importance of these contributions.

On the other hand, it should be remembered that the Council is increasingly more acting as a forum for policy-shaping and as a decision-making space for its members.[51] Since 2011, with the adoption of the first regional agreement negotiated under the auspices of the Council,[52] the contribution of Arctic IPs has also been key to the adoption of sectoral regional agreements and this will likely continue in the future. Thus, the capacity of indigenous peoples to influence the decision- and law-making process undoubtedly reverberates in

50 Adopted by the Arctic Council and the Permanent Participants in 2015. Available at: http://www.saamicouncil.net/fileadmin/user_upload/Documents/Eara_dokumeanttat/Ottawa_TK_Principles.pdf (Last access, 11 August 2019).

51 In addition to the special importance accorded to indigenous peoples, perhaps the most interesting feature of this forum for cooperation is the quasi-normative role that it has come to play in serving as a forum for the negotiation of regional agreements. Indeed, the following binding regional treaties have been adopted under the auspices of the Arctic Council: Agreement on Cooperation on Aeronautical and Maritime Search and Rescue in the Arctic (SAR), adopted on 12 May 2011, entered into force on 19 January 2013; Agreement on Cooperation on Marine Oil Pollution Preparedness and Response in the Arctic (OPPRA), adopted on 15 May 2013, entered into force on 25 March 2016; Agreement on Enhancing International Arctic Scientific Cooperation, adopted on 11 May 2017, entered into force on 23 May 2018. On this, see L. HEININEN, H. EXNER PIROT and J. PLOUFFE (eds.) *The Arctic Council: 20 Years of Regional Cooperation and Policy-Shaping*, Arctic Yearbook 2016. Akureyri: Northern Research Forum, 2016.

52 See, on the AC agreements, S.V. ROTTEM, "A Note on the Arctic Council Agreements", *Ocean Development & International Law*, Vol. 46, No. 1, 2015, pp. 50–59.

regional negotiations, being reflected in binding agreements that include their perspectives and concerns. According to Poelzer, in fact:

> [The Arctic Council] offers Indigenous Peoples' organizations and regional governments with unprecedented access to high-level international diplomatic conversations, providing a global model for indigenous engagement in the process. Although the Arctic Council operates in the realm of soft power, rather than hard power, there is no denying the enormous impact that indigenous people have played in shaping Arctic policy.[53]

Finally, the documents and declarations adopted by the Council following this pattern assume growing importance on the international level too. Each new State applying for observer status to the Council is obliged, through the above-mentioned Nuuk rules, to transmit and uphold an "Arctic message" in any international institution, bringing the concerns of its indigenous peoples to the attention of global decision-making bodies, in partnership with the Arctic States and the PPs.

As the above demonstrates, the participation of Arctic indigenous peoples in the Arctic Council under the status of Permanent Participants has resulted in the recognition of Arctic indigenous peoples' interests, knowledge and normative weight as (limited) subjects of international law in this regional context. Over the past decades, the Council has made the participation and representation of Arctic IPs one of its most distinguished and distinguishing features, indirectly endorsing and implementing those international instruments that, not always ratified by its Member States, enshrine indigenous rights. This, in turn, has significantly contributed to the advancement of Arctic IPs' rights regionally and internationally. Their representation under a unique category, has had the effect of rendering their status and weight in circumpolar governance uniform, regardless of the fact that their actual legal status may vary from State to State.[54] This ultimately, and as it will be shown in the following section, has contributed to their empowerment and positioning on the international scene.

4.4 Going global: Arctic Indigenous internationalism against climate change

Together with the land claims settlements of Canada and the self-government agreement achieved in Greenland, the exceptional degree of participation that

53 G. POELZER, "Governance in the Arctic: Political Systems and Geopolitics", in J. NYMAND LARSEN and G. FONDAHL (eds.) *Arctic Human Development Report: Regional Processes and Global Linkages*. Copenhagen: Nordic Council of Ministers, 2014, pp. 185–220, at 213.

54 As of August 2019, only Norway and Denmark have ratified the ILO Convention No. 169. The USA has voted against the adoption of the UNDRIP and the Russian Federation has abstained from voting. On the other hand, Canada has signed the UNDRIP on May 2016.

the indigenous peoples of the Arctic enjoy within the largest forum devoted to circumpolar affairs, is arguably the feature that distinguishes them most from other indigenous peoples and non-governmental actors alike. The status of Permanent Participants has allowed them to influence the regional cooperation and has been, in parallel with the influence of a wider indigenous movement, a factor that has substantiated their actions, aimed at strengthening the link between indigenous peoples' and self-determination, human rights and environmental protection at the transnational and international levels.

As it will be discussed below, the ability of these peoples to influence different international political processes has manifested through their ability to expand the political space in which they operate so as to accommodate their interests and rights, to make the traditional knowledge recognised and endorsed by the AC essential to the success of intergovernmental negotiations and, where this has not been sufficient, to internationalise their cause by filing complaints before human rights courts.

4.4.1 Beyond Westphalia: an Arctic indigenous diplomacy?

The nation state has traditionally been the primary unit for the conduct of international political and legal affairs. From this standpoint, the conduct of international law and relations is an attribute of statehood which will mostly reflect the interests of State entities, mainly focused on the maintenance of their sovereignty, security and national interests. While this has not necessarily changed over the last decades, the dawn of human rights and environmental movements were largely characterised by the emergence of new political actors: individual advocates, non-profit organisations and indigenous peoples, among others.

Considered the fundamental importance that nature has for the realisation of individual and collective rights in an indigenous perspective, it is no surprise that the protection of the environment, the achievement of self-determination and the upholding of human rights coalesced under an indigenous movement in the Arctic and elsewhere. In this regard, the current Chair of the ICC and legal scholar Dalee Sambo Dorough, has recalled the key role that the Sámi Council and the ICC have played in the negotiation of the UNDRIP,[55] which enshrines the rights of IPs to environmental integrity, to culture and economic development *inter alia*, signalling the emergence of an Arctic indigenous diplomacy as early as in 1982 with the establishment of a United Nations Working Group on Indigenous Populations. Contextually to climate change, Ben Powless has given an account of the emergence of a global indigenous movement and diplomacy in a recent contribution.[56]

55 D. S. DOROUGH, *supra* note 47.

56 B. POWLESS, "The Indigenous Rights Framework and Climate Change", in S. DUYCK, S. JODOIN and A. JOHL (eds.) *Routledge Handbook of Human Rights and Climate Governance*. New York: Routledge, 2018, pp. 213–221.

It follows that trying to answer the question of whether an indigenous diplomacy exists implies, first of all, abandoning a state-centric conception of law and politics to consider a broader political space that accommodates and confers relevance to both State and non-State entities,[57] in this specific case indigenous peoples. In relation to this, the acknowledgement that the traditional idea of sovereignty as an unconditioned prerogative of States has been largely eroded by the emergence of new political agents, finds support in the context of indigenous advocacy. In her account of sovereignty, indigeneity and Inuit governance, Shadian has pointed that: "While states may remain a dominant political reality, examples of indigenous agency, such as the ICC, highlight the need to abstract, relocate and reconceptualize sovereignty altogether".[58]

Answering this question also requires understanding the importance of the transnational cooperation of these groups, which has enabled them to extend their efforts beyond borders, to gain greater weight on the international stage and, through this, to influence the national, regional and international politics of the States they inhabit. In this sense, Shadian has underlined that: "Indigenous diplomacies do not operate abstracted from global politics, namely interstate politics. The structures which they have created to engage in interstate politics are themselves manifestations of their historical interactions with global politics".[59] As a consequence of the above, and assuming the existence of an indigenous diplomacy, the Arctic experience and especially the advocacy of the Inuit Circumpolar Council is a case in point.

In a recent publication on circumpolar governance, Gamble and Shadian have highlighted how the Arctic Council is entering a new phase of *westphalianisation*, meaning a stage in which this forum is increasingly becoming a conventional intergovernmental regime. It is beyond doubt that, since 2008 and following the progressive geopolitical relevance assumed by the Arctic, the region has increasingly become the subject of the political claims of the Arctic coastal states (Canada, Denmark, Norway, Russia and the USA).[60] Evidence

57 In this regard, *Shadian* uses the notion of *polities*, entities that have the political capacity to mobilise people and resources for political ends. These units therefore represent an alternative to the model of sovereign states, often conceptualised as Eurocentric, ahistorical and exclusive. In this sense, these political entities help to rethink the boundaries of political space and action. See J. SHADIAN, *supra* note 22.

58 *Ibid*, at 494.

59 J. SHADIAN, "Reimagining Political Space: The Limits of Arctic Indigenous Self-Determination in International Governance", in K. KEIL and S. KNECHT (eds.) *Governing Arctic Change: Global Perspectives*. London: Palgrave Macmillan, 2017, pp. 43–58.

60 Although following a peaceful fashion and the provisions of the LOS Convention, most Arctic coastal States have issued a claim to the Commission on the Limits of the Continental Shelf for extending their continental platforms beyond the 200 nautical miles. See, on the state of Arctic marine jurisdictions: https://www.dur.ac.uk/ibru/resources/arctic/ (Last access, 20 August 2019). For more on this topic, see: E. CONDE PÉREZ and Z. VALERIEVA YANEVA, "Outer Arctic Continental Shelf", in E. CONDE and S. SÁNCHEZ IGLESIAS (eds.) *Global Challenges in the Arctic Region*. London: Routledge, 2017, pp. 19–41 and E. CONDE PÉREZ, "Delimitaciones marítimas

and culmination of this process has been, in fact, the celebration of the Ilulissat Summit in 2008,[61] where the five Arctic coastal states (A5) met to discuss the future of the region outside the framework of the Arctic Council, thus at the exclusion of the remaining Arctic countries (Finland, Iceland and Sweden) and all Permanent Participants. The publication of the Ilulissat Declaration the same year – by means of which the A5 reaffirmed their sovereign rights in the region and their adherence to the Law of the Sea in the settlement of any disputes – led to the mobilisation of the ICC against what was perceived as a claim to exclusive sovereignty over their ancestral territories and resources, due to their marginalisation from the regional decision-making process.

The *Inuit Circumpolar Declaration on Sovereignty in the Arctic*[62] and the *Inuit Declaration on Resources Development Principles in the Arctic*[63] represent, in this sense, the Inuit diplomatic responses to the attempt of minimising their participatory rights in the regional governance. Indeed, these declarations have provided yet another opportunity to challenge the predominance of a westphalian concept of sovereignty in the region and to reaffirm the principle of self-determination on which a legitimate Inuit participation in regional cooperation is based.[64] Thus, by claiming the need to reconcile the right to self-determination with the need for nation states to maintain their sovereignty, the Inuit have

y territoriales en el Ártico: Desarrollo y Tendencias", *Revista Española de Derecho Internacional*, Vol. 68, No. 1, 2016, pp. 235–239.

61 The 2008 Arctic Ocean Conference was held among the five Arctic coastal states, at the exclusion of the remaining Arctic countries and Arctic indigenous peoples. After its conclusion, the Ilulissat Declaration was issued. This is a document in which the Arctic coastal states have made clear their opposition to the possibility of negotiating a binding regional treaty, reaffirming their adherence to the Law of the Sea as the legal framework that applies to the region. See, Arctic Ocean Conference, *The Ilulissat Declaration*, Greenland, 2008. Available at http://www.oceanlaw.org/downloads/arctic/Ilulissat_Declaration.pdf (Last access, 20 August 2019).

62 The declaration reaffirms the indigenous' will to be part of the complex system of Arctic governance that, articulated at multiple levels, requires their inclusion. In this sense, the Inuit are presented as ideal partners for the conduct of international relations in the Arctic, who can help States achieving sustainable development in the region through their resilience strategies and knowledge of polar ecosystems. See Inuit Circumpolar Council, *"Circumpolar Inuit Declaration on Sovereignty in the Arctic"*, 2009. Available at: http://www.inuitcircumpolar.com/sovereignty-in-the-arctic.html (Last access, 20 August 2019).

63 This second document, which expressly refers to the development and use of regional resources and territories, advocates the obligation for Arctic States to include indigenous peoples in any decision that relates to the exploitation of resources and lands in the region. By recalling the principles enshrined in the Rio Declaration of 1992 and in the Aarhus Convention of 1998, and reminding that Arctic IPs will likely face the greatest changes in the Arctic, they advocate for playing a prominent role in any decision that will impact their livelihoods. Inuit Circumpolar Council, "*A Circumpolar Inuit Declaration on Resources Development Principles in Inuit Nunaat*", 2011. Available at: http://www.inuitcircumpolar.com/uploads/3/0/5/4/30542564/declaration_on_on_resource_development_a3_final.pdf (Last access, 20 August 2019).

64 N. C. FABBI, "Inuit Foreign Policy and International Relations in the Arctic", in L. C. JENSEN and G. HONNELAND (eds.) *Handbook of the Politics of the Arctic*. Cheltenham: Edward Elgar, 2015, pp. 482–500.

claimed their role as peoples and citizens of the Arctic, as well as the enjoyment of their rights and the use of the resources of the territory in which they have traditionally lived.[65]

While the above statements represent a manifestation of indigenous diplomacy at the primarily regional level – insofar as they reject any form of regional cooperation that fails to secure their inclusion in Arctic political, economic and developmental processes – these documents have been fundamental to the construction of a rights-based discourse and narrative, on which subsequent Inuit (and Arctic IPs) actions and claims have been built. Primarily, the claim of a right to participate in regional policy-making by virtue of their status as *right-holders*[66] and not as mere *stakeholders*. This discourse, already incorporated by the Convention on Biological Diversity of 1993 and which will later be transferred by Inuit peoples in their legal claims on climate change,[67] is relevant to the objectives of this analysis. Adopting a rights-based framework (in the specific case based on human rights) can serve as a tool to address climate change and, above all, to improve the position of other non-State entities in the governance of this environmental problem. While this idea will be recalled and further analysed in the final chapter of this work, there are two other aspects of indigenous practice that, the author believes, are worth analysing for the purposes of this research.

4.4.2 Arctic Indigenous Peoples and International Environmental Law-Making

Different authors acknowledge the fundamental role that Arctic indigenous peoples have played, through their position in the Arctic Council and transnational cooperation, in the negotiation and conclusion of international agreements that, due to its environmental and fragile ecologic balance, have direct application in and relevance for the Arctic.[68] In an environmental context, this

65 See, on a revised concept of sovereignty as proposed by Inuit people, F. BORGIA and P. VARGIU, "The Inuit Declaration on Sovereignty in the Arctic Between the Right to Self-Determination and a New Concept of Sovereignty?", in G. ALFREDSSON and T. KOIVUROVA (eds.) *The Yearbook of Polar Law IV*, 2012, pp. 189–204.

66 In this regard, as recalled by Dalee Dorough and other authors, the status of IPs as right-holders has been recognised through different national constitutions, national legislation, agreements and other instruments in which they are addressed as peoples. Moreover, despite the non-legally binding nature of the UNDRIP, it must be recalled here that the provisions set in the UN Declaration correspond to customary law and therefore create legal obligations for all States. As described by Borgia and Vargiu: "The UNDRIP is indeed an example of how international instruments lacking binding force can nonetheless contribute to consolidate customary international law by means of recognition and state practice, taking the principles enunciated in them to a new, and legally relevant, level". F. BORGIA and P. VARGIU, *supra* note 65, at 197.

67 See, on the subject, B. POWLESS, *supra* note 56.

68 See, T. FENGE and D. DOWNIE (eds.) *Northern Lights Against POPs*. Montreal: McGill- Queen's University Press, 2003 and D. S. DOROUGH, *supra* note 47.

has happened for the first time with the negotiation of an international agreement on persistent organic pollutants (POPs).

Persistent organic pollutants are toxic chemicals that abound in the Arctic, as they are carried to the region by a process of volatilisation and consequent condensation at high latitudes, and are able to accumulate in Arctic species influencing the food chain and lives of human beings. When the Working Group *Arctic Monitoring and Assessment Programme* (AMAP) was established as a scientific programme to assess pollution in the Arctic, three indigenous organisations were already participating in the AEPS programs as observers and could contribute to the AMAP *Assessment Report: Arctic Pollution Issues*. The document informed the international community about the effects that pollutants have on Arctic nature and on the well-being of its populations.[69] Especially the discovery of high percentages of these contaminants in the breast milk of Inuit women alarmed about a public health problem for Arctic peoples, which would affect their well-being and culture. The pressure of the indigenous peoples of the North on their national governments, made it possible to initiate the negotiations that led to the conclusion of the Stockholm Convention in 2001,[70] which specifically mentions the Arctic and its peoples in its Preamble.[71]

In his analysis of the process that led to the conclusion of the above-mentioned agreement, Fenge highlights three aspects that have particularly empowered Arctic indigenous peoples prior to and as a result of their participation in intergovernmental negotiations. First, their inclusion in the development of pre-negotiation scientific programs, such as the AMAP Report, has allowed them to acquire a knowledge that, in addition to their traditional experience, has enabled them to act credibly and effectively in circumpolar and international negotiation forums. In fact, representatives of several Arctic IPs had the possibility to participate directly in the bargain of the agreement as members of the national delegations of the USA and Canada.

Second, the status of PPs within the Arctic Council has allowed them to put pressure on the respective national governments so as to negotiate common positions that they would maintain throughout the international law-making process. Finally, the recognition of the significant indigenous influence on this

69 The document has indeed made it possible to estimate the exposure of the Arctic region to these pollutants. Although, as in the case of short-lived pollutants and black carbon, these pollutants are not produced in the Arctic, they are transported in the region through the atmosphere, as well as deposited and accumulated in the natural environment. Particularly serious was the detection of these contaminants in the breast milk of different Arctic indigenous women and in Arctic IPs food chain due to the consumption of fish and marine mammals.

70 See, T. FENGE, "POPs and Inuit: Influencing the Global Agenda", in T. FENGE and D. DOWNIE (eds.) *Northern Lights Against POPs*. Montreal: McGill- Queen's University Press, 2003, pp. 193–213.

71 A detailed analysis of the process that has led to the conclusion of the 2001 Stockholm Convention on Persistent Organic Pollutants and other environmental convention can be found in H. SELIN, "Global Environmental Governance and Treaty-Making: The Arctic's Fragmented Voice", in K. KEIL and S. KNECHT (eds.) *Governing Arctic Change. Global Perspectives*. London: Palgrave Macmillan, 2017, pp. 101–120.

international process has set a precedent for addressing other pressing regional and international environmental issues with their contribution.

Indeed, this experience of engagement and advocacy has fed into the negotiation of the Minamata Convention on Mercury (2017) too.[72] As for POPs, this chemical is long transported to the Arctic from external sources and represents a severe health and environmental harm in the region. This clearly explains the engagement of the AMAP in this issue and the contribution that Permanent Participants have made by partaking in its work, which includes the report *Mercury in the Arctic* of 2011, with a section assessing the impacts of mercury on human health and in Arctic inhabitants' food webs. In an informative article on the role of the AC in the negotiation of the Minamata Convention, Platjouw, and others have qualified the AC "as a provider, broker and communicator of science related to the environmental problem of mercury".[73]

Although successful because they are primarily supported by Arctic States, the above demonstrates that the indigenous peoples of the region have been able to contribute to the scientific research carried out within the AEPS and AC, supporting the formation of scientific evidence that has catalysed the consensus and political action necessary for the negotiation of international environmental treaties. Interestingly, this practice demonstrates the importance of an effective exercise of Arctic IPs procedural and participatory rights at the international level.

4.4.3 The inuit petition before the Inter-American Commission on Human Rights.

> Arctic countries and non-state groups invoke the fact that the Arctic is a highly ecologically sensitive place where signs of important changes can be detected early to expand regional cooperation to reduce environmental and human health risks from hazardous substances and climate change. In parallel, they seek to promote an Arctic agenda in international forums. However, the success of these external efforts has been mixed at best.[74]

In the comparative analysis of the processes that have led to the conclusion of several binding agreements relevant to the protection of the Arctic environment, Selin discusses the peculiarities of the climate change regime case. Due to the highly politicised nature of climate change and the relatively late involvement of the Arctic Council in this issue,[75] the regulation of global warming has

72 *Minamata Convention on Mercury* of 10 October 2013 (55 ILM 582).

73 F. M. PLATJOUW, E. H. STEINDAL and T. BORCH, "From Arctic Science to International Law: The Road towards the Minamata Convention and the Role of the Arctic Council", *Arctic Review on Law and Politics*, Vol. 9, 2018, pp. 226–243, at 238.

74 H. SELIN, *supra* note 71, at 102.

75 The work of the Arctic Council on climate change has been primarily done at the regional level, including the establishment of an Expert Group on short-lived climate pollutants. Although

been the international process in which the different Arctic actors have found it most difficult to successfully influence intergovernmental negotiations. The indigenous peoples of the region, largely involved in the negotiation of the Convention on Biological Diversity, did not take part in the climate decision-making process before 1998. It was only in 2001 that they were effectively recognised as one of the stakeholders along with other indigenous groups, primarily alarmed by the implementation of mitigation projects through sustainable forest management programmes.[76] Since then, and for long unsuccessfully, the Arctic caucus operating within the UN Permanent Forum on Indigenous Issues has recommended the creation of a seat reserved to IPs at the negotiating table of the UNFCCC.

Arguably for these reasons, the strategy chosen by Arctic indigenous peoples to influence the creation, extent and implementation of an international climate regime that could effectively counteract the impacts of global warming, has resorted on all the instruments analysed so far but has also been complemented by the actions taken outside the UNFCCC process. For instance, recurring to a regional human rights court to advance the development and implementation of international environmental and human rights law on the subject.[77]

This chapter has previously referred to the impacts that climate change is having on the indigenous populations living in the Arctic which, along with Amazonia, the Sahel and Central Asia, is one of the regions of the planet most dramatically affected by global warming. Faced with the impossibility to see their rights to life, health and land, *inter alia*, comprehensively guaranteed by

---

different declarations of the Council explicitly refer to the need of addressing this environmental problem which, today, is also among the main priorities of the Finnish Chairmanship, the Council doesn't hold an observer status to UN climate negotiations. Nonetheless, the Council has organised several side events showcasing the impact of climate change on the Arctic natural and human environment.

76 For more details on this topic, see C. BETZOLD, *Non-State Actors in International Climate Change Negotiations*, Doctoral dissertation, 1984.

77 While the Inuit petition to the IACHR is among the most visible legal actions undertaken by Arctic IPs at the international level, it should be recalled here that lawsuits related with environmental issues and human rights have also been filed to national courts. In Canada, for instance, the Supreme Court has ruled in favour of the Inuit community of Clyde River, Nunavut, who initiated legal proceedings against the decision to allow a 5-year seismic blasting project. Remarkable is that the case focused on the governmental duty to consult and accommodate Inuit peoples' concerns when permits for industrial activities that might impact on Inuit rights are issued, highlighting the IPs' human right to free, prior and informed consent. See, Supreme Court of Canada, *Clyde River (Hamlet) v. Petroleum Geo-Services Inc.* (Judgement). [2017] 1 SCR 1069 of 26 July 2017. Other cases related to the Canadian duty to consult with indigenous peoples prior to the authorisation of projects with negative environmental impacts have been reported in the IWGIA report on indigenous peoples. See, P. J. ANDERSEN, *supra* note 23, at 65. The possibility for similar litigations to take hold in the USA, as for example in the case of the Pebble Mine in Alaska, has been favoured by the start of the Trump administration, which reversed several of the decisions made by the administration Obama in the context of resources exploitation and environmental policy.

conventional instruments, in December 2005 the then president of the ICC, Sheila Watt-Cloutier, filed a petition before the Inter-American Commission on Human Rights against the United States on behalf of herself and other Inuit living in the Arctic regions of the United States of America and Canada.[78] By alleging the violation of a number of human rights recognised in the American Declaration of the Rights and Duties of Man[79] and other international instruments (ICCPR; UNFCCC), the claimants have sought to hold the US accountable for the acts and omissions related to its greenhouse gases emissions' policy,[80] as well as to demonstrate the existence of a correlation between global warming and the (impaired) enjoyment of human rights.

As a regional human right body established by the Organisation of American States (OAS), the IACHR has a jurisdiction that extends over the territories of the American and Canadian Arctic. While this explains why the petition does not represent the Inuit living in Greenland and Russia, the IACHR was also considered to be a suitable forum for the analysis of a complaint of this kind because, in terms of standing, it allows the reception of petitions from private citizens. Moreover, while the exhaustion of domestic remedies is usually determinant for the admission of an international litigation, the Commission allows a number of exceptions to this criterion when, as claimed in the case in point, the petitioners lack the resources necessary to exhaust domestic legal procedures or allege the absence of effective remedies at the national level. In the latter case, the burden to prove that existing remedies are in place but have not been used rests on the respondent government. Nonetheless, it should be recalled that any declaration from the Commission is not directly enforceable; the IACHR exclusively has the authority to establish human rights violations and prepare a report with recommendations. In any case, this did not conflict with the spirit of the petition. In the words of Ms. Watt-Cloutier:

> Protecting human rights is ground occupied by both reasonable governments and civil society, including Inuit and other Indigenous peoples. This petition is our means of inviting the United States to talk with us and to

78 "Petition to the Inter-American Commission on Human Rights Seeking Relief from Violations Resulting from Global Warming Caused by Acts and Omissions ofThe United States". Available at: http://www.inuitcircumpolar.com/uploads/3/0/5/4/30542564/finalpetitionicc.pdf (Last access, 21 August 2019). For an analysis of the petition, see M. CASTILLO DAUDÍ, "Cambio Climático y Derechos Humanos: El Asunto de los Inuit Ante la Comisión Interamericana de Derechos Humanos", in R. GILES CARNERO (coord.) *Cambio Climático, Energía y Derecho Internacional: Perspectivas de Futuro*. Cizur Menor: Aranzadi, 2012, pp. 207–218.

79 American Declaration of the Rights and Duties of Man, entered into force on 2 May 1948. Adopted by the Ninth International Conference of American States, Bogotá, 1948.

80 Although a US policy on climate change is certainly the sum of the different policies adopted at the subnational and federal level, it was key for the petition that the USA decided to withdraw from the Kyoto Protocol under the Bush administration, in 2001.

> put this global issue into a broader human and human rights context. Our intent is to encourage and to inform.[81]

In its substance, the relation between a human rights violation and the acts and omission of the American states was built on three main assumptions: (1) The USA substantially contributed and still contributes to the global greenhouse gases emissions but is not taking adequate steps to reduce them. Quite the opposite, the US withdrawal from the Kyoto Protocol points to the fact that this will not likely change in the future. In this sense, the State's conduct is considered to be negligent. (2) The impacts derived from climate change have negative effects on Inuit livelihoods and on the environment in which they live and subsist on. To this end, the findings of the 2004 Arctic Climate Impact Assessment Report were largely cited in the petition. (3) The impact that human-induced climate change is having on Inuit lives amounts to a human rights violation. Arguably the most innovative aspect of this lawsuit, this argument has reframed the environmental problem of climate change through using the lenses of human rights.

Sustaining that the evidence provided in the case was not sufficient to ascertain a violation of human rights, the Commission refused to consider the case in November 2006 but conducted a public hearing on the relationship between global warming and human rights in March 2007. Nevertheless, this case should be noted for several reasons. First of all, it is beyond doubt that the petition has had a major impact in giving a "human face" to climate change, hitherto exclusively considered as an abstract environmental problem and mainly addressed through market-based instruments, such as the European emissions trading system. In this respect, it has undoubtedly contributed to the international publicity of the indigenous cause too. Notwithstanding the accuracy of certain criticisms moved to the Inuit petition by some commentators,[82] the case has been praised for being "an important example of creative lawyering in both substance and form".[83] The case, at the intersection between an environmental rights litigation and a human rights petition, is a mix of a legal action aimed at securing the respect of human rights and an advocacy strategy targeted at addressing pressing environmental issues. In this regard, and particularly relevant in terms of participation of the public, Koivurova and others have maintained that:

81 S. WATT-CLOUTIER, *The Climate Change Petition by the Inuit Circumpolar Conference to the Inter-American Commission on Human Rights*, Presentation held at the Eleventh Conference of Parties to the UN Framework Convention on Climate Change. Montreal: 2005. Available at: http://www.inuitcircumpolar.com/inuit-petition-inter-american-commission-on-human-rights-to-oppose-climate-change-caused-by-the-united-states-of-america.html (Last access, 22 August 2019).

82 M.CASTILLO DAUDÍ, *supra* note 78

83 H., M. OSOFSKY, "The Inuit Petition as a Bridge? Beyond Dialectic of Climate Change and Indigenous Peoples' Rights", *American Indian Law Review*, Vol. 31, No. 2, 2007, pp. 675–697, at 267.

> The ICC's actions demonstrate how to effectively challenge both the basic rules prescribed by the climate change and the structure upheld by international law as a society of states. By raising the human rights petition against the US, the Inuit expanded society's notion of who is entitled to participate in the fight against climate change.[84]

In the framework of this work, the petition is of great value for the contribution that it has made to the legal doctrine exploring a climate change-human rights nexus, and for its capacity to generate a debate on the relationship between global warming and human rights within the legal scholarship and in UN bodies. Indeed, and primarily driven by the Inuit petition, since 2005 the issue of human rights has been a key element in the debate on global climate change, embodied in various resolutions of the Human Rights Council.[85] As Duyck, Jodoin and Johl have reported: "This petition, in combination with the Inuit Circumpolar Council's advocacy efforts in the UN climate negotiations, is generally considered to have played a critical role in raising awareness of the human rights dimension of climate change".[86] Indeed, the Inuit efforts were joined in 2007 by the Small Island Developing States (SIDS), which called for the commitment of the United Nations Human Rights Council to recognise the negative implications of climate change for human rights.

The petition, a pioneer in specifically linking human rights and global warming, has finally set a relevant precedent for other climate litigation that has taken place in different jurisdictions and judicial systems. In this regard, Arctic indigenous peoples have been the first to use the human rights framework to address a global environmental problem, paving the way for similar legal actions and advocacy strategies in the Arctic and elsewhere.[87] For instance, in 2013 a new petition was filed before the IACHR by the Athabaskan peoples of Canada and the United States. Although the case is still pending, the Commission has progressively recognised and expressed concern for the impacts of climate

84 T. KOIVUROVA, S. DUYCK and L. HEINÄMÄKI, "Climate Change and Human Rights", in E. J. HOLLO, K. KUVOLESI and M. MEHLING (eds.) *Climate Change and the Law*. Dordrecht: Springer, 2013, pp. 287–325, at 324.

85 A. JOHL and S. DUYCK, "Promoting Human Rights in the Future Climate Regime", *Ethics, Policy and Environment*, Vol. 15, No. 3, 2012, pp. 298–302. The role of UN bodies in the affirmation of such a relationship will be detailed in the last chapter of this research.

86 S. DUYCK, S. JODOIN and A. JOHL (eds.) *Routledge Handbook of Human Rights and Climate Change*. London: Routledge, 2018, at 5.

87 Although it has attracted less media and public attention than the first Inuit petition, several authors have analysed the case. See, for example, V. DE LA ROSA JAIMES, "The Arctic Athabaskan Petition: Where Accelerated Arctic Warming Meets Human Rights", *California Western International Law Journal*, Vol. 2, No. 45, 2015, pp. 213–260; D. McCRIMMON, "The Athabaskan Petition to the Inter-American Human Rights Commission: Using Human Rights to Respond Climate Change", *The Polar Journal*, Vol. 2, No. 16, 2016, pp. 398–416.

change on the enjoyment of human rights in the region, something that might influence its future decision on this case.[88]

In conclusion, the resort to a petition as a means to obtain effective legal remedies against the detrimental impact that climate change has on human rights, has arguably been the most pioneering expression of indigenous diplomacy in the Arctic and internationally, also proving the ICC's ability to stand up for a broad international indigenous climate movement, which the Inuit petition has undoubtedly promoted and strengthened. Indeed, although unsuccessful from a strictly legal perspective, the case has at least called into question the premises on which the negotiation of a climate change regime has largely relied. Not only the Paris Agreement today expressively acknowledges the relationship between climate change and human rights in its Preamble, but climate litigation has surged as a transnational phenomenon aimed at promoting regulatory change and upholding procedural rights in the context of climate change law.

4.5 Concluding remarks

The decision to analyse the practice of Arctic indigenous peoples in the Arctic Council and at the international level aimed at highlighting the value of their model of participation, inspired by and constructed on the acknowledgement of their specific status as *peoples* who, under international law, are holders of specific collective and individual human rights.

The description of indigenous practice in the Arctic has shown that most of their actions as Permanent Participants and transnational non-governmental organisations have primarily relied upon their capacity to transmit their knowledge to political actors, as well as to influence the scientific research and decision- and law-making process. Likewise, and most importantly, they have resorted to their ability to claim, project and uphold their status as *right-holders* in regional and international negotiation forums, promoting their rights to participation through rights-based discourses and claims. As Aponte Miranda explains:

> For indigenous peoples, the human rights discourse has offered a normative framework potentially capable of lending increased legitimacy to their local, anti-subordination struggles and to translating their contemporary claims into recognizable rights.[89]

88 ORGANIZATION OF AMERICAN STATES, "IACHR Expresses Concern Regarding Effects of Climate Change on Human Rights", *OAS*, 2 December 2015. Available at: http://www.oas.org/en/iachr/media_center/preleases/2015/140.asp (Last access, 27 August 2019).

89 L. APONTE MIRANDA, "Introduction to Indigenous Peoples' Status and Rights under International Human Rights Law", in R. S. ABATE and E. A. KRONK WARNER (eds.) *Climate Change and Indigenous Peoples. The Search for Legal Remedies.* Cheltenham: Edward Elgar, 2013, pp. 39–62, at 41.

The possibility of considering and proposing the Arctic case as a model for the participation of other non-State actors – primarily individuals and the non-governmental organisations representing them – for their participation in the process of climate change law-making may seem *prima facie* unsuitable. A reasonable commentator would object that it is primarily because of their status as *peoples* within States, that indigenous peoples enjoy specific rights, as the right to self-determination. Yet, most of their claims have resorted upon the respect of international human rights which, by definition, pertain to and are inherent to all individuals. In the specific case of climate change then, both the theory and practice of law have evolved towards a more sensible approach to a human rights dimension, as demonstrated by the integration of a rights-based perspective in the regime tackling global warming and by those climate litigation cases that have relied on this body of law for their determination.[90] This, in turn, makes relying on the rights-based approach practice adopted by Arctic IPs a more plausible and acceptable option.

Far from being an easy task, the possibility to draw a legal analogy between the model of participation of Arctic IPs and that of other non-State actors so that they can enjoy improved rights of participation in international climate governance, is also related to the question of whether the consideration of climate change as a human rights issue has sufficiently affirmed internationally.

While answering this question, the final part of this work will more broadly look at a set of international law instruments that may be suitable to the improvement of procedural rights in the climate change context, primarily climate change litigation but also the emergence of an autonomous and independent right to a healthy and safe environment.

Bibliography

Abate, R. S. and E. A. Kronk Warner. "Commonality among Unique Indigenous Communities: An Introduction to Climate Change and its Impacts on Indigenous Peoples", in R. S. Abate and E. A. Kronk Warner (eds.) *Climate Change and Indigenous Peoples. The Search for Legal Remedies*. Cheltenham: Edward Elgar, 2013, pp. 3–18.

Anaya, J. *Indigenous Peoples in International Law*. Oxford: Oxford University Press, 2004.

Andersen, P. J. (ed.) *The Indigenous World 2018*. Copenhagen: The International Work Group for Indigenous Affairs, 2018.

Aponte Miranda, L. "Introduction to Indigenous Peoples' Status and Rights under International Human Rights Law", in R. S. Abate and E. A. Kronk Warner (eds.) *Climate Change and Indigenous Peoples. The Search for Legal Remedies*. Cheltenham: Edward Elgar, 2013.

Arctic Council. *Declaration on the Establishment of the Arctic Council of 19 September 1996* (35 ILM 1382).

90 See, e.g., P. DE VILCHEZ MORAGUES, "Broadening the Scope: The Urgenda Case, the Oslo Principles and the Role of National Courts in Advancing Environmental Protection Concerning Climate Change", *The Spanish Yearbook of International Law*, Vol. 20, 2016, pp. 71–92.

Arctic Environmental Protection Strategy. *The Nuuk Declaration on Environment and Development in the Arctic of 16 September 1993*. Available at http://arcticcircle.uconn.edu/NatResources/Policy/nuuk.html.

Arena Hidalgo, N. "Climate Change Induced Displacement: Migration as an Adaptation Strategy Also in the Arctic?", in E. Conde and S. Sánchez Iglesias (eds.) *Global Challenges in the Arctic Region*. London: Routledge, 2017, pp. 254–277.

Barnabas, S. G. "The Legal Status of the United Nations Declaration on the Rights of Indigenous Peoples (2007) in Contemporary International Human Rights Law", *International Human Rights Law Review*, Vol. 6, 2017, pp. 242–261.

Betzold, C. *Non-State Actors in International Climate Change Negotiations*, Doctoral dissertation, 1984.

Borgia, F. and P. Vargiu. "The Inuit Declaration on Sovereignty in the Arctic Between the Right to Self-Determination and a New Concept of Sovereignty?", in G. Alfredsson and T. Koivurova (eds.) *The Yearbook of Polar Law IV*, 2012, pp. 189–204.

Byers, M. *International Law and the Arctic*. Cambridge: Cambridge University Press, 2014.

Cassese, A. *Self-Determination of Peoples. A Legal Reappraisal*. Cambridge: Cambridge University Press, 1995.

Castillo Daudí, M. "Cambio Climático y Derechos Humanos: El Asunto de los Inuit Ante la Comisión Interamericana de Derechos Humanos", in R. Giles Carnero (coord.) *Cambio Climático, Energía y Derecho Internacional: Perspectivas de Futuro*. Cizur Menor: Aranzadi, 2012, pp. 207–218.

Conde Pérez, E. "Delimitaciones marítimas y territoriales en el Ártico: Desarrollo y Tendencias", *Revista Española de Derecho Internacional* Vol. 68, No. 1, 2016, pp. 235–239.

Conde Pérez, E. and Z. Valerieva Yaneva. "Outer Arctic Continental Shelf", in E. Conde and S. Sánchez Iglesias (eds.) *Global Challenges in the Arctic Region*. London: Routledge, 2017, pp. 19–41.

Coppes, M. "Canada's Acceptance of the United Nations Declaration on the Rights of Indigenous Peoples: Implications for the Inuit", *The Arctic Institute*, 09 August 2016. Available at: https://www.thearcticinstitute.org/canadas-acceptance-declaration-rights-indigenous-peoples/.

Dahl, J. *IWGIA: A History*. Copenhagen: International Work Group on Indigenous Affairs, 2009.

De La Rosa Jaimes, V. "The Arctic Athabaskan Petition: Where Accelerated Arctic Warming Meets Human Rights", *California Western International Law Journal*, Vol. 2, No. 45, 2015, pp. 213–260.

De Vilchez Moragues, P. "Broadening the Scope: The Urgenda Case, the Oslo Principles and the Role of National Courts in Advancing Environmental Protection Concerning Climate Change", *Spanish Yearbook of International Law*, Vol. 20, 2016, pp. 71–92.

Dorough, D. S. "The Rights, Interests and Role of the Arctic Council Permanent Participants", in R. Beckman, T. Henriksen, K. Dalaker Kraabel And Others (eds.) *Governing Arctic Shipping*. Leiden: Brill, 2017, pp. 68–103.

Dorough, D. S. "Our Homeland. Arctic Indigenous Peoples' Perspectives on Non-Arctic States", in A. Shibata, L. Zou, N. Sellheim and M. Scopelliti (eds.) *Emerging Legal Orders in the Arctic: The Role of non-Arctic Actors*. New York: Routledge, 2019, pp. 69–90.

Duyck, S. "Which Canary in the Coalmine? The Arctic in the International Climate Change Regime", in T. Koivurova, G. Alfredsson and W. Hasanat (eds.) *The Yearbook of Polar Law, Volume 4*. Leiden: Brill, 2012.

Duyck, S. *The Arctic Voice at the UNFCCC Negotiations. Interplay Between Arctic & Climate Governance*. LL.M. programme dissertation, 2015.

Duyck, S., Jodoin, S. and A. Johl (eds.) *Routledge Handbook of Human Rights and Climate Change*. London: Routledge, 2018.

Fabbi, N. C. "Inuit Foreign Policy and International Relations in the Arctic", in L. C. Jensen and G. Honneland (eds.) *Handbook of the Politics of the Arctic*. Cheltenham: Edward Elgar, 2015, pp. 482–500.

Fenge, T. and D. Downie (eds.) *Northern Lights Against POPs*. Montreal: McGill- Queen's University Press, 2003.

Gamble, J. and J. Shadian. "One Arctic…But Uneven Capacity: The Arctic Council Permanent Participants", in W. Lackenbauer, N. Heather and W. Graves (eds.) *One Arctic. The Arctic Council and Circumpolar Governance*. Ottawa: Canadian Arctic Resources Committee and Centre on Foreign Policy and Federalism, 2017, pp. 142–156.

Graczyk, P. and T. Koivurova. "A new era in the Arctic Council's External Relations? Broader Consequences of the Nuuk Observer Rules for Arctic Governance", *Polar Record*, Vol. 50, No. 254, 2014, pp. 225–236.

Hassol, S. J. *Impacts of a Warming Arctic. Arctic Climate Impact Assessment*. Cambridge: Cambridge University Press, 2004.

Heinämäki, L. *The Right to Be a Part of Nature – Indigenous Peoples and the Environment*. Rovaniemi: Lapland University Press, 2010.

Heininen, L., Exner Pirot, H. and J. Plouffe (eds.) *Arctic Council: 20 Years of Regional Cooperation and Policy-Shaping, Arctic Yearbook 2016*. Akureyri: Northern Research Forum, 2016.

Heleniak, T. "Arctic Populations and Migration", in J. Nymand Larsen and G. Fondahl (eds.) *Arctic Human Development Report. Regional Processes and Global Linkages*. Copenhagen: Nordic Council of Ministers, 2014, pp. 53–103.

Hussain, K. and A. Petrétei (eds.) *Understanding the Many Faces of Human Security: Perspectives of Northern Indigenous Peoples*. Leiden: Brill Nijhoff, 2016.

International Labour Organisation. *Indigenous and Tribal Peoples Convention, C 169, of 27 June 1989* (28 ILM 1382).

Johl, A. and S. Duyck. "Promoting Human Rights in the Future Climate Regime", *Ethics, Policy and Environment*, Vol. 15, No. 3, 2012, pp. 298–302.

Keil, K. and S. Knecht (eds.) *Governing Arctic Change. Global Perspectives*. London: Palgrave Macmillan, 2017.

Koivurova, T. "The Draft for A Nordic Saami Convention", *European Yearbook of Minority Issues*, Vol. 6, 2006, pp. 103–136.

Koivurova, T. and A. Stepien. "How International Law Has Influenced the National Policy and Law Related to Indigenous Peoples in the Arctic", *Waikato Law Review*, Vol. 19, No. 1, 2011, pp. 123–143.

Koivurova, T., Duyck, S. and L. Heinämäki. "Climate Change and Human Rights", in E. J. Hollo, K. Kuvolesi and M. Mehling (eds.) *Climate Change and the Law*. Dordrecht: Springer, 2013, pp. 287–325.

Loukacheva, N. "Arctic Indigenous Peoples' Internationalism: In Search of a Legal Justification", *Polar Record*, Vol. 45, No. 23, 2009, pp. 51–58.

Mccrimmon, D. "The Athabaskan Petition to the Inter-American Human Rights Commission: Using Human Rights to Respond Climate Change", *The Polar Journal*, Vol. 2, No.16, 2016, pp. 398–416.

Molenaar, E. J. "Current and Prospective Roles of the Arctic Council System Within the Context of the Law of the Sea", *The International Journal of Marine and Coastal Law*, Vol. 27, No. 3, 2014, pp. 553–595.

Nord, D. *The Arctic Council: Governance Within the Far North*. New York: Routledge, 2016.

Organization of American States. "IACHR Expresses Concern Regarding Effects of Climate Change on Human Rights", *OAS*, 2 December 2015. Available at: http://www.oas.org/en/iachr/media_center/preleases/2015/140.asp.

Osofsky, H. M. "The Inuit Petition as a Bridge? Beyond Dialectic of Climate Change and Indigenous Peoples' Rights", *American Indian Law Review*, Vol. 31, No. 2, 2007, pp. 675–697.

Platjouw, F., M., Steindal, E. H. and T. Borch. "From Arctic Science to International Law: The Road Towards the Minamata Convention and the Role of the Arctic Council", *Arctic Review on Law and Politics*, Vol. 9, 2018, pp. 226–243.

Plaut, S. "Cooperation Is the Story: Best Practices of Transnational Indigenous Activism in the North", *The International Journal of Human Rights*, Vol. 16, No. 1, 2012, pp. 193–215.

Poelzer, G. "Governance in the Arctic: Political Systems and Geopolitics", in J. Nymand Larsen and G. Fondahl (eds.) *Arctic Human Development Report. Regional Processes and Global Linkages*. Copenhagen: Nordic Council of Ministers, 2014, pp. 185–220.

Poto, M. P. and L. Fornabaio. "Participation as the Essence of Good Governance: Some General Reflections and a Case Study on the Arctic Council", *Arctic Review on Law and Politics*, Vol. 8, 2017, pp. 139–159.

Powless, B. "The Indigenous Rights Framework and Climate Change", in S. Duyck, S. Jodoin and A. Johl (eds.) *Routledge Handbook of Human Rights and Climate Governance*. New York: Routledge, 2018, pp. 213–221.

Rottem, S. V. "A Note on the Arctic Council Agreements", *Ocean Development & International Law*, Vol. 46, No. 1, 2015, pp. 50–59.

Scopelliti, M. and N. Sellheim. "Sustaining a Conservationist Agenda? NGO-Influence on Arctic Sealing, Whaling and Hydrocarbon Regimes", in A. Shibata, L. Zou, N. Sellheim and M. Scopelliti (eds.) *Emerging Legal Orders in the Arctic: The Role of non-Arctic Actors*. New York: Routledge, 2019, pp. 91–106.

Selin, H. "Global Environmental Governance and Treaty-Making: The Arctic's Fragmented Voice", in K. Keil and S. Knecht (eds.) *Governing Arctic Change. Global Perspectives*. London: Palgrave Macmillan, 2017, pp. 101–120.

Shadian, J. "From States to Polities: Reconceptualizing Sovereignty through Inuit Governance", *European Journal of International Relations*, Vol. 16, No. 3, 2010, pp. 485–510.

Shadian, J. "Rethinking Westphalian Sovereignty: The Inuit Circumpolar Council and the Future of Arctic Governance", *Working Papers on Arctic Security*, Vol. 8, 2013, pp. 1–58.

Shadian, J. *The Politics of Arctic Sovereignty. Oil, Ice and Inuit Governance*. New York: Routledge, 2014.

Steinberg, P., Tasch, J., Gerhardt, H. and A. Keul. *Contesting the Arctic. Rethinking Politics in the Circumpolar North*. London: I.B. Tauris, 2015.

Stephen, K. "Arctic Indigenous Cookbook Wins Gourmand World Cookbook Award", *High North News*, 30 May 2018. Available at: http://www.highnorthnews.com/arctic-indigenous-cookbook-wins-gourmand-world-cookbook-award/.

Taylor, M. "Antarctic ice Melting Faster Than Ever, Studies Show", *The Guardian*, 13 June 2018. Available at: https://www.theguardian.com/environment/2018/jun/13/antarctic-ice-melting-faster-than-ever-studies-show.

Tennberg, M. "Indigenous Peoples as International Political Actors: A Summary", *Polar Record*, Vol. 46, No. 238, 2010, pp. 264–270.

Torrecuadrada García-Lozano, S. *Los Pueblos Indígenas en el Orden Internacional*. Madrid: Dykinson, 2001.

Torrecuadrada García-Lozano, S. and R. M. Fernández Egea. "Environmental Challenges for Arctic Peoples", in E. Conde and S. Sánchez Iglesias (eds.) *Global Challenges in the Arctic Region*. London: Routledge, 2017, pp. 236–253.

United Nations General Assembly. *United Nations Declaration on the Rights of Indigenous People of 02 October 2007* (UN Doc. A/Res/61/295).

Vanderzwaag, D., Huebert, R. and S. Ferrara, "The Arctic Environmental Protection Strategy, Arctic Council and Multilateral Environmental Initiatives: Tinkering While the Arctic Marine Environment Totters", in A. G. Oude Elerink and D. R. Rothwell (eds.) *The Law of the Sea and Polar Maritime Delimitation and Jurisdiction*. The Hague: Martinus Nijhoff, 2001, pp. 225–248.

Watt-Cloutier, S. *The Climate Change Petition by the Inuit Circumpolar Conference to the Inter-American Commission on Human Rights*. Presentation held at the Eleventh Conference of Parties to the UN Framework Convention on Climate Change. Montreal: 2005. Available at: http://www.inuitcircumpolar.com/inuit-petition-inter-american-commission-on-human-rights-to-oppose-climate-change-caused-by-the-united-states-of-america.html.

Watts, J. "Arctic's Strongest Sea Ice Break Up for First Time on Record", *The Guardian*, 21 August 2018. Available at: https://www.theguardian.com/world/2018/aug/21/arctics-strongest-sea-ice-breaks-up-for-first-time-on-record.

Young, O. "The Arctic Council at Twenty: How to Remain Effective in a Rapidly Changing Environment", *UC Irvine Law Review*, Vol. 6, No. 99, 2016, pp. 99–120.

Part III

Improving public participation in climate change law-making

International law instruments

5 Climate change litigation

A bottom-up approach to climate change governance

5.1 Introduction

A UNEP report surveying the state of climate change litigation counted that, as of March 2017, over 800 climate change-related cases were filed in 24 countries.[1] In September 2020, this number doubled, reaching 1665 cases across different jurisdictions, 200 of which have been filed across European countries. At least to some extent, this trend relates and points to the fact that the number of national and international laws aimed at redressing climate change has grown in recent years.[2] Yet, the rise in the number of litigation cases challenges the content and application of those regulations in different ways. As a matter of fact, albeit a minority of cases involves private actors such as major companies or carbon producers, governments appear in courts as defendants in the vast majority of lawsuits.

By taking a closer look at the reality of climate litigation, it will be noticed that just a small pool of these cases aims at challenging the implementation of specific projects, such as the extraction of resources in environmentally sensitive areas or the construction of invasive structures in territories at risk from erosion. On the contrary, corporations bring to court around half of the registered claims in order to overturn administrative decisions and sustain climate deregulation, in the interests of the projects they aim at implementing. Notwithstanding this, most of the scholarly analysis looking at the emergence of this new trend has rather focused on those cases that are brought by individuals, NGOs or subnational authorities. In the claims registered outside the USA until 2018, 68 of the lawsuits have been initiated by an individual,

1 UNITED NATIONS ENVIRONMENT PROGRAMME, *The Status of Climate Change Litigation – A Global Review*. Nairobi: UNEP, 2017, p. 10. The Sabin Center for Climate Change Law maintains a database on US and non-US climate change litigation. The databases are available at: http://climatecasechart.com/ (Last access, 28 August 2020).

2 Indeed, all of the signatories of the Paris Agreement have enacted at least one law or policy on climate change. The Grantham Research Institute on Climate Change and the Environment, in collaboration with the London School of Economics, maintains a database on world climate change legislation and periodically publishes a report on the global progresses and setbacks found in this

Table 5.1 Number of Climate Change Litigation Cases by Country

Region	*Country*	*Number of Cases**
Inter-American Commission on Human Rights		3
Inter-American Court of Human Rights		1
International Court of Justice		2
OECD		7
UN Committee on the Rights of the Child		1
UN Framework Convention on Climate Change		11
UN Human Rights Committee		2
UN Special Rapporteurs		1
Africa		
	Kenya	1
	Nigeria	1
	South Africa	4
	Uganda	1
	Pakistan	4
Asia Pacific		
	Australia	112
	India	2
	Indonesia	1
	Japan	4
	New Zealand	18
	Philippines	1
	South Korea	1
Europe		
	European Union	55
	European Committee on Social Rights	1
	European Court of Human Rights	1
	Austria	2
	Belgium	1
	Czech Republic	1
	Estonia	1
	France	11
	Germany	7
	Ireland	4
	Luxembourg	1
	Netherlands	3
	Norway	2

(*Continued*)

field. The report is available in Spanish too, see: M. NACHMANY and S. FANKHAUSER, *Estudio sobre legislación de cambio climático 2015. Informe sobre la legislación de cambio climático en 99 países.* London: London School of Economics, 2015. While the database is available at: http://www.lse.ac.uk/GranthamInstitute/climate-change-laws-of-the-world/ (Last access, 28 August 2020). For a detailed and overreaching analysis of climate change legislations, see: A. AVERCHENKOVA, S. FANKHAUSER and M. NACHMANY (eds.) *Trends in Climate Change Litigation.* Cheltenham: Edward Elgar, 2017.

Table 5.1 (*Continued*)

Region	*Country*	*Number of Cases**
	Poland	4
	Slovenia	1
	Spain	14
	Sweden	1
	Switzerland	2
	Ukraine	2
	United Kingdom	59
Latin America and Caribbean		
	Argentina	8
	Brazil	8
	Chile	2
	Colombia	2
	Ecuador	1
	Peru	1
North America		
	Canada	25
	Mexico	2
	United States	1267
TOTAL		**1665**

* The numbers shown here reflect our tally of climate change cases across jurisdictions as of September 2020. It is possible that these numbers omit one or more cases that have already been filed or decided but have not yet come to our attention.

Source: Sabin Center for Climate Change Law, Columbia Law School.

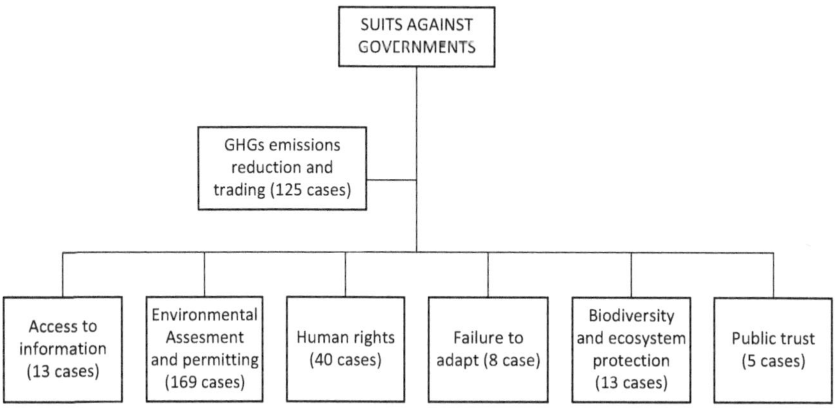

Figure 5.1 Non-U.S. Climate Change Litigation, Suits Against Governments Credit: 2020 Sabin Center for Climate Change Law U.S. Litigation Chart made in collaboration with Arnold & Porter Kaye Scholer LLP. Reproduced with permission. Retrieved from: http://climatecasechart.com/non-us-climatechange-litigation/

while NGOs have acted as representatives of groups of individuals around 48 times.[3] As said, this account does not consider those litigations initiated in the USA where, usually based on the doctrine of public trust and due to different standing requirements, [groups of] individuals appear as plaintiffs in the majority of cases.

The reason for such academic interest arguably rests on the relevance that climate change litigation may have as a mechanism for climate governance at the national and, alternatively, international levels. While the use of litigation in environmental contexts has usually related to the quest of environmental justice, several climate change-related litigations today maintain this characteristic but contemporarily assume a more strategic meaning too. Borrowing the definition used by the Grantham Research Institute on Climate Change:

> strategic litigation is a method that can bring about significant changes in the law, practice or public awareness via taking carefully-selected cases to court. In this way, strategic litigation focuses on an individual case in order to bring about social change.[4]

It follows that, as argued elsewhere, these cases stand at the intersection between legal actions aimed at obtaining remedies and a broader advocacy strategy promoted by climate advocates.[5]

In the context of the present research, climate change litigation is considered exactly for this specific feature, as a bottom-up strategy to climate governance, in which adjudication is used to push the improvement and reform of climate change laws and policies, as well as the defence and advancement of different rights, including procedural rights. By looking at how climate litigation has developed becoming an increasingly influent trend, this chapter aims at answering the question of whether – and how successfully – the resort to climate litigation is used as an instrument to redress the lack of participation in international climate change law-making, thus as an instrument to uphold participatory rights in this environmental context. While different international law instruments could be an object of scrutiny in this sense, the decision to focus on climate change litigation is motivated by the relatively new inception of this instrument and by its potential relevance as a trend that is developing

3 M. NACHMANY and J. SETZER, "Global Trends in Climate Change Legislation and Litigation: 2018 Snapshot". Grantham Research Institute on Climate Change and the Environment and Centre for Climate Change Economics and Policy, 2018.

4 *Ibid.*

5 See, e.g., S. JODOIN, R. FAUCHER and K. LOFTS, "Look before You Jump: Assessing the Potential Influence of the Human Rights Bandwagon on Domestic Climate Policy", in S. DUYCK, S. JODOIN and A. JOHL (eds.) *Routledge Handbook of Human Rights and Climate Governance*. New York: Routledge, 2018, pp. 167–182; H. M. OSOFSKY, "The Inuit Petition as a Bridge? Beyond Dialectic of Climate Change and Indigenous Peoples' Rights", *American Indian Law Review*, Vol. 31, No. 2, 2007, pp. 675–697.

in a transnational fashion. With this aim, the first section of this chapter will introduce the topic of litigation more broadly and try to bring some clarity on the main characteristics and elements that constitute climate-related litigations.

5.2 Litigation in International Environmental Law

The affirmation of an environmental justice movement in the USA during the 1980s was mostly concerned with how to address disproportionate environmental harms to humans. The idea of achieving justice, in this sense, stemmed from the need to address inequalities in how the burdens and benefits derived from economic development had to be carried by different communities. A manifest discrimination would be constituted, for instance, by the concentration of toxic and hazardous waste in socio-economically fragile communities. The latter being a common practice during the 1970s and 80s, this spurred the inception of the environmental justice movement, given that the degradation of the environment was adding another layer of vulnerability to the lack of resources and poor living conditions of those communities. It follows that the achievement of justice in an environmental context requires the reconciliation of the social, environmental and economic dimensions that constitute the modern understanding of sustainable development:[6] an objective to be pursued by ensuring equal protection of people(s) against any environmental and health hazard, as well as by securing their equal access to decision-making processes.

In recent decades, the emergence of climate change as a global, transnational and transgenerational environmental problem has given new impetus to environmental justice, primarily due to the ethical questions raised by this issue. The anthropogenic nature of climate change as a human-caused harm has turned public attention towards questions regarding human-nature interactions and relationships. For example, is it possible – and if so, how – to strike a balance between the rights and duties carried by different generations? Is there any nation that is to be considered more responsible for the negative consequences of greenhouse gases emissions? While most of these interrogatives remain largely unanswered to date, a clear question of justice and equity refers to the fact that those countries and communities that will likely be more affected by climate change have contributed the least to causing this environmental harm. In this regard, climate change acts as an amplifier of pre-existing vulnerabilities and largely diminishes the resilience capacity of most developing States and communities.[7]

6 See, on the idea of sustainable development and its dimensions, the report of the Brundtland commission: WORLD COMMISSION ON ENVIRONMENT AND DEVELOPMENT, *Our Common Future. Report of the World Commission on Environment and Development*. Oxford: Oxford University Press, 1987.

7 See, S. HALLEGATTE, M. BANGALORE, L. BONZANIGO and others, *Shock Waves: Managing the Impacts of Climate Change on Poverty: Climate Change and Development*. Washington, DC: World Bank Group, 2016. The report has estimated that, between 2015 and 2030, around 100 million

Against this background, the idea of environmental justice is reflected in that of climate justice,[8] the latter being the response of those countries and communities that have been – and will likely be in the future – more exposed and disproportionally affected by the impacts of climate change. Counting on fewer resources to adapt, they are demanding a change in the way in which this environmental problem is being addressed, both in terms of equal distribution and enjoyment of resources, or with reference to procedural rights and compensation.[9] It is particularly in the context of these last dimensions of climate justice, the defence of procedural rights and remediation, that climate litigation has been used to strategically advance different rights. Although these same issues have been brought to the attention of climate change law negotiators on different occasions,[10] and have been partially enshrined in the principles of common but differentiated responsibilities, intergenerational responsibilities or addressed in a loss and damage mechanism, the nature of negotiation is essentially political and rarely helps to achieve a redistributive objective.[11]

Against this backdrop, climate change litigation is a relatively novel phenomenon, which has nonetheless exponentially increased since the mid-2000s. Preston reports that the first American decision relating to climate change dates back to 1990 and that, since then, climate change arguments have been primarily litigated in different national American and Australian courts[12] and

people will end in poverty due to climate-related causes (damages in crops, raise in the prices of goods, etc.). On the other hand, these factors are likely to impact on the growth of the so-called climate-induced migrations. See, on this topic, R. McLEMAN and F. GEMENNE (eds.) *Routledge Handbook of Environmental Displacement and Migration*. New York: Routledge, 2018.

8 See, D. ROSER and C. SEIDEL, *Climate Justice: An Introduction*. New York: Routledge, 2013; D. STABINSKY, "Climate Justice and Human Rights", in S. DUYCK, S. JODOIN and A. JOHL (eds.) *Routledge Handbook of Human Rights and Climate Governance*. New York: Routledge, 2018, pp. 280–291; U. BAXI, "Towards a Climate Change Justice Theory?", *Journal of Human Rights and the Environment*, Vol. 7, No. 1, 2016, pp. 7–31. In the context of climate change negotiation, particularly the Small Island Developing States have been promoting an agenda on climate justice and a qualified reference to the latter is today included in the Preamble of the Paris Agreement which recognises the importance "for some" of the concept of climate justice.

9 See, on this issue, S. BORRÁS PENTINAT, "Movimientos para la justicia climática global: replanteando el escenario internacional del cambio climático", *Relaciones Internacionales*, Vol. 33, 2017, pp. 97–119.

10 See, S. BORRÁS PENTINAT, "Los litigios climáticos: Entre la tutela climática y la fiscalización de las responsabilidades por daños climáticos", in R. GILES CARNERO (coord.) *Cambio Climático, Energía y Derecho Internacional: Perspectivas de Futuro*. Cizur Menor: Aranzadi, 2012, pp. 91–104, at 103.

11 It should be noted though that, in the framework of the Paris Agreement, the principle of common but differentiated responsibilities is less prominent than in the UNFCCC or the Kyoto Protocol. This answers for the willingness of imposing emission reductions targets on all Parties based on their NDCs, which are largely established on a voluntary basis. As regards the loss and damage mechanism established at the Warsaw Conference of 2013 and included in the Paris Agreement then, article 8 of the treaty expressively tells that the reference to loss and damage does not provide a basis for any liability or compensation. It follows that the content of the article is largely symbolic.

12 B., J. PRESTON, "Climate Change Litigation (Part 1)", *Carbon & Climate Law Review*, Vol. 5, No. 1, 2011, pp. 3–14, at 4.

are, increasingly more, considered under different national, regional and international jurisdictions beyond the USA. This, consequently, reflects the increasingly more prominent role that courts and tribunals have come to play in domestic and international climate change governance. Due to the great variety of actors, jurisdictions and legal sources that the analysis of climate change litigation entails, however, some preliminary questions related to the characteristics and legal elements of this new phenomenon are considered below.

5.3 Introducing climate change litigation: characteristics and legal elements

The appearance of climate-related suits in different national, regional and international jurisdictions has been attributed to the fact that nobody has legal jurisdiction and authority over the global scope of the climate change problem. Likewise, frustration has been caused by the slow pace at which climate negotiations have developed, as well as by the lack of adequate means to adjudicate the obligations of States in relation to climate change mitigation.

Indeed, the UNFCCC does not foresee strong mechanisms for sanctioning the countries that are acting in violation of its provisions and exclusively affirms the competence of the ICJ to address climate change-related cases in article 14.[13] In this regard, a possible avenue to assess the negligence of States would rely on the possibility to establish their responsibility in violation of the no-harm rule, which prescribes the obligation of a State to prevent, reduce and control the risk of environmental harm coming from its own territory to other States.[14] The first attempt in this sense was made in 2002 by the insular State of Tuvalu (Polynesia), who advanced the possibility to denounce the USA

13 Under the UNFCCC, compliance was assessed through a relatively weak pledge and review system. As detailed in the second chapter of this research, the latter has been also included in the Paris Agreement but in legally binding terms. As for dispute settlement mechanisms, instead, article 14 of the UNFCCC provides the possibility to resort to negotiation, conciliation and non-compulsory arbitration or adjudication. In the latter case, the International Court of Justice may be invoked exclusively if the Parties to a dispute have previously accepted its jurisdiction. To date, none of the mentioned mechanisms has been invoked.

14 Primarily established in the Trail Smelter Arbitration, *United States v. Canada*, 16 April 1938 and 11 March 1941. 3 UNRIAA 1905, Principle 21 of the Stockholm Declaration of 1972 established that: "States have, in accordance with the Charter of the United Nations and the principles of international law, the sovereign right to exploit their own resources pursuant to their own environmental policies, and the responsibility to ensure that activities within their jurisdiction or control do not cause damage to the environment of other States or of areas beyond the limits of national jurisdiction". See, Declaration of the United Nations Conference on the Human Environment, *Principle 21* of 16 June 1972 (UN Doc. A/CONF/48/14/Rev.1). Although there is no agreement as if the rule reflects customary international law, the ICJ has reaffirmed the relevance of this principle in relevant case law. Although the rule is originally based on a clear separation of sovereign competencies between States, it has acquired the identity in environmental law of a principle aimed at preserving a healthy environment. See, for a detailed analysis, D. BODANSKY, J. BRUNNÉE and L. RAJAMANI, *International Climate Change Law*. Oxford: Oxford University Press, 2017, p. 40.

and Australia before the International Court of Justice for the non-ratification of the Kyoto Protocol.[15] Ultimately, Tuvalu acknowledged the difficulty of bringing such a case and the claim was not submitted. Similarly, in 2011, the Pacific island of Palau proposed to the UN General Assembly to request an advisory opinion from the ICJ concerning the duties of States in the application of the no-harm rule.[16] Also in the latter case, however, the initiative was eventually not carried out. As a result, no climate case has been heard by the International Court of Justice to date and most climate-related litigation claims have been addressed in other international fora or presented at the national level. Notwithstanding this, the role of the ICJ and the potential for international adjudication in the context of climate change more broadly is still discussed in the scholarly debate.[17]

Other attempts to obtain successful adjudication at the international level include the already cited Inuit and Athabaskan petitions before the IACHR, as well as cases filed to the World Heritage Committee for violation of the 1972 Convention Concerning the Protection of the World Cultural and Natural Heritage, the result of which has been the listing of several sites affected by climate change within the List of World Heritage in Danger.[18]

Since most international jurisdictions are closed to individuals and are instead relevant to inter-state disputes, more proliferate and somewhat successful have been the claims raised before national courts. While, as already said, the USA is the country where most of these petitions have been presented,

15 See, M. GROMILOVA, "Rescuing the People of Tuvalu: Towards an I.C.J. Advisory Opinion on the International Legal Obligations to Protect the Environment and Human Rights of Populations Affected by Climate Change", *Intercultural Human Rights Law Review*, Vol. 10, 2015, pp. 233–289.

16 UNITED NATIONS NEWS, "Palau seeks UN World Court Opinion on Damage Caused by Greenhouse Gases", *UN NEWS*, 22 September 2011. Available at: https://news.un.org/en/story/2011/09/388202 (Last access, 28 August 2019).

17 See, e.g., D. BODANSKY, "The Role of the International Court of Justice in Addressing Climate Change: Some Preliminary Reflections", *Arizona State Law Journal*, Vol. 49, 2017, pp. 689–712; P. SANDS, "Climate Change and the Rule of Law: Adjudicating the Future in International Law", *Journal of Environmental Law*, Vol. 28, No. 19, 2016, pp. 19–35. Involved in the adjudication of several cases related to environmental problems, the ICJ established a chamber for environmental disputes in 1993, although the latter has stopped operating in 2006 when no new judges where elected to the chamber. For a more general analysis of the ICJ role in environmental dispute settlement, see: R. GILES CARNERO, "La Corte International de Justicia frente a las controversias internacionales de carácter medioambiental", in E., M. VÁZQUEZ GÓMEZ, M., D. ADAM MUÑOZ and N. CORNAGO-PRIETO (coord.) *El arreglo pacífico de las controversias internacionales: XXIV Jornadas de la Asociación Española de Profesores de Derecho internacional y Relaciones internacionales*. Valencia: Tirant lo Blanch, 2013, pp. 159–168; J. KLABBERS, *International Law*. Cambridge: Cambridge University Press, 2017, at 279.

18 UNITED NATIONS EDUCATIONAL, SCIENTIFIC AND CULTURAL ORGANISATION, *Convention Concerning the Protection of the World Cultural and Natural Heritage* of 16 November 1972 (1037 UNTS 151). See, World Heritage Committee, "Threats to World Heritage Properties", Decision 29 COM 7B.a, 2005; World Heritage Committee, Conservation of the World Heritage Properties: The Impacts of Climate Change on World Heritage Properties, Decision 30 COM 7.1, 2006.

civil suits have succeeded in Europe and the Middle East.[19] In the latter case, a mix of domestic (civil) law and international (human rights) law and principles have been relevant to adjudication. In fact, as this brief account has shown, the characteristics of climate-related litigation largely vary on the involved sources of law and the body, national or international, in which a claim is heard. Therefore, before assessing the potential relevance of these instruments and before going into the details or relevant cases, the following section of this chapter will explore the legal elements on which climate change litigation builds or can be constructed.

5.3.1 Commonalities among climate change litigation: legal elements

Climate change litigation is a very general term and different adjudication cases have been qualified using this one-size-fits-all category. Quite intuitively, this is primarily because, beyond the heterogeneity of rights at stake and the broad spectrum of involved actors, these cases have climate-related claims at their centre. Furthermore, although the objectives pursued by a petition are to be considered on a case by case basis, there are at least a number of legal elements that are common to most adjudications. The latter are exposed and detailed below.

5.3.1.1 Justiciability

In general terms, justiciability refers to the possibility of a legal case to be heard and adjudicated in a court, in order to ensure the protection of recognised rights or redress their actual or potential violation. It follows that not all legal issues are justiciable, as well as not all courts are appropriate forums for adjudication. A test for justiciability entails the existence of an actual controversy between two or more parties and that their interest is adverse. Moreover, and differently from the request for an advisory opinion, the controversy must lead to a practical relief. Finally, the judicial authority of a specific court relates to its ability and entitlement to decide on a specific matter (competent body). Even when this authority is uncontested, a court has discretion in deciding whether or not it should adjudicate on a specific matter.

Standards of justiciability may vary from one jurisdiction to the other and, of course, differences are to be found in national and international legal systems too. At both of these levels, however, climate change has been a rather conflicting issue as far as standing requirements and separation of powers are concerned. The latter are, in fact, two of the main requirements to be satisfied when a claim is to be presented before an international court or a national

19 *Supreme Court of the USA, Massachusetts v. Environmental Protection Agency, 549 U.S. 497, Judgement of 2 April 2007*. More details on the case are available at: http://climatecasechart.com/case/massachusetts-v-epa/ (Last access, 28 August 2019).

tribunal. The satisfaction of these requirements in climate change litigation is here considered in more detail:

- The separation of powers doctrine

  Due to the highly politicised nature of climate change and because of the key role that the legislative and executive powers maintain in this field, the exercise of what has been referred to as "judicial governance" in this realm has been contentious. The respect of the principle of separation of powers must be maintained when a court is considering to admit a climate change litigation. In different instances this has constituted the basis for the rejection of a claim. Yet, cases heard both in American and European courts have established groundbreaking precedents in this sense. For example, in the Urgenda case that will be detailed below, a district court found that Dutch law requires the judiciary to assess the actions of political bodies when the rights of citizens are at stake.[20] The same principle has been established by the US Supreme Court in its consideration of the case *Connecticut v. AEP*.[21] It follows that in a number of climate claims, the judicial power has shown willingness to assume a progressively more prominent role in the determination of which are to be considered effective actions to address and revert climate change, as well as in establishing that climate change may entail a violation of rights. It is no coincidence that, as maintained by Bodansky and others, the regulation of climate change is increasingly influenced by judicial governance and that the latter will likely become a complement of climate negotiations in the future.[22] Directly related to the doctrine of balance of powers is the satisfaction of standing requirements by those presenting a claim to a tribunal. In fact, the latter has often been interposed as the circumstance to prevent the consideration of contentious hearings.

- Standing requirements (or *locus standi*)

  The requirement of standing is used to ascertain who, based on the rules applied by different jurisdictions and legal systems, has sufficient interest in – and thus is allowed to – filing a claim before a court or tribunal. Requirements for initiating legal proceeding may be more or less restrictive but usually refer to the ability to demonstrate causation – the existence of a relationship between an injury and the unlawful or negligent behaviour of the defendants – and injury – particularised or to the detriment of

20 See, District Court of the Hague, *Urgenda Foundation v. the State of the Netherlands*, HAZA C/09/00456689, Judgement of 24 June 2015. Available at: http://climatecasechart.com/non-us-case/urgenda-foundation-v-kingdom-of-the-netherlands/ (Last access, 06 September 2019); UNEP, 2017, *op cit.*, at 30.

21 United States Court of Appeals, Second Circuit, *Connecticut v. American Electric Power Company Inc.*, 582 F.3d 309, 39 ELR 20215 (2d Cir. 2009), Judgement of 21 September 2009.

22 See, D. BODANSKY, J. BRUNNÉE and L. RAJAMANI, *supra* note 14, at 285; D. BODANSKY, *supra* note 17, at 705.

the public interest – something that, in the specific case of climate change, has proved challenging.

Given that climate change may be combined with other factors in producing its impacts, it may be difficult to prove a clear causal link between global warming and the violation of a right. Yet, several legal systems allow the consideration of cases on the basis of the so-called Public Interest Litigation (PIL), meaning that a lawsuit is brought to court to ascertain on an issue of public concern. PIL, as its denomination tells, is largely used to advance public interests and policy change, the reason for which no injury or causation need to be alleged when bringing a case to court. Therefore, and being the second common element to different climate litigation cases, different NGOs and individuals have been able to access courts by bringing public interest claims. Very common in these cases is also to file a petition as a class action, where the representatives of a group of people affected by the same alleged violations, will act as plaintiff on behalf of all class members.

5.3.1.2 Sources of legal rights and obligations

After the exhaustion of procedural requirements and when a matter is eventually considered judiciable, the analysis of substantive merits will entail the consideration of which legal theories and legal sources have been used to frame the alleged violations, as well as their applicability to a determined case. Climate litigation is interesting in this sense because a broad range of legal arguments, doctrines, international legal principles or a mix thereof, have provided the basis for adjudication. Some of the most prominent and innovative features are considered here:

- Rights-based claims

Rights-based claims have been constructed to allege that the constitutional or fundamental human rights of citizens have been violated by those national climate laws and policies that are not able to adequately address climate change. In this regard, today more than 90 States directly protect the rights to a healthy environment in their constitutions.[23] Even when no express protection is given to such a right, the latter can be protected by relying on the right to life, health or property, among others. In national climate change litigation, therefore, the alleged violation of constitutional rights has been used as an instrument to hold governments accountable for their climate policies. Likewise, to challenge those legislations that are not always ambitious may prove to be incompatible with the protection of the above-mentioned rights. Once again in the

23 D. R. BOYD, *The Environmental Right Revolution: A Global Study of Constitutions, Human Rights, and the Environment.* Vancouver: University of British Columbia Press, 2012.

Urgenda case, the plaintiffs claimed that the Dutch climate policy was in violation of article 21 of the Dutch constitution, which enshrines the authorities' competence to keep the country habitable and to protect and improve the environment.

Similarly, human rights law has largely been used as an argument in support of national and international claims. In the latter case, the Inuit and Athabaskan petitions invoked the rights enshrined in the American system of human rights to denounce the inadequate regulation of climate change by the USA and Canada, respectively.[24] Extensive has also been the appeal to human rights law in national contexts, where a State violation of regional and international human rights instruments is often put forward alongside the violation of constitutional rights.[25] This is, for instance, the case in *The People v. Arctic Oil*,[26] in which the infringement of articles 2 and 8 of the European Convention on Human Rights (ECHR) – concerning the rights to life and the right to private and family life, respectively – was complained along with the breach of article 112 of the Norwegian constitution (right to environment). Since a good number of climate change litigation have occurred in European countries, the provisions of the ECHR have been largely invoked. Likewise, the procedural rights enshrined in the Aarhus Convention (1998) have assumed relevance in climate change cases.[27]

24 For a detailed analysis of human rights-based climate change litigation cases, see A. RUBINSON VOLLMER, "Mobilizing Human Rights to Combat Climate Change Through Litigation", in S. DUYCK, S. JODOIN and A. JOHL, (eds.) *Routledge Handbook of Human Rights and Climate Governance*. New York: Routledge, 2018, pp. 359–371.

25 Traditionally, socio-economic and cultural rights have been considered non-judiciable in national and international tribunals, meaning that they primarily constituted moral principles instead of being directly enforceable rights. In this sense, adjudication and enforcement of such rights are considered to be a competence of the legislative and executive powers, what brings back this issue to the separation of powers doctrine described above. Notwithstanding, it should be noted that these rights have in practice been adjudicated in a number of cases. See, as a general reference, D. McGOLRICK, "The Boundaries of Justiciability", *The International and Comparative Law Quarterly*, Vol. 59, No. 4, 2010, pp. 981–1019.

26 Oslo Tingrett (Oslo District Court), *Föreningen Greenpeace Norden & Natur og Ungdom vs Staten ved Olje- og energidepartementet*, 16-166674TVI-OTIR/06, Judgement of 4 January 2018. At the time of writing, an appeal has been filed to the Norwegian Supreme Court by the NGOs Nature and Youth/Young FoE Norway and Greenpeace Norway, after the Oslo District Court has ruled in favour of the Norwegian government. See, M. SCOPELLITI and N. SELLHEIM, "Sustaining a Conservationist Agenda? NGO-Influence on Arctic Sealing, Whaling and Hydrocarbon Regimes", in A. SHIBATA, L. ZOU, N. SELLHEIM and M. SCOPELLITI (eds.) *Emerging Legal Orders in the Arctic: The Role of non-Arctic Actors*. New York: Routledge, 2019, pp. 91–106.

27 The relevance of such rights has to be understood for their intrinsic value, thus for the rights and duties created by the Aarhus Convention and, in the context of Latin American countries, by the Escazú Agreement (2018), but also as a complement to substantive considerations. In this regards, Klabbers has underlined the relevance of two dissenting opinions issued by judges Al-Khasawneh and Simma in the resolution of the Pulp Mills case of 2010 by the ICJ. The author has underlined that the violation of procedural rights can help determine a substantive violation when particularly ambiguous concepts – such as sustainable development or the equitable and rational use of

Exception to this is the case *Ashgar Leghari v. Federation of Pakistan*, in which a Pakistani farmer sued the national government for the violation of its constitutional and fundamental rights, relying on the international human rights instruments ratified by Pakistan.[28] Different but equally interesting is the case *Greenpeace Southeast Asia et al. v. Carbon Majors*,[29] in which several individuals and organisations filed a claim against carbon producers and, among other requests, sought more engagement from policy- and law-makers in assessing that corporations are acting according to their human rights obligations.

Although different hurdles remain in terms of causation, these cases well illustrate why human rights-based claims can be relevant. First, this body of law usually provides individuals with direct standing to complain about a violation of their human rights. Moreover, when a violation has been caused by private actors, human rights law can be relevant in establishing States' duty to verify and monitor that those private actors are not acting in violation of its citizens' fundamental rights related to the environment.

- International law

Interestingly, international law has been used as a supportive argument in different national climate litigation cases. For instance, international treaties have provided the basis for reasserting that States have international obligations when it comes to addressing climate change. To this end, often employed have been the three instruments that constitute the international legal framework on climate change: the UNFCCC, but also the Kyoto Protocol and the Paris Agreement. For example, in *The People v. Arctic Oil*, the plaintiffs alleged that the decision of the Norwegian Government to grant new licences for the exploitation of oil in the Barents Sea was primarily in breach of article 112 of the Norwegian Constitution, but also in opposition to the *spirit* of the Paris Agreement, ratified by Norway shortly before the licences were issued.[30]

resources – are at stake. A substantive violation could be discernible because of the procedural obligations that such concepts bear. See, J. KLABBERS, *supra* note 17, at 283.

28 Lahore High Court Green Bench, *Asghar Leghari v. Federation of Pakistan* (W.P. No. 255501/2015), Judgement of 4 September 2015. The ruling is available at: https://elaw.org/system/files/pk.leghari.090415_0.pdf (Last access, 30 August 2019).

29 Greenpeace Southeast Asia and Philippine Rural Reconstruction Movement, *Petition to the Commission on Human Rights of the Philippines Requesting for Investigation of the Responsibility of the Carbon Majors for Human Rights Violations or Threats of Violations Resulting from the Impacts of Climate Change*. 2015. Available at: http://www.greenpeace.org/seasia/ph/PageFiles/105904/Climate-Change-and-Human-Rights-Complaint.pdf (Last access, 30 August 2019).

30 At the time of writing, an appeal has been filed by Nature and Youth/Young FoE Norway and Greenpeace Norway to the Norwegian Supreme Court, after the Oslo District Court has ruled in favour of the Norwegian government. See, Friends of the Earth Europe, "YFoE Norway takes government to supreme court over Arctic oil" *Friends of the Earth Europe*, 5 February 2018. Available at: http://www.foeeurope.org/yfoee/yfoe-norway-takes-government-supreme-court-050218 (Last access, 20 August 2019).

Ratification, indeed, entails refraining from any action that would undermine the object and purpose of a treaty.

In relation to this, Corsi has noted the potentially revolutionary impact that a positive adjudication of the case *Thomson v. Minister for Climate Change Issues* would have had if not dismissed by the High Court of New Zealand in 2017.[31] The petition alleged the illegality of New Zealand's NDCs under the Paris Agreement since, as argued by the plaintiff, the provisional reduction targets established in the national plan would not have stabilised the concentration of GHGs in the atmosphere to a safe level. The reliance on NDCs is interesting because, as maintained by the author: "This type of argument may open the doors to a new use of international law in climate change litigation, as it could be derived that NDCs represent an intention, and as such international law may have a reflex effect creating full-fledged obligations to the State".[32] Although the mentioned case was not successful, it could serve as a roadmap for future claims as States further define and implement their NDCs under the framework of the Paris Agreement. Finally, principles of international environmental law, *inter alia* the principles of precaution – which puts an emphasis on mitigation measures – prevention, intergenerational equity and sustainable development – which are used to claim more ambitious climate laws and policies – have been employed to support the existence of States' duties in protecting their citizens from climate-related violations.[33]

- European law

In the European Member States, EU law and treaties provided a further basis for climate change litigation. The EU Directive on Emission Trading System (ETS), alongside with articles 191.1 and 191.2 of the Treaty on the Functioning of the European Union (TFEU) – constituting the basis of an EU environmental policy – have been used as a basis to prove States' responsibility in relation to climate change mitigation.[34] At the moment of writing, the *People's Climate Case* has been admitted by the European General Court. The case concerns the suing of the European Parliament and the Council of

31 A review of the case is available at: http://climatecasechart.com/non-us-case/thomson-v-minister-for-climate-change-issues/ (Last access, 30 August 2019).

32 G. CORSI, "A Bottom-Up Approach to Climate Governance: The New Wave of Climate Change Litigation", *ICCG Reflection*, Vol. 57, 2017, pp. 1–12, at 7.

33 See, as a general reference, P. BIRNE, A. BOYLE and C. REDGWELL, *International Law and the Environment*. Oxford: Oxford University Press, 2009.

34 *Directive 2003/87/EC of the European Parliament and of the Council of 13 October 2003 establishing a scheme for greenhouse gas emission allowance trading within the Community and amending Council Directive 96/61/EC*, OJ L 275, 2003; *Consolidated version of the Treaty on the Functioning of the European Union*, OJ C 326, 2012. See, as a general reference, M. SCOPELLITI, "El Liderazgo Climático Europeo: ¿Qué Está En Juego?" in E. CONDE PÉREZ (coord.) *Occasional Paper ICEI OP03/18:* Proyecto Jean Monnet - La Unión Europea y la seguridad: defensa de los espacios e intereses comunes, Madrid: ICEI Occasional Papers OP03/18, 2018, pp. 32–39.

the European Union by different families living in EU countries, on the basis of the ETS, the Effort Sharing Regulation (ESR) and the Regulation on the inclusion of greenhouse gas emissions and removals from land use, land use change and forestry (LULUCF).[35] At the core of the case is the demand for the EU to accelerate its climate action and upscale its 2030 climate target.

- Tort law

Particularly in common law jurisdictions, tort law has been used to prove the negligence of States in relation to climate change. Under this argument, the non-fulfilment of a State duty of care – for example, related to the protection of its citizens from climate impacts – is used to prove its tort or negligence.[36] Far from being straightforward, such claims entail the existence and proof of four elements: (1) a duty held by public authorities; (2) the breach of such an obligation; (3) causation and (4) the existence of an injury. Primarily applied in the USA, although with difficulties in proving causation, claims of negligence have found prolific ground in civil law jurisdictions too. Always in the Urgenda case, the duty of care of the Dutch authorities has been inferred from the Dutch Civil Code and the definition of tortuous act found therein.

- Public trust

Always deriving from common law systems is the doctrine of public trust, according to which certain natural elements – including land, water and the atmosphere – inherently belong to people and are administered by public authorities who are, in turn, guardians of such elements and trust. It follows that, whenever a State is failing to take adequate care of the entrusted duties, it can be found in breach of the public trust doctrine. The latter was largely used in the USA and raised international attention in the case *Juliana v. United States*, in which a group of 21 young American plaintiffs and the climate scientist J. Hanses (on behalf of future generations) have brought a case against the USA and the Government of Oregon, claiming that the Federal and national states' actions and inaction were jeopardising the right to life and liberty of future generations.[37] To date, the case has been admitted and permitted to proceed on trial by a US district court, but it has not yet been heard on its merit.

- The use of climate science

35 More details on the case are available at: https://peoplesclimatecase.caneurope.org/ (Last access, 01 September 2019).

36 See, e.g., D. HUNTER and J. SALZMAN, "Negligence in the Air: The Duty of Care in Climate Change Litigation", *University of Pennsylvania Law Review*, Vol. 155, 2007, pp. 1741–1794.

37 *Juliana v. United States*, case no.: 6:15-cv-01517-TC. More details on the case are available at: https://www.ourchildrenstrust.org/us/federal-lawsuit/ (Last access, 01 September 2019).

Finally, although not a strictly legal element, modern climate science has been a determinant in most climate change litigation cases and reference to solid scientific evidence has been made to sustain causation in most of the cases considered so far. Particularly the IPCC assessment reports and national climate science research findings have been used as a basis in support of different legal arguments. For example, in order to establish and to prove the causal relationship between climate change and its anthropogenic nature, but also to show evidence of the impacts of climate change on human and natural life and thus support the existence of an injury. Moreover, as the Paris Agreement indicates for the first time a temperature threshold under which global temperature should be kept to avoid environmental disruption, climate science offers now a specific parameter against which the effectiveness or ambition of national policies and laws can be contrasted and decided upon.

5.3.1.3 The strategic choice of the relevant legal forum

Together with the applicable sources of law and legal doctrines, the forum in which a climate-related litigation is brought may also change from one case to the other and influence its adjudication. Besides the great variety of national courts and tribunals, also at the international level the fora where climate change cases may be heard are numerous. As already discussed above, the International Court of Justice could be a forum for adjudication or for the request of an advisory opinion on climate change-related violations. As Bodansky has rightly pointed, the ICJ has the most general subject matter jurisdiction of any international tribunal and it could address climate change in a very comprehensive manner.[38] Given the small number of states currently accepting the compulsory jurisdiction of the ICJ, however, the request of an advisory opinion will be more likely than adjudication on a contentious case.

Besides the many international and regional human rights tribunals, among which are the Inter-American Court of Human Rights or the ECtHR, climate change litigation could be filed in different international tribunals that, due to their competence, are likely to exert their jurisdiction on the topic. The latter include, just to name a few, the International Tribunal for the Law of the Sea, where claims concerning the damage to the marine environment could be brought; or the World Trade Organisation Appellative Body, in which a case on how national climate policies impinge on economic rights could be considered.

5.3.2 Building on climate change litigation: main problems

Despite the enthusiasm and euphoria generated by successful climate change litigation cases, many difficult issues pend on those willing to undertake such

38 D. BODANSKY, *supra* note 17, at 701. See, also on this topic, J. KLABBERS, *supra* note 17, at 158.

an avenue to address climate change-related violations. Some of these difficulties have been outlined in the section above. Yet, further delving into these issues may help considering potential solutions to overcome these hurdles.

- Causation and liability

Arguably together with the overcoming of standing requirements, proving causation has been one of the most challenging features of climate-related litigation, particularly so when global warming is to be proved as being the source of violation of fundamental or constitutional rights. Equally challenging can be to demonstrate the existence of a nexus between the injuries claimed by the plaintiff and the conduct (active or omissive) of the defendant. In fact, characteristic of such environmental harm is its cumulative nature, global origin and reach, where the evidence of local impacts may be difficult to prove, especially since the effects of climate change may be amplified by different factors. In this regard, some courts have nonetheless resorted to the assessment of contributory action as a basis for liability, looking at the impact that, for instance, fossil fuel and transportation as publicly regulated sectors have in determining climate change and amplifying its impacts.[39] Moreover, albeit not yet widespread, studies of climate attribution have been conducted recently. Their future appreciation is likely to be fundamental in the determination of historic contributions and also for the attribution of responsibility for specific emissions to different countries or companies.[40]

- The legitimacy of the judiciary power

At both the international and the domestic level, the rise in climate change litigation numbers has created some concern. Different commentators have argued on the legitimacy of what has been perceived, at least to some extent, as the *de facto* exercise of a policy- or law-making function by the judiciary power.[41] Despite the limited success of climate litigation which, in any case, does not amount to a frustration of the legislative or executive powers, the foreseen increase in such cases makes the question of legitimacy worth considering.

39 See, on causation and other problems, J. PEEL, "Issues in Climate Change Litigation", *Carbon & Climate Law Review*, Vol. 5, No. 1, 2011, pp. 15–24.

40 See, on this, P. GRIFFIN, *The Carbon Majors Database. CDP Carbon Majors Report 2017*. London: CDP Report, 2017. Available at: https://6fefcbb86e61af1b2fc4-c70d8ead6ced550b4d987d7c03fcdd1d.ssl.cf3.rackcdn.com/cms/reports/documents/000/002/327/original/Carbon-Majors-Report-2017.pdf?1501833772 (Last access, 03 September 2019).

41 See, e.g., M. PEETERS, "Urgenda Foundation and 886 Individuals v. The State of the Netherlands: The Dilemma of More Ambitious Greenhouse Gas Reduction Action by EU Member States", *Review of European Community & International Environmental Law*, Vol. 25, No. 1, 2016, pp. 123–129; PEEL, *supra* note 39.

At the international level, the problem of global climate change has been handled since its inception through the negotiation of multilateral environmental agreements, which shall evolve on the basis of scientific knowledge development. In this context, state negotiators and diplomats act – in democratic circumstances at least – as legitimate representatives of their electorate. Legitimacy in this sense is primarily reduced to a procedural question or to how ambitiously and fast decision-making evolves in relation to the electorate expectations. The judiciary seems *prima facie* having no role to play on this ground beside law enforcement or redress. Yet, the specific nature of climate change as a transboundary environmental harm may put into question this assumption, challenging the authority of international negotiations too. As Bodansky has pointed with reference to national climate policies that are likely to have an impact beyond national borders: "In addressing problems of global externalities, such as climate change, the deference that negotiations afford to state sovereignty thus does not have a democratic justification".[42] It follows that, when the legitimacy of international negotiations and international adjudication are compared, no process has intrinsically more authority than the other. Thus, international adjudication may well form part of the most conventional legal governance approach that has characterised the creation of a climate regime to date, and adjudication in international contexts raises fewer legitimacy problems if compared with national adjudication.

The proliferation of climate change litigation at the domestic level, in fact, raises a question of legitimacy too, although with differences depending on the legal system under analysis. Particularly in countries of common law tradition, where judicial rulings constitute a source of law, the adjudication of climate change-related cases becomes relevant. As Peel has pointed out with reference to such systems: "In the absence of strong government action to address climate change, rulings in climate change litigation may serve as a de facto source of national climate policy with very real impacts on the regulatory landscape".[43] Therefore, in this context, a legitimacy question is raised by the fact that the judiciary is not primarily acting in its natural realm – law enforcement – but rather expanding its function by directly forcing the creation of laws and policies and contributing to regulatory change and development with a strategic purpose, notwithstanding the existence of a clearer division of powers in domestic contexts. In civil law systems instead, where adjudication is made on a case by case basis, legitimacy problems are less pronounced, although the emergence and maintenance of case law will likely influence adjudications in

42 D. BODANSKY, *supra* note 17, at 703.

43 J. PEEL, 2011, *supra* note 39, at 23. The author is also considering what can make adjudication by the judiciary more legitimate. For instance, the fact that adjudication is grounded in scientific evidence and clear reasoning, instead of political considerations, will likely increase the authority of climate change judgement. Moreover, there is the possibility that, in addressing climate change, the judiciary power will overall gain legitimacy by finding innovative solutions to such an urgent environmental problem.

different jurisdictions. Altogether, these problems are amplified by the direct applicability of judicial decisions at the national level, since compliance with the ruling is usually higher than in international contexts.

- Limited authority of international courts as opposed to decisions made by national tribunals

Indeed, the limited applicability of international courts' decisions is another problem that, far from being new, has been discussed in relation to climate change litigation cases heard in international fora. This question was first raised by the Inuit petition in which, even if the case would have been admitted, the IACHR could only have prepared a report with recommendations for the USA and have set a deadline for compliance. Although international adjudication might, in principle, be more legitimate than the resolution of climate change litigation cases by national tribunals, the enforcement of international rulings is far more complex at the international level. A potentially innovative aspect of national adjudication in this sense would be determined by the adjudication of claims related to States' nationally determined contributions. The establishment of what constitutes acceptable (even lawful) standards of GHGs emission reduction targets in one jurisdiction could have more diffuse impacts elsewhere. For instance, it could be adopted by other courts deciding on future cases and serve as a relevant precedent, influencing the assessment of the review mechanisms established by the Paris Agreement at articles 13, 14 and 15. Altogether, it would constitute a common basis for the evaluation of NDCs. On the contrary, however, the possibility of NDCs to be upheld and confirmed by national courts, should not be ruled out.

5.4 Functions and potentially positive impacts of litigation in the context of a changing climate

As already pointed out in the introduction to this chapter, climate change litigation cases may serve very different purposes, are built with very different characteristics and include a great variety of actors. Assessing who is acting as plaintiff or defendant in a specific case may, in fact, already tell about the purpose that a claim aims at satisfying. As the objective of this chapter is to consider which implications climate change litigation cases may have for the improvement of procedural rights in the context of climate change law-making, this section will mostly consider those cases in which individuals or civil society representatives are acting as plaintiffs. Relevant to this research is therefore the analysis of the functions that climate change litigation may assume when a petition is filed by individuals or NGOs against governments, a trend that is increasing in Europe and the USA following the successful outcome of some trials, which will be analysed at a later stage. Indeed, while these cases may pursue very specific goals (ranging from the assessment of national mitigation and adaptation policies, to the redress of human rights violations), they all have a very strategic connotation and resonance, with impacts that extend to national and international environmental law-making and beyond it. In this regard, the above-mentioned UNEP report on climate change litigation has identified the following as the main issues that climate change litigation aims at achieving:

(1) Holding governments to their legislative and policy commitments;
(2) Linking the impacts of resource extraction to climate change and resilience;
(3) Establishing that particular emissions are the proximate cause of adverse climate change impacts;
(4) Establishing liability for failures to adapt to climate change.

Comprised of all these – potentially overlapping – objectives, litigation can be conceived as a bottom-up strategy to climate governance because it is used to push compliance or regulatory change in the realms of climate mitigation and adaptation, pushing governmental action towards the development, adoption and implementation of more ambitious policies and laws to tackle climate change. In this sense, litigation may be considered as a form of advocacy aimed at influencing regulation at the national level and decision-making at the international one. Likewise, judicial governance is but another expression of the polycentric governance arisen around the problem of global warming, since policy or regulatory developments will likely follow to the obtainment of an enforceable court order.[44] As a matter of fact, the assessment that Osofsky has made of the Inuit petition as a "bridge" (between environmental protection and rights' defence, as well as among the multiscale level of climate governance), can be extended to other cases filed at the national and international levels.[45] In both contexts, climate litigation can be referred to as something in between advocacy and litigation as a strategy that aims at finding innovative and multilevel solutions to the problem of global warming.

Even if the impacts of climate change litigation cases should be assessed primarily on the basis of their real success, Hunter has noted the awareness-building impacts of climate litigation and the influence that such strategies may have on the development of climate change law and policy, even when claims are eventually dismissed. Particularly relevant in this sense is the impact that climate litigation may have in creating "mechanisms for the integration of the climate regime with other institutions, such as human rights tribunals or other treaty regimes".[46] This, in turn, could help understanding climate change as primarily theorised by Keohane and Victor, a regime complex to

44 On the idea of polycentric governance, see: A. JORDAN, D. HUITEMA, H. VAN ASSELT and J. FORSTER (eds.) *Governing Climate Change: Polycentricity in Action?* Cambridge: Cambridge University Press, 2018.

45 See, H. M. OSOFSKY, *supra* note 5, at 686.

46 D. B. HUNTER, "The Implications of Climate Change Litigations for International Environmental Law-Making", *Washington College of Law Research Paper*, No. 14, 2007, pp. 1–19, at 10.

be informed and complemented by the interaction with different regimes, mainly human rights or migration law.[47] Given the negative influence that climate change has and will have on the enjoyment of human rights, and being the trigger of climate-induced migrations, adopting such a framework of analysis may improve the overall effectiveness of the international climate change regime.

Another positive effect that climate litigation may have on climate change law, and international law more broadly, is the promotion of its development into new directions. While international environmental law has developed fairly recently and with a rather modest involvement and contribution by courts, today the judiciary power is increasingly driving the advancement of environmental law at the national and international levels. This is exemplified, for example, by the extensive scholarly debate that has revolved around the potential for human rights law to address global warming after the Inuit petition, as well as over the existence of a free-standing human right to a healthy environment.[48] The same can be said for the relationship between climate change law and international trade law or the law of the sea.[49] In relation to this, the framing of climate change as a legal problem could, at least in principle and particularly at the international level, improve the suitability of courts to deal with environmental issues, potentially reinvigorating the practice of instituting special environmental chambers or of inviting external experts' opinions.

Finally, and arguably an effect of at least all successful climate-related cases, is the indirect validation of the science base upon which plaintiffs build links of causation or provide evidence of the alleged infringement of fundamental rights. In the context of the present US administration's position on climate change, for instance, the validation of the scientific basis of global warming in a courtroom may challenge the assumptions of climate change denials and, in turn, influence public opinion. At the same time, the assessment of national climate policies that are required to establish the existence of a wrongful act or to express a reasoned judgement may entail the closure of important scientific knowledge gaps, what might set new standards for environmental impact

47 See, R. O. KEOHANE and D. G.VICTOR, "The Regime Complex for Climate Change", *Perspective on Politics*, Vol. 9, No. 1, 2011, pp. 7–23.

48 See, e.g., S. DUYCK, S. JODOIN and A. JOHL (eds.) *Routledge Handbook of Human Rights and Climate Governance*. New York: Routledge, 2018; D. BODANSKY, "Introduction: Climate Change and Human Rights: Unpacking the Issues", *Georgia Journal of International and Comparative Law*, Vol. 38, No. 3, 2010, pp. 551–524; J. H. KNOX, "Climate Change and Human Rights Law", *Virginia Journal of International Law*, Vol. 50, No. 1, 2009, pp. 1–59; S. McINERNEY-LANKFORD, M. DARROW and L. RAJAMANI, *Human Rights and Climate Change: A Review of the International Legal Dimensions*. Washington: The International Bank for Reconstruction and Development, 2011.

49 See, e.g., W. BURNS, "Potential Causes of Action for Climate Change Damages in International Fora: The Law of the Sea Convention", *Sustainable Development Law & Policy*, Vol. 1, No. 2, 2006, pp. 27–51.

assessments, the allocation of licences and the authorisation of projects with foreseeable externalities.

5.5 Climate change litigation: analysis of relevant case law

Although not directly concerned with the respect of procedural rights in a climate change law-making context, the successful outcome of particularly two climate change litigation cases has put emphasis on how domestic litigation can be conceived as a relevant instrument for the reaffirmation and upholding of public participation. While the improvement of procedural rights through litigation could be the direct or indirect outcome of climate litigation at all levels, inasmuch as litigation is conceived and used as a bottom-up and advocacy strategy, the following cases are detailed here for several reasons. Even though they have been heard in different jurisdictions and on the basis of different legal arguments, they involve similar allegations and outcomes and are, for such reasons, among the cases that have best underlined that shortcomings still exist in how public participation is realised and secured in the making of climate change law at the international level.

- *Urgenda Foundation v. the State of the Netherlands*[50]

In 2013 the Dutch Foundation Urgenda sued, together with other 886 Dutch citizens, the Government of the Netherlands for its inaction on climate change. As a consequence of such inertia, the plaintiffs argued, the Government was to be judged responsible for the infringements of its citizens' constitutional and fundamental rights, violated by the allowed greenhouse gases' emission levels. The claimants considered that the States' inaction on climate change amounted to a breach of its duty of care and invoked liability under tort law based on article 21 of the Dutch Constitution and article 6:162 of the Dutch Civil Code. Alleged were also the violation of different international rights, including articles 2 and 8 of the European Convention on Human Rights, the rights of future generations, the TFEU and the no-harm principle. Against these allegations, the Dutch State underlined the lack of causation between the Dutch emissions and the impacts of climate change against which the Urgenda Foundation sought protection, and also underlined the minor contribution that the national emissions make to the global climate change problem, thus arguing that the question could not be assessed on a national basis.

The requirement of standing didn't suppose a challenge to the case because, under the Dutch Civil Code, a foundation can bring an action pertaining to the protection of collective interests to courts. Being the primary objective of the Urgenda Foundation to foster "a fast transition towards a sustainable

50 *Urgenda Foundation v. the State of the Netherlands*, HAZA C/09/00456689, 2015.

society",[51] the Court considered that the Urgenda had *locus standi* and could also act in representation of current and future generations. Nonetheless, the Court acknowledged that being a legal person, the Foundation could not directly rely on the ECHR's provisions and exclusively considered the jurisprudence of the ECtHR on articles 2 and 8 as relevant to its interpretation of the Dutch civil law.[52]

By combining these sources of law in a unique precedent, the Hague District Court ordered the Dutch Government in June 2015 to reduce the country's emission by at least 25% by 2020 compared to the 1990 levels, in order to fulfil its obligation to protect and improve the living environment against the dangers caused by climate change. As such, the court considered insufficient the original pledge of a 17% reduction rate decided by the Government. Its climate policy was judged inadequate and unlawful and the State conduct negligent.

In the words of Roger Cox, who issued proceedings against the Dutch Government on behalf of the Urgenda Foundation and concerned citizens,

> the ruling marks the first successful climate change action founded in tort law as well as the first time a court has determined the appropriate emission-reduction target for a developed state, based on the duty of care and regardless of arguments that the solution to global climate problem does not depend on one country's efforts alone.[53]

While the judgment was provisionally enforceable, the Dutch Government appealed the ruling in October 2015 objecting to the interference of the District Court with the work of the Dutch Parliament. In May 2018 the appeal hearing took place before the Hague Court of Appeal, which rejected on 9 October 2018 the State's objection in a remarkable sentence.[54] By fully upholding the judgement of 2015, the Court concluded that

> the State is acting unlawfully (because in contravention of the duty of care under Articles 2 and 8 ECHR) by failing to pursue a more ambitious

51 See the website of the Urgenda Foundation. Available at: http://www.urgenda.nl/en/home-en/ (Last access, 10 September 2019).

52 For extensive and detailed reference to the resolution of the case, see R. COX, "A Climate Change Litigation Precedent: Urgenda Foundation v The State of the Netherlands", *Journal of Energy & Natural Resources Law*, Vol. 34, No. 2, 2016, pp. 143–163. For a comparative perspective, see S. ROY and E. WOERDMAN, "Situating Urgenda v The Netherlands within Comparative Climate Change Litigation", *Journal of Energy & Natural Resources Law*, Vol. 34, No. 2, 2016, pp. 165–189.

53 R. COX, *supra* note 52, at 144.

54 Hague Court of Appeal, *The State of The Netherlands v. Urgenda Foundation*, case 200.178.245/01, judgement of 9 October 2018. Available at: https://uitspraken.rechtspraak.nl/inziendocument?id=ECLI:NL:GHDHA:2018:2610 (Last access, 21 October 2019).

reduction as of end-2020, and that the State should reduce emissions by at least 25% by end-2020.[55]

Despite the result of the appeal, several authors have especially questioned the competence of a District court to rule (somehow indirectly) over the adequacy of European climate law, since exclusively the Court of Justice of the European Union is entitled to such a function.[56] Likewise, objections have been raised as to the respect of the separation of powers doctrine, arguing that the decision is contrary to the State discretionary power to regulate climate change. Despite this, the case has had great international resonance and most of the climate change litigation cases brought before European courts resemble the claims of the Urgenda case.[57] As it will be recalled below, this somewhat signals to the emergence of a transnational climate change litigation movement that has implications on how procedural rights are exercised in the context of climate change law-making.

- *Asghar Leghari v. Federation of Pakistan*

Differently from the Urgenda case, this litigation case was initiated by a natural person, Asghar Leghari, a Pakistani subsistence farmer. The latter decided to sue the Government of Pakistan in 2015 for the violation of its fundamental constitutional rights. As for the case above, this was allegedly caused by the governmental inaction towards global climate change. More specifically, the plaintiff denounced the inaction of the Government in implementing its National Climate Change Policy of 2012 and the Framework for Implementation of Climate Change Policy for the period 2014–2030, asserting the violation of articles 9, 14, 19a and 23 of the Pakistani Constitution concerning the right to life, human dignity, information and property, respectively.

Brought by a natural person asserting the violation of his rights, the *locus standi* did not suppose much hurdles for the admission of the case. In fact, no great discussion of the issue of standing was given by the Court, besides acknowledging that the petitioner was a citizen seeking the enforcement of his fundamental rights.

Contrarily to what ruled in the Urgenda case, where the court left to the Dutch Government discretion on how to pursue the prescribed emission

55 *Ibid*, final statement.

56 M. PEETERS, *supra* note 41, at 125; L. BERGKAMP and J. C. HANEKAMP, "Climate Change Litigation against States: The Perils of Court-made Climate Policies", *European Energy and Environmental Law Review*, Vol. 24, No. 5, 2015, pp. 102–114.

57 Based on similar allegations are the following cases: *Plan B v. UK* (2018); *VZW Klimatzaak v. Kingdom of Belgium* (2015); *PUSH Sweden, Nature and Youth Sweden and Others v. Government of Sweden* (2016); *Union of Swiss Senior Women for Climate Protection v. Swiss Federal Council* (2016). A review of these case is maintained by the NGO Our Children Trust. Available at: https://www.ourchildrenstrust.org/global-legal-actions/ (Last access, 06 September 2019).

reduction target, the Lahore High Court clearly identified a violation in that "the delay and lethargy of the State in implementing the Framework offends the fundamental rights of the citizens which need to be safeguarded" and prescribed very specific action as a remedy to the plaintiff.[58] Among those are: the nomination by different Ministries of a climate change focal person, who will ensure the correct and smooth application of the above-mentioned Framework for Implementation; the presentation by each Ministry of a list of action points against climate change; and, finally, the creation of a Climate Change Commission composed of representatives of the relevant Ministries, NGOs, individuals and technical experts, in charge of monitoring the Government's project on the implementation of its climate change policy. Although it is impossible to determine whether these measures will be incisive and effectively implemented by the Pakistani Government, at the moment of writing no appellation has been presented by the Federal Government.

5.6 Climate change litigation as an instrument to uphold procedural rights?

The decision to examine, among all successful climate change litigation claims, these two cases brings this research back to its main purpose, considering *whether* and *how* the participation of non-governmental entities in international climate change law-making should be enhanced. It is sustained here that the consideration of climate change litigation may provide an answer to the *if* and *how* of this research question. A common characteristic of the analysed claims is that they aim at redressing States' inactions in climate change mitigation and adaptation policies. As such, the examined cases may be envisioned in at least two ways. First, simply because of their having been filed, they stem as an evidence of civil society disaffection with the regime created to tackle climate change. Therefore, they constitute a further argument in support of a more open international decision-making process. Second, the proliferation of these cases in a transnational fashion and their foreseeable increase in the future, can be linked to an increasingly widespread discomfort within society – or at least big portions of it – that feels underrepresented, frustrated and even excluded from the climate change national and international decision- and law-making processes and thus aims at reverting this direction by going to courts. In this sense, these cases open new views on how the enhancement of public participation can be pursued in national and international courts. This once again underlines, as also discussed in the third chapter of this research, that the measures taken to date to enhance public participation in the context of climate change law as required in article 12 of the Paris Agreement, have not been satisfactory.

58 *Asghar Leghari v. Federation of Pakistan* (W.P. No. 255501/2015), 2015, paragraph 8. The ruling is available at: https://elaw.org/system/files/pk.leghari.090415_0.pdf (Last access, 06 September 2019).

Concerning the *how*, the question to be answered is whether climate change litigation, as a bottom-up strategy to climate governance, can be considered as an adequate instrument to improve the participatory rights of non-governmental entities in the context of climate change law-making. A query that requires very accurate consideration. As argued elsewhere, climate litigation certainly aims at democratising climate change law and policy-making. It does so by questioning the largely undisputed role that States and State-based entities maintain in different phases of the decision- and law-making process. Primarily, but not exclusively, litigation helps to shape the agenda of international negotiations by putting at the centre of discussion rights-based concerns, as well as by moving the debate on international climate change beyond the institutional framework of the UNFCCC. As maintained by Hunter:

> Although the scale, scope, and methods of participation by civil society in the formal climate negotiations have been substantial, at the end of the day everything from the agenda to the final outcome of international treaty negotiations is appropriately monopolized by governments. Civil society can observe, propose, pressure, prod, and even parody, but ultimately its role in international negotiations is limited. Not so in terms of litigation.[59]

In this sense, climate change litigation cases have had, at least indirectly, the effect of empowering different climate advocates at the national and subnational levels, allowing them to better place their concerns at the international level too.

Although innovative in the use of the law – since it alternates the use of national, European and international law, and resorts to public interest litigation to overcome standing requirements – it is maintained here that litigation should be regarded as a second-best option to climate change governance and as an instrument to secure public participation in this context. Albeit, as seen above, litigation may be the driver of new developments in international environmental law, as well as relevant in pushing more ambitious responses to one of the most challenging issues that international environmental law has ever faced, judicial governance is but a distortion of the primary role of the judiciary power. The adoption of ambitious and effective legislation should be the central function of the legislative power. Therefore, even though litigation might be an ill-suited instrument to improve procedural rights in the making of international climate change law due to its largely remedial character, the surge of climate litigation in a transnational fashion certainly has emphasised the need for more public participation in climate change law-making at the national and international level. Finally, the positive adjudication of rights-based claims has served to legitimise and underscored a rights-based discourse on which, instead, the improvement of public participation could be built.

59 D., B HUNTER, *supra* note 46, at 14.

5.7 Concluding remarks

This chapter has considered the emergence of climate change litigation as a new phenomenon in the governance of international climate change. By analysing the broad range of actors involved in litigation, the different applicable sources of law and the potentially relevant fora of adjudication, the very diverse nature of climate-related cases have been spelled out.

Out of a growing number of climate change petitions filed against States and companies, this research has particularly focused on those strategic litigation cases in which individuals or NGOs are bringing claims against governments. This is primarily done in order to require and set more ambitious mitigations and adaptation law and policies, as well as to demand the implementation of existing pledges. In this sense, litigation is seen as a bottom-up (and often rights-based) approach to climate governance, in which both climate advocates and courts play an increasingly prominent role.

Despite the scholarly debate and interest generated by this trend, largely overlooked has been the significance that strategic litigation may have for upholding the participatory rights of non-governmental actors in the making of international climate change law. In this sense, litigation may be considered as an argument in support of a more open international decision-making process, since it unveils the disaffection created by a largely State-centred international decision-making system. By the same token, it may be considered as a way to empower those advocating for a more rights-based approach to climate change. In this regard, the relevance of this instrument rests in its transnational character and in the possibility of replication in different countries and judicial systems. Despite not having public participation issues at their core, the expected increase and increasingly successful outcome of these cases may have the effect of opening up the international decision-making space to non-State entities in a way that their interests can be better represented in the negotiation phase, rather than in judicial fora.

Bibliography

Averchenkova, A., Fankhauser, S. and M. Nachmany (eds.) *Trends in Climate Change Litigation*. Cheltenham: Edward Elgar, 2017.

Baxi, U. "Towards a Climate Change Justice Theory?", *Journal of Human Rights and the Environment*, Vol. 7, No. 1, 2016, pp. 7–31.

Bergkamp, L. and J. C. Hanekamp. "Climate Change Litigation against States: The Perils of Court-made Climate Policies", *European Energy and Environmental Law Review*, Vol. 24, No. 5, 2015, pp. 102–114.

Birne, P., Boyle, A. and C. Redgwell. *International Law and the Environment*. Oxford: Oxford University Press, 2009.

Bodansky, D. "Introduction: Climate Change and Human Rights: Unpacking the Issues", *Georgia Journal of International and Comparative Law*, Vol. 38, No. 3, 2010, pp. 551–524.

Bodansky, D. "The Role of the International Court of Justice in Addressing Climate Change: Some Preliminary Reflections", *Arizona State Law Journal*, Vol. 49, 2017, pp. 689–712.

Bodansky, D., Brunnée, J. and L. Rajamani. *International Climate Change Law*. Oxford: Oxford University Press, 2017.

Borrás Pentinat, S. "Los litigios climáticos: Entre la tutela climática y la fiscalización de las responsabilidades por daños climáticos", in R. Giles Carnero (coord.) *Cambio Climático, Energía y Derecho Internacional: Perspectivas de Futuro*. Cizur Menor: Aranzadi, 2012, pp. 91–104.

Borrás Pentinat, S. "Movimientos para la justicia climática global: replanteando el escenario internacional del cambio climático", *Relaciones Internacionales*, No. 33, 2017, pp. 97–119.

Boyd, D. R. *The Environmental Right Revolution: A Global Study of Constitutions, Human Rights, and the Environment*. Vancouver: University of British Columbia Press, 2012.

Burns, W. "Potential Causes of Action for Climate Change Damages in International Fora: The Law of the Sea Convention", *Sustainable Development Law & Policy*, Vol. 1, No. 2, 2006, pp. 27–51.

Consolidated Version of the Treaty on the Functioning of the European Union, OJ C 326, 2012.

Corsi, G. "A Bottom-Up Approach to Climate Governance: The New Wave of Climate Change Litigation", *ICCG Reflection*, Vol. 57, 2017, pp. 1–12.

Cox, R. "A Climate Change Litigation Precedent: Urgenda Foundation v The State of the Netherlands", *Journal of Energy & Natural Resources Law*, Vol. 34, No. 2, 2016, pp. 143–163.

Directive 2003/87/EC of the European Parliament and of the Council of 13 October 2003 Establishing a Scheme for Greenhouse Gas Emission Allowance Trading Within the Community and Amending Council Directive 96/61/EC, OJ L 275, 2003.

Duyck, S., Jodoin, S. and A. Johl (eds.) *Routledge Handbook of Human Rights and Climate Governance*. New York: Routledge, 2018.

Giles Carnero, R. "La Corte International de Justicia frente a las controversias internacionales de carácter medioambiental", in E. M. Vázquez Gómez, M. D. Adam Muñoz and N. Cornago-Prieto (coord.) *El arreglo pacífico de las controversias internacionales: XXIV Jornadas de la Asociación Española de Profesores de Derecho internacional y Relaciones internacionales*. Valencia: Tirant lo Blanch, 2013, pp. 159–168.

Griffin, P. *The Carbon Majors Database. CDP Carbon Majors Report 2017*. London: CDP Report, 2017.

Gromilova, M. "Rescuing the People of Tuvalu: Towards an I.C.J. Advisory Opinion on the International Legal Obligations to Protect the Environment and Human Rights of Populations Affected by Climate Change", *Intercultural Human Rights Law Review*, Vol. 10, 2015, pp. 233–289.

Hallegatte, S., Bangalore, M., Bonzanigo, L. and Others. *Shock Waves. Managing the Impacts of Climate Change on Poverty. Climate Change and Development*. Washington, DC: World Bank Group, 2016.

Hunter, D. B. "The Implications of Climate Change Litigations for International Environmental Law-Making", *Washington College of Law Research Paper*, No. 14, 2007, pp. 1–19.

Hunter, D. B. and J. Salzman. "Negligence in the Air: The Duty of Care in Climate Change Litigation", *University of Pennsylvania Law Review*, Vol. 155, 2007, pp. 1741–1794.

Jodoin, S., Faucher, R. and K. Lofts. "Look before You Jump: Assessing the Potential Influence of the Human Rights Bandwagon on Domestic Climate Policy", in S. Duyck, S. Jodoin and A. Johl, (eds.) *Routledge Handbook of Human Rights and Climate Governance*. New York: Routledge, 2018, pp. 167–182.

Jordan, A., Huitema, D., Van Asselt, H. and J. Forster (eds.) *Governing Climate Change. Polycentricity in Action?* Cambridge: Cambridge University Press, 2018.

Keohane, R. O. and D. G. Victor. "The Regime Complex for Climate Change", *Perspectives on Politics*, Vol. 9, No. 1, 2011, pp. 7–23.

Klabbers, J. *International law*. Cambridge: Cambridge University Press, 2017.

Knox, J. H. "Climate Change and Human Rights Law", *Virginia Journal of International Law*, Vol. 50, No. 1, 2009, pp. 1–59.

Mcgolrick, D. "The Boundaries of Justiciability", *International and Comparative Law Quarterly*, Vol. 59, No. 4, 2010, pp. 981–1019.

Mcinerney-Lankford, S., Darrow, M. and L. Rajamani. *Human Rights and Climate Change: A Review of the International Legal Dimensions*. Washington: International Bank for Reconstruction and Development, 2011.

Mcleman, R. and F. Gemenne (eds.) *Routledge Handbook of Environmental Displacement and Migration*. New York: Routledge, 2018.

Nachmany, M. and S. Fankhauser. *Estudio sobre Legislación de cambio climático 2015. Informe sobre la legislación de cambio climático en 99 países*. London: London School of Economics, 2015.

Nachmany, M. and J. Setzer. "Global Trends in Climate Change Legislation and Litigation: 2018 Snapshot", *Grantham Research Institute on Climate Change and the Environment and Centre for Climate Change Economics and Policy*, 2018.

Osofsky, H. M. "The Inuit Petition as a Bridge? Beyond Dialectic of Climate Change and Indigenous Peoples' Rights", *American Indian Law Review*, Vol. 31, No. 2, 2007, pp. 675–697.

Peel, J. "Issues in Climate Change Litigation" *Carbon & Climate Law Review*, Vol. 5, No. 1, 2011, pp. 15–24.

Peeters, M. "Urgenda Foundation and 886 Individuals v. The State of the Netherlands: The Dilemma of More Ambitious Greenhouse Gas Reduction Action by EU Member States", *Review of European Community & International Environmental Law*, Vol. 25, No. 1, 2016, pp. 123–129.

Preston, B. J. "Climate Change Litigation (Part 1)", *Carbon & Climate Law Review*, Vol. 5, No. 1, 2011, pp. 3–14.

Roser, D. and C. Seidel. *Climate Justice. An Introduction*. New York, London: Routledge, 2013; D. Stabinsky, "Climate Justice and Human Rights", in S. Duyck, S. Jodoin and A. Johl, (eds.) *Routledge Handbook of Human Rights and Climate Governance*. New York: Routledge, 2018, pp. 280–291.

Roy, S. and E. Woerdman. "Situating Urgenda v The Netherlands within Comparative Climate Change Litigation", *Journal of Energy & Natural Resources Law*, Vol. 34, No. 2, 2016, pp. 165–189.

Rubinson Vollmer, A. "Mobilizing Human Rights to Combat Climate Change Through Litigation", in S. Duyck, S. Jodoin and A. Johl, (eds.) *Routledge Handbook of Human Rights and Climate Governance*. New York: Routledge, 2018, pp. 359–371.

Sands, P. "Climate Change and the Rule of Law: Adjudicating the Future in International Law", *Journal of Environmental Law*, Vol. 28, No. 19, 2016, pp. 19–35.

Scopelliti, M. "El Liderazgo Climático Europeo: ¿Qué Está En Juego?", in E. Conde Pérez (coord.) *Occasional Paper ICEI OP03/18: Proyecto Jean Monnet - La Unión Europea y la seguridad: defensa de los espacios e intereses comunes*. Madrid: ICEI Occasional Papers OP03/18, 2018, pp. 32–39.

Scopelliti, M. and N. Sellheim. "Sustaining a Conservationist Agenda? NGO-Influence on Arctic Sealing, Whaling and Hydrocarbon Regimes", in A. Shibata, L. Zou, N. Sellheim and M. Scopelliti (eds.) *Emerging Legal Orders in the Arctic: The Role of non-Arctic Actors*. New York: Routledge, 2019, pp. 91–106.

United Nations Educational, Scientific and Cultural Organisation. *Convention Concerning the Protection of the World Cultural and Natural Heritage of 16 November 1972* (1037 UNTS 151).

United Nations Environment Programme. *The Status of Climate Change Litigation – A Global Review*. Nairobi: UNEP, 2017.

United Nations News, "Palau Seeks UN World Court Opinion on Damage Caused by Greenhouse Gases", *NEW South*, 22 September 2011. Available at: https://news.un.org/en/story/2011/09/388202.

World Commission on Environment and Development. *Our Common Future. Report of the World Commission on Environment and Development*. Oxford: Oxford University Press, 1987.

6 A human rights-based approach to climate change

Improving the participation of non-governmental actors in international climate change law-making

6.1 Introduction

After the Inuit petition was filed to the IACHR in 2005, the possibility to envision and address global warming as a question of human rights has gained ground internationally, becoming not only an academically debated question but also the basis for the actions of diverse climate advocates and practitioners, as the previous chapter has discussed. As already stressed, the petition has had the major effect of giving a human face to a problem that, before so, had exclusively been addressed as an economic or an environmental question.

From 2008 onwards the existence of a relationship between human rights and global warming has been considered and established by UN bodies too. Particularly the Human Rights Council and the Special Rapporteur on human rights and the environment have worked on emphasising and reaffirming that climate change has implications on a range of human rights, as well as the implementation of mitigation and adaptation projects have the potential to further impinge on human dignity.[1] These correlations have also been the object of debate of intergovernmental negotiations. As a result of such efforts, today the Paris Agreement is the first global environmental treaty that makes an explicit reference to human rights in its Preamble. Nonetheless, the interaction between human rights law and international environmental law is not clear-cut and several questions remain open concerning the meaning of human rights obligations in an environmental context.

Against this background, the first sections of this chapter will discuss the relationship between human rights and the environment. After a brief introduction on human rights and human rights law, the relationship between human dignity and environmental protection will be explored. Besides the emergence of a converging jurisprudence pointing to the idea that environmental harm can trump the enjoyment of fundamental rights, the link between the respect

1 The Special Rapporteur was created in 2012 by resolution 19/10 of the Human Rights Council, with the mandate to study human rights obligations related to the enjoyment of the environment and to identify best practices regarding States' performance on human rights obligations in this area and in the formulation of environmental policies.

of human rights and environmental protection is not always evident. In this sense, a common approach has been that of introducing environmental considerations within human rights law by "greening" human rights obligations more than by recognising a human right to environment, which so far has been enshrined in just a few regional human rights instruments. The hurdles that the recognition of a stand-alone right to a safe environment raises showcase the main problems of a human rights-based approach to climate change and environmental protection more broadly, while also allowing one to consider the advantages of such a proposal from the perspective of the right to public participation.

6.2 Introducing Human Rights and International Human Rights Law: The Emergence of Third Generation Rights

After World War II and particularly with the adoption of the *Universal Declaration of Human Rights* by the General Assembly (1948), the ground was set for the development of human rights internationally.[2] Whereas the UN Charter contains just a few references to human rights, the UNGA competence in this area is based on article 55 of the Charter, which gives the UN the ability to formulate human rights policies, something it first accomplished with the establishment of a Commission on Human-Rights, out of which the Universal Human Rights Declaration emerged in 1948.[3] Seventy years after its adoption as an UNGA recommendation – thus with no formal legally binding value – its content is considered customary law. As a matter of fact, the non-binding nature of the Declaration has not prevented the individual human rights contained therein to be elaborated in subsequent international and regional treaties, as well as in national constitutions and legislation.

Whereas first- and second-generation rights are primarily concerned with the protection of individuals against their governments,[4] thus with the obligations that States owe to individuals, with the emergence of new needs – among which the concerns for the protection of the environment – also the affirmation of new rights came into being. With the progressive development

2 United Nations General Assembly, *Universal Declaration of Human Rights* of 10 December 1948 (217 A (III)).

3 Following strong critics for allowing States with poor human rights records to become its members, the UN Commission on Human Rights has been dismantled and substituted in 2006 by the UN Human Rights Council (UNHRC) by the UNGA Resolution A/RES/60/251. The UNHRC is today responsible for investigating allegations of human rights violations within UN member States.

4 The so-called first-generation rights, largely influenced by a liberal tradition, are mainly civil and political rights. The right to life, property, freedom of expression and liberty are enunciated in the International Covenant on Civil and Political Rights of 1966. Second generation rights attain, instead, to a more social tradition and are thus concerned with ensuring adequate standards of living for humans, including the right to education, health and social security. The International Covenant on Economic, Social and Cultural Rights of 1966 has established the content of social rights.

of the so-called third generation rights, the focus of attention has increasingly displaced from the individual to the rights of society or social groups and thus supposed the possibility that also actors other than States are to be considered duty-bearers under human rights law. While this is novel, the relevance of third generation rights is often questioned and their content criticised for being indefinite. Besides the observance of the procedural rights that the respect of third generation rights may imply, in fact, there are difficulties in determining which substantive obligations these provisions suppose and how they should be applied as not to weaken the protection of other, arguably more relevant, human rights.[5]

6.2.1 Applying Human Rights Law: particular reference to the Right to a Healthy Environment

The application of human rights law, both internationally and regionally, entails the account and balancing of different considerations, among which are the nature of duties and obligations under human rights instruments, but also the balancing of different rights and interests at stake. Concerning the nature of duties, three main general obligations primarily loom on States due to human rights law: the duty to respect, protect and fulfil human rights. As a result, the respect of such rights entails the prohibition for States to engage in activities that may deprive individuals of their dignity and freedoms. As well explained by the prohibition of torture as a fundamental right, the duty on each States to refrain from torturing its citizens is typified as a negative duty. Conversely, a positive duty usually characterises the responsibility of States to protect their citizens from human rights' violations. In this sense, States are not only required to abstain from human rights' violations themselves, but also obliged by human rights law to take actions aimed at protecting the rights of individuals against possible violations. It follows that a breach of the duty to protect will happen by omission, rather than by a State action. Finally, the duty to fulfil human rights' obligations refers to the State duty to facilitate the satisfaction of human rights. As such, it is usually linked with the protection of second and third generations' rights, which might require, for their effective realisation, the enactment of specific legislation at the national level, the adoption and allocation of specific budget lines or any other possible measures aimed at facilitating and enabling the realisation of these rights.

By reviewing relevant case law, Bodansky, Brunnée, and Rajamani have well explained this point by considering the different ways in which the right to life

5 In this regard, different authors fear that the increasing emphasis on the protection of third generation rights, whose scope, content and justiciability is usually more difficult to identify, may divert international attention from the protection of individuals from crimes against humanity, genocide or torture. See, e.g., H. HANNUM, "Reinvigorating Human Rights for the Twenty-First Century", *Human Rights Law Review*,Vol. 16, 2016, pp. 409–451.

may be put at risk by a polluted environment.[6] For instance, a State can violate the right to life by directly taking actions that will cause environmental harm, as it could be the construction of invasive infrastructures in an environmentally sensitive area. On the other hand, a State can infringe such a right by failing to prevent the disruption of the environment by private actors. Finally, the human right to life can be violated when a State fails to take positive actions aimed at protecting the environment, as increasingly is being established by the national case law on climate change.[7]

The existence of obligations under international law also entails the existence of rights- holders and duty-bearers. While this is certainly true for human rights law, the spectrum of rights and duties holders under this body of law has evolved in recent decades. Since human rights law first developed to ensure the protection of individuals against their government, States have traditionally been considered the only entities holding human rights obligations. More recently, however, the possibility to hold private actors (and particularly corporations) accountable for their negative human rights records has been discussed in the literature and partially adjudicated in courtrooms.[8] On the other hand, the emergence of new rights, based on the assumption that their satisfactory enjoyment may be only carried out within a specific group or community, has spurred the emergence of collective rights. The central idea here is that individuals cannot be considered apart from the community in which they live, enjoy and exercise their rights. While this line of thought mostly applies in the context of second- and third-generation rights, slightly different is the case of minority rights, in which the main aim is to secure particularly vulnerable sections of society – such as women, children and indigenous peoples – and the final scope of protection is to ensure the continued existence of these groups.

Whether or not human rights law may find extraterritorial application will also determine who holds human rights obligations – and towards whom – in a particular context. While the scholarship and case law have recognised that human rights law can apply beyond national borders where a State exercises effective control over a territory or people abroad – as in the case of occupied territories and cross-border activities by States' agents – the geographic scope of human rights duties is less clear when private or public activities are the cause of transnational environmental harm.[9] In general terms, the conflict is given by the need to reconcile

6 See, D. BODANSKY, J. BRUNNÉE and L. RAJAMANI, *International Climate Change Law*. Oxford: Oxford University Press, 2017, p. 306.

7 See, Chapter 5.

8 See, e.g., A. CLAPHAM, "Human Rights Obligations for Non-State-Actors: Where are We Now?", in F. LAFONTAINE and F. LAROCQUE (eds.) *Doing Peace the Rights Way: Essays in International Law and Relations in Honour of Louise Arbour*. Cambridge: Intersentia, 2018, pp. 1–18; A. CLAPHAM, *Human Rights Obligations of Non-State Actors*. Oxford: Oxford University Press, 2006.

9 See, as a general reference, S. JOSEPH, "Extraterritorial Human Rights Duties", in S. JOSEPH, *Blame it on the WTO?: A Human Rights Critique*. Oxford: Oxford University Press, 2011, pp. 245–264; J. ABRISKETA and M. NAGORE CASAS, "Extraterritorial Application of Human Rights

the universal nature of human rights with the requirement to give to them actual application within the jurisdiction of determined States, while preserving the equal rights of individuals on the basis of the principles of non-discrimination and equality. The extraterritorial application of human rights in environmental context supposes in this sense more hurdles for the need to establish a link of causation between the activity (or the omission) of a State, the transnational environmental harm and the violation of rights. Jurisdiction is also a problem at stake. For instance, does the protection of human rights exclusively fall within the jurisdiction of the State in which the polluting activity is taking place and the victims happen to live? Or, conversely, the responsibility to protect human rights can also be attached to the polluting State since the latter holds control over the source of harm? As it will be recalled below, the issue of extraterritorial applicability is being discussed with regard to the transboundary impacts of climate change.

Finally, the application of human rights law may require the balancing between different and potentially conflicting rights. Generally speaking, the freedom of expression, religion and speech are often said to find limitations in the respect and exercise of the freedoms of someone else. Likewise, the right to economic development pursued by States as an attribute of their sovereignty comes with certain limitations when lucrative activities are likely to impair, for instance, the rights to life or health of their citizens. Although the notion of balancing is somehow hampered in the context of environmental harm, since few human rights instruments recognise the right to an environment of a certain quality, a balancing between the protection of socio-economic rights and the protection of the environment is increasingly gaining foothold in the literature. This considers the environment to have a value in itself, as well as in application of the concept of sustainable development in which the protection of the environment as a precondition to prosperous societies is implied.

While these key questions have been only briefly introduced here, they will be resumed and further analysed below, when discussing the possibility of approaching climate change from the perspective of human rights.

6.3 Human rights and the environment

The interconnection between climate change and human rights is fairly recent. However, more established is the link between environmental integrity and the enjoyment of human rights. A sound environment is considered to be a precondition for the enjoyment of very fundamental human rights, including the right to life and health.[10] This idea was first considered by the

Treaties", *Oxford Bibliographies in International Law*, 2016; J. E. VIÑUALES, "A Human Rights Approach to Extraterritorial Environmental Protection? An Assessment", in N. BHUTA (ed.) *The Frontiers of Human Rights*. Oxford: Oxford University Press, 2016, pp. 177–221.

10 The term "sound" could be interchangeably exchanged with the following qualifications: secure, healthy, stable and safe. The problem of defining uniform standards and definition of what constitutes

General Assembly in 1968[11] and lately affirmed in the Stockholm Declaration on the Human Environment of 1972, Principle 1, which establishes that: "Man has the fundamental right to freedom, equality and adequate conditions of life, in an environment of a quality that permits a life of dignity and well-being, and he bears a solemn responsibility to protect and improve the environment for present and future generations".[12]

Principle 1 was re-taken in 1994 by the UN Sub-Commission on the Prevention of Discrimination and Protection of Minorities, which proposed the adoption of a Declaration of Principles on Human Rights and the Environment.[13] The latter document somehow recalled the Stockholm Declaration as it put emphasis on the value of a sound environment as well as on intergenerational responsibility, but it also went a step further by envisioning for the first time the possibility to establish at the international level an autonomous human right to a healthy and decent environment. Nonetheless, the proposal was not substantially discussed at the UN level and was finally abandoned.[14] It follows that the relationship between a secure environment and human rights is not always straightforward. While a great number of national constitutions appreciate a right to the environment, human rights law instruments differ in their recognition of such a right and, as explained below, largely derive its protection from the defence of other human rights. John Knox has qualified as anomalous such a trend while affirming that the absence of a universally acknowledged right to a healthy environment is rather irrelevant to the application of human rights to the environment, since there is well-established evidence that environmental harm can interfere with the enjoyment of human rights.[15] Another section of this chapter will discuss the work done by the former UN Special Rapporteur and the United Nations General Assembly on the subject.

To date, exclusively four regional human rights instruments explicitly recognise the right to an environment of some kind. Fairly recent is the inclusion of such a provision in the 2004 Arab Charter on Human Rights and in the 2012 Association of Southeast Asian Nations' (ASEAN) Human Rights

environmental integrity will be recalled later on in this chapter, when assessing the possibility of affirming a stand-alone human rights to the environment.

11 Resolution adopted by the UN General Assembly on 3 December 1968 on Problems of the Human Environment, UNGA Res. 2398 (XXIII).

12 Declaration of the United Nations Conference on the Human Environment, *Principle 1,* of 16 June 1972 (UN Doc. A/CONF/48/14/Rev.1).

13 Draft Principles On Human Rights and the Environment, E/CN.4/Sub.2/1994/9, Annex I (1994). Available at: http://hrlibrary.umn.edu/instree/1994-dec.htm (Last access, 19 September 2020).

14 K. WOLFE, "Greening the International Human Rights Sphere? Environmental Rights and the Draft Declaration Principles on Human Rights and the Environment", *APPEAL Review of Current Law and Law Reform,* Vol. 9, No. 1, 2003, pp. 45–58.

15 J. H. KNOX, "Human Rights Principles and Climate Change", in C. P. CARLARNE, K. R. GRAY and R. TARASOFSKY (eds.) *The Oxford Handbook of International Climate Change Law,* 2016, pp. 214–235.

Declaration. In both instruments, the right to environment is set as a part of the right to an adequate standard of living and has not given rise, thus far, to relevant case law. Somehow more established is this right in the other two regional systems. The Additional Protocol to the American Convention on Human Rights, provides at article 11 that "Everyone shall have the right to live in a healthy environment and to have access to basic public services"[16], while the 1981 African Charter of Human Rights and Peoples' Rights recognises a more substantive right in article 24 by establishing that: "All peoples shall have the right to a general satisfactory environment favourable to their development".[17] While the former right refers to an obligation owed to individuals, it is worth noting that the African Charter expresses the right in collective terms. A limited, though relevant, case law has also developed under these two instruments.

A well-known decision is the *Ogoniland case*,[18] which clarified both procedural and substantive obligations as to how such a broad provision as the one established in article 24 of the African Charter, should be interpreted and applied in practice. This ruling assessed both the violation of article 16 (right to health) and article 24 (right to a satisfactory environment) of the Charter, recognising that the latter imposes obligations on States "to prevent pollution and ecological degradation, to promote conservation and to secure an ecologically sustainable development and use of natural resources"[19]. The assessment made in 2012 by the Economic Community of West African States (ECOWAS) has had even more relevant implications for the ascertainment of a free-standing human right to the environment.[20] As noted by Adinolfi: "The autonomy of the right to a healthy environment from other human rights has been acknowledged, and its violation has been ascertained without assessing whether poor environmental quality has undermined human health or life".[21] In effect, the judgement represents a precedent concerning the justiciability of a right to environment. By the same token, the Inter-American Court of Human Rights

16 Organisation of American States, *American Convention on Human Rights* of 22 January 1969 (1144 UNTS 123), article 11.

17 Organisation of African Unity, *African Charter on Human and Peoples' Rights* of 27 June 1981 (21 ILM 58), article 24.

18 *Social and Economic Rights Action Center and Center for Economic and Social Rights v. Nigeria*, ACHPR SERAC Decision, Comm. 155, 2001. The case relates to the widespread environmental contamination and consequent health problems caused to the Ogoni people by oil exploitation activities carried out by the Nigerian National Company and the Shell Petroleum Development Corporation in the region of the Niger River delta. See, for a detailed account of the case, F. COOMANS, "The Ogoni Case Before the African Commission on Human and Peoples' Rights", *International and Comparative Law Quarterly*, Vol. 52, No. 3, 2003, pp. 749–760.

19 SERAC Decision, par. 52.

20 Case *Socio-Economic Rights and Accountability Project v. Federal Republic of Nigeria*, ECW/CCJ/JUD/18/12, 2012.

21 G. ADINOLFI, "The Right to a Healthy Environment. Delineating the content (and contours) of a slippery notion", in F. F. ZORZI GIUSTINIANI, E. SOMMARIO, F. CASOLARI and others (eds.) *Routledge Handbook of Human Rights and Disasters*. New York: Routledge, 2018, pp. 211–227.

(IACtHR) has recognised in a recent advisory opinion the possibility of invoking the right to a healthy environment, clarifying its content and reach upon request of the Republic of Colombia.[22] In what Fernández Egea has defined as one of the most important international decisions in the environmental fields of the last decades, the IACtHR has expressively mentioned that "Environmental degradation may cause irreparable harm to human beings; thus, a healthy environment is a fundamental right for the existence of humankind".[23]

Concerning universal human rights instruments where, as already said, no autonomous human right to the environment has been recognised up to the moment of writing, the environmental dimension of different human rights has nevertheless been indirectly ascertained. As discussed above, this is largely due to the failure of adopting the Draft Declaration of Principles on Human Rights and the Environment of 1994, in which one of the first principles declared that: "All persons have the right to a secure, healthy and ecologically sound environment. This right and other human rights, including civil, cultural, economic, political and social rights, are universal, interdependent and indivisible". The interdependency of different human rights has been also underlined by the Committee on Economic, Social and Cultural Rights of the UN with regard, for instance, to the right to food and health and the need to prevent or avoid environmental contamination or detriment. Likewise, the Human Rights Committee has underlined the relevance that the use of land resources has for different communities and with regard to the enjoyment of minority rights.

Alan Boyle has maintained that environmental rights can be found and tracked down in all generations of human rights.[24] For example, the exercise of civil and political rights can empower individuals and favour their participation in environmental decision-making – particularly in those countries that have ratified the Aarhus Convention – as well as force States to meet standards of protection for their citizens' right to life, securing them from environmental harm, as it is now increasingly the case in the European jurisprudence. In this sense, different authors have signalled the existence of a substantial case law that has, in fact, "greened" general human rights. Indeed, also when no direct mention of a right to the environment is found in universal or regional human rights treaties, the case law has pointed to an indirect protection of the environment or of environmental rights. This practice has been so extensive in the case of the European Convention on Human Rights that the adoption of an environmental protocol to the ECHR was recommended by the Parliamentary Assembly of the Council of Europe in 2005. Nonetheless, up to the point of

22 The advisory opinion is available at: https://www.corteidh.or.cr/docs/opiniones/seriea_23_ing.pdf (Last access, 02 October 2020).

23 Inter-American Court of Human Rights, Advisory Opinion OC-23/17 of 15 November 2017, p. 26.

24 A BOYLE, "Human Rights or Environmental Rights? A Reassessment", *Fordham Environmental Law Review*, Vol. 18, No. 3, 2008, pp. 471–551.

writing, only the Courts' decisions on this subject have been summarised in a Manual on Human Rights and the Environment, adopted by the Council of Europe the same year.[25] As some landmark cases, including *Lopez Ostra v. Spain*[26] or *Guerra v Italy*[27] have showed, the ECtHR jurisprudence on the environment has mainly relied on the substantive obligations included in articles 2 (right to life) and 8 (right to private and family life) of the ECHR, as well as on the procedural duties established by the Aarhus Convention of 1998. Extensive reference and analysis of this case law have been made in previous research works.[28]

Another option would be to treat the environment as a social and economic right, thus as a specific public good to be protected and balanced against other human rights' obligations in its own value. As it will be discussed when assessing the potential affirmation of a free-standing right to the environment, the advantage of such an approach rests on the possibility of adequately balancing its protection against the still largely pre-eminence of other social and economic rights. As again Boyle has rightly maintained: "Lacking the status of a right means that the environment can be trumped by those values which do have that status, including economic development and natural resources exploitation".[29] In this sense, the establishment of such a right would close what seems to be a still pending normative gap. Finally, as already said, the environment as a third generation right would put more emphasis on how communities – and not only individuals – exercise a right to determine the quality of the environment in which they live, sustain their lives and activities. This is a perspective that holds great value for indigenous peoples and local communities, for instance in the management of biodiversity.

Interestingly, all these approaches also highlight an ongoing debate on how the relationship between human rights and the environment should be reconsidered, arguably putting more emphasis on the intrinsic value that the environment has in itself and not exclusively as an attributed for the flourishing and prosperity of human life, namely, as Davies and others have put it, *as a resource base to meet human needs*.[30] In this sense, several commentators have been critical towards what is considered to be a purely anthropocentric view and approach to the protection of the environment through human rights' lenses. Nature, so the

25 The Manual is available at: https://www.echr.coe.int/LibraryDocs/DH_DEV_Manual_Environment_Eng.pdf (Last access, 25 September 2020).

26 *Lopez Ostra v. Spain*, 20 Eur. Ct. H.R. 277, 1994.

27 *Guerra v. Italy*, 26 Eur. Ct. H.R. 357, 1998.

28 See, e.g., A BOYLE, *supra* note 24; L. LOUCAIDES, "Environmental Protection through the Jurisprudence of the European Convention on Human Rights", in L. LOUCAIDES (ed.) *The European Convention on Human Rights. Collected Essays*. Leiden: Brill, 2005, pp. 167–191.

29 A. BOYLE, "Human Rights and the Environment: Where Next?", in B. BOER (ed.) *Environmental Law Dimensions of Human Rights*. Oxford: Oxford University Press, 2015, pp. 201–239, at 222.

30 K. DAVIES, S. ADELMAN, A. GREAR and others, "The Declaration on Human Rights and Climate Change: A New Legal Tool for Global Policy Change", *Journal of Human Rights and the Environment*, Vol. 8, No. 2, 2017, pp. 217–253, at 233.

argument goes, should be valued for itself, as an essential element of social life of which humans are but one part. While the promotion of a more biocentric – as opposed to anthropocentric – perspective holds great ethical value, it seems problematic to construct solid legal arguments on such a basis. Part of such limitations certainly derives from the Eurocentric conception of law, which builds on a clear separation of categories – such as human and non-human – and on the distinction between objects and subjects of law. While, in this regard, the idea of stewardship as exercised in indigenous peoples' cultures may prove relevant, it seems too far a development for international law as a State-centred discipline to allocate duties and rights to non-human entities.[31] Also in the context of climate change, an anthropocentric viewpoint has been prominent and this environmental harm has been framed as a common concern of mankind or as a threat to human rights at best. In this regard, a more balanced perspective may be found in the *Framework Principles on Human Rights and the Environment*, elaborated by the former UN Special Rapporteur J. Knox, which establish:

> Human rights and environmental protection are interdependent. A safe, clean, healthy and sustainable environment is necessary for the full enjoyment of human rights […]. At the same time, the exercise of human rights, including rights to freedom of expression and association, to education and information, and to participation and effective remedies, is vital to the protection of the environment.[32]

Although still largely anthropocentric, the latter perspective of interdependency between the exercise of human rights and the protection of the environment seems the most adequate framework of analysis for this research.

6.4 When climate change became a human rights issue: the role of the United Nations in establishing the climate change-human rights nexus

"It is now beyond debate that the adverse effects of climate change will, in their severity, threaten a range of human rights, including the right to life, health, food and housing".[33]

31 On the other hand, the increasing research focused on the potential establishment or existence of animal rights is in opposition with this assumption. See, e.g., A. PETERS, "Global Animal Law: What It Is and Why We Need It", *Transnational Environmental Law*, Vol. 5, No. 1, 2016, pp. 9–23. Different, although still debated, is the consideration of the rights of future generations as "humans to be".

32 The Framework Principles on Human Rights and the Environment have been elaborated by the former Special Rapporteur on human rights and the environment, John Knox, in his last annual report of 2018, UN Doc. A/HRC/37/59. The Principles are available at: https://www.ohchr.org/en/issues/environment/srenvironment/pages/annualreports.aspx (Last access, 18 September 2020).

33 D. BODANSKY, J. BRUNNÉE and L. RAJAMANI, *supra* note 6, at 296.

Bodansky, Brunné, and Rajamani recognised this in 2017 at the opening of a chapter on the intersection between climate change regulation and human rights law. The implication that climate change is and will likely have on human rights was nonetheless discussed and made public much earlier than 2017. As already underlined, the Inuit Petition to the Inter-American Commission on Human Rights has served as a springboard for framing climate change in terms of human rights violations. By linking rising temperatures to the US failure to take effective steps to reduce its GHGs' emissions – what, in turn, resulted in the alleged violation of Inuit's human rights – these populations tried to make the USA accountable for such omissions. Therefore, the case was framed to demonstrate that the USA failed to protect the rights of this population, and also to ascertain whether the State fulfilled their rights by enacting adequate federal legislation.

Since then, the analysis and assessment of climate-induced human rights violations have gained momentum and, also thanks to the scientific evidence gathered by the IPCC from 1988 onwards, there is now consensus on the idea that rising temperatures impinge on the exercise and enjoyment of general human rights. Certainly, such a development has also been the result of a lively academic debate, of the active work of several UN human rights bodies, international and non-governmental organisations and of a few committed nation states.[34] In this sense, particularly remarkable is the case of the Small Island Developing States. As for the Arctic region, SIDS are highly vulnerable to the impacts of climate change and since 2007 have voiced their concerns on this issue. This same year, SIDS adopted the first-ever intergovernmental statement on the human dimension of climate change, requesting to the UN Human Rights Council to hold a discussion on this topic and that the Office of the UN High Commissioner for Human Rights (OHCHR) studied the impacts of rising temperatures on human rights.[35] Once the debate on climate change and human rights had been opened by the SIDS, UN human rights bodies assumed a very prominent and central role in studying and making public the interconnections between climate change and human rights.[36] The first resolution of the Human Rights Council was issued in 2008 and, while expressing its concern that *climate change poses immediate and far-reaching threat to people and*

34 For instance, the Center for International Environmental Law have issued several publications on the topic, as well as a Declaration on Human Rights and Climate Change was developed in 2016 by the Global Network for the Study of Human Rights and the Environment. See, on the latter, K. DAVIES, S. ADELMAN, A. GREAR and others, *supra* note 30.

35 The full text of the Malé Declaration on the Human Dimension of Global Climate Change, adopted on 14 November 2007, is available at: http://www.ciel.org/Publications/Male_Declaration_Nov07.pdf (Last access, 25 September 2018).

36 Such a role has to be understood in a broader context in which, more generally, the Human Rights Council and different appointed Special Rapporteurs have continued to investigate and report on the relationship human rights-environment. Under such a perspective, in fact, climate change is but one – although especially disruptive – of many environmental harms that may impair human rights.

has implications for the full enjoyment of human rights, it requested the OHCHR to conduct a detailed study on the relationship between climate change and human rights.[37]

Already in 2009, the Office of the High Commissioner for Human Rights reported that an increase in global temperatures could interfere with the exercise and enjoyment of different human rights. Likewise, the implementation of mitigation and adaptation projects under the Clean Development Mechanism could further undermine these rights, for instance by failing to respect the right of free, prior and informed consent of indigenous communities that are usually affected by the projects developed under the scheme.[38] The report was followed by another Human Rights Council resolution, in which the Council more specifically noted that climate change-related impacts have implications for the effective enjoyment of human rights including, *inter alia*, the right to life, to adequate food, to the highest attainable standard of health, and also recognised that these implications will be felt most acutely by those segment of the population who are already in vulnerable situations. Remarkable is that the Council affirmed that human rights obligations and commitment have the potential to inform and strengthen international and national policy-making in the area of climate change.[39] Since the presentation of the first OHCHR report, the Human Rights Council has warned in subsequent resolutions about the correlation between climate change and human rights.[40] It also decided in 2012 to appoint an independent expert (later renamed Special Rapporteur) to assess and report on human rights and the environment. Parallel to such developments, the discussion on the relationship climate change-human rights also entered the 2010 climate negotiations and, with more force, the 2015 climate talks.

37 Resolution adopted by Human Rights Council on 28 March 2008 on Human rights and climate change, Res. 7/23, UN Doc. A/HRC/RES/7/23.

38 See, for a discussion of CMD projects and REDD initiatives, S. DUYCK, "The Paris Agreement and the Protection of Human Rights in a Changing Climate", *Yearbook of international Environmental Law*, Vol. 26, No. 1, 2015, pp. 3–45.

39 Resolution adopted by the Human Rights Council on 25 March 2009 on Human rights and climate change, Res. 10/4, UN Doc. A/HRC/10/4.

40 The following UN Human Rights Council resolutions have considered the relationship human rights-climate change: Resolution adopted by the Human Rights Council on 17 October 2011 on Human rights and climate change, Res. 18/22, UN Doc. A/HRC/RES/18/22; Resolution adopted by the Human Rights Council on 15 July 2014 on Human rights and climate change, Res. 26/27, UN Doc. A/HRC/RES/26/27; Resolution adopted by the Human Rights Council on 30 June 2015 on Human rights and climate change, Res. 29/15, UN Doc. A/HRC/RES/29/15; Resolution adopted by the Human Rights Council on 1 July 2016 on Human rights and climate change, Res 32/33 UN Doc. A/HRC/RES/32/33; Resolution adopted by the Human Rights Council in 7 July 2017 on Human rights and climate change, Res. 35/20, UN Doc. A/HRC/RES/35/20; Resolution adopted by the Human Rights Council on 5 July 2018 on Human rights and climate change, Res. 38/4, UN Doc. A/HRC/RES/38/4.

As a matter of fact, the Cancun Agreement of 2010 incorporated for the first time a direct reference to the Human Rights Council Resolution 10/4 on human rights and climate change. Kirchmeier and Lador have carefully reconstructed the steps that have favoured the recognition of human rights' obligations in the text of the Paris Agreement which, to date, is the first international environmental treaty to make explicit reference to human rights in its preamble:

> Parties should, when taking action to address climate change, respect, promote and consider their respective obligations on human rights, the right to health, the rights of indigenous peoples, local communities, migrants, children, persons with disabilities and people in vulnerable situations and the right to development, as well as gender equality, empowerment of women and intergenerational equity. [41]

Whereas, *prima facie*, the reference made to human rights in the Paris Agreement may seem irrelevant in such a wording and because exclusively included in the Preamble, its potential impact deserves further discussion. In a previous draft of the climate accord, a reference to human rights was to appear in both the preamble and in article 2 in the following form: "This Agreement shall be implemented [...] while ensuring [...] and the respect, protection, promotion and fulfilment of human rights for all, including the right to health and sustainable development [...]".[42] Nonetheless, due to the opposition of different States, among which particularly Norway and the USA, the reference was finally relegated to the Preamble.[43] Arguments concerning the discretion of States in choosing how to implement their international obligations, together with the discrepant adherence of States to international or regional human rights legal instruments, have been brought against the inclusion of a stronger and more demanding reference to human rights in the body of the text. Albeit the reference to human rights as made in the Preamble of the agreement does not create new rights for its parties and besides being articulated with little legal force (in that the word "should" resembles more a declaration of intentions

41 See, F. KIRCHMEIER and Y. LADOR, "From Copenhagen to Paris at the UN Human Rights Council: When Climate Change Became a Human Rights Issue", in S. DUYCK, S. JODOIN and A. JOHL (eds.) *Routledge Handbook of Human Rights and Climate Governance*. New York: Routledge, 2018, pp. 145–164; *Paris Agreement* of 12 December 2015, Preamble.

42 S. ATAPATTU, "The Paris Agreement and Human Rights: Is Sustainable Development the 'New Human Right'?", *Journal of Human Rights and the Environment*, Vol. 9, No. 1, 2018, pp. 68–88, at 72.

43 According to Ferreira, USA and Norway agreed to champion the position of those States that feared that the inclusion of a human rights language in the Paris Agreement would open the door to legal liability mechanisms for human rights violations derived from climate change. See. P. G. FERREIRA, "Did the Paris Agreement Fail to Incorporate Human Rights in Operative Provisions? Not if You Consider the 2016 SDGs", *Centre for International Governance Innovation Paper*, No. 113, 2016, pp. 1–11, at 5.

rather than a full obligation for its signatories), such a reference is important for several reasons. It should be recalled at this point that, under the Vienna Convention on the Law of Treaties, the Preamble to each agreement has great interpretative value and carries weight when enforcing the obligations contained therein. Therefore, apart from having a great symbolic value, different authors have referred to the Paris Agreement as potentially innovative, insofar as it could help to substantiate the obligations of the parties to the agreement, having paved the way for the adoption of a human rights-based approach to climate governance.

Indeed, well-established legal experts and scholars have underlined the importance of the agreement. In his analysis of how human rights should be internalised in the climate change regime in order to cope with one of the most pressing challenges of the twenty-first century, John Knox has directly equated the agreement to a human rights treaty. As he has noted: "The Paris Agreement will be remembered not only as the first major climate agreement of the century, but also as the first international environmental agreement to recognize that human rights are part of the framework it creates".[44] In a very acute reflection that discusses the human rights provisions included in the Paris Agreement in the wider context of sustainable development, Atapattu underlines how the binding nature of the climate treaty (in which the link between human rights and global warming is recognised) gives significance to such a reference.[45] First, it definitely recognises that human rights are relevant when addressing climate change – something criticised by those sceptical towards this approach – and also because it underlines the legal duty that States have under human rights law when acting against climate change.

Looking at the intersection between human rights law and international environmental law, Savaresi has assessed the potential that the Paris Agreement Preamble may have in redirecting the fragmentation between different branches of international law.[46] In this sense, human rights law and climate change law are increasingly less compartmentalised and the emergence of environmental human rights law specific to climate change may be on the rise. This, in turn, will likely have positive effects on other fields of international law, for instance on refugees' law. Likewise, the process that has led to the inclusion of a human rights language into the Paris Agreement has certainly promoted institutional cooperation between UN human rights bodies and the UNFCCC system, something that will likely continue in the future.

44 J., H. KNOX, "The Paris Agreement as a Human Rights Treaty", in D. AKANDE, J. KUOSMANEN, H. McDERMOTT and others (eds.) *Human Rights and 21st Century Challenges: Poverty, Conflict, and the Environment*. Oxford: Oxford University Press, 2019, pp. 1–26, at 26.

45 S. ATAPATTU, *supra* note 42.

46 A. SAVARESI, "Climate change and Human Rights. Fragmentation, Interplay, and Institutional Linkages", in S. DUYCK, S. JODOIN and A. JOHL (eds.) *Routledge Handbook of Human Rights and Climate Governance*. New York: Routledge, 2018, pp. 31–42.

Finally, it is maintained here that, while the actual reference made in the Preamble exclusively concerns the human rights obligations that States have assumed already or will assume in the future, nothing precludes the possibility that it will gain more normative relevance and enforceability as the relationship between climate change and human rights develops. In this sense, as it will be resumed when talking about the opportunities derivable from a human rights-based approach to climate change, the inclusion of a human rights language in the Paris Agreement marks an important turning point in the establishment of a climate change-human rights nexus.

6.5 Framing climate change as a human rights issue: limitations and opportunities

While the existence of a relationship between the effects of global warming and human rights is now well affirmed, more complicated is to ascertain what this actually means in terms of rights and obligations. In other words, what does it mean to frame climate change as a human rights issue? And, equally important, which problems does the adoption of such a framework supposes?

As a base argument, it follows from the recognition of climate change as a threat to human rights that global warming constitutes a severe enough environmental harm to be framed as a human rights problem. As emerged by converging case law, the disruption of the environment is increasingly considered as having a negative impact on human rights. Furthermore, the essence of climate change as a global, intergenerational and particularly severe environmental problem makes it stand out as a particularly dangerous threat to these rights and thus allows the application of such jurisprudence to this environmental harm. It follows that, even in the context of climate change, States human rights' duties will relate to the respect of procedural and substantive obligations, particularly so in the case of most vulnerable people.[47] As maintained by Atapattu, human rights law imposes a general obligation on States to respect, protect and fulfil their human rights obligations when taking action relating to climate change, including mitigation and adaptation law and strategies.[48]

Nonetheless, the interference of a particularly serious environmental harm may not be sufficient for determining the violation of human rights' provisions. To be established as a violation of human rights, any disturbance must be traced back to the action or inaction of a certain State or non-State entity holding

47 In this regard, procedural obligations may require the conduct of environmental impact assessments, that the full and effective participation of all concerned people within the decision-making process is guaranteed and that effective remedies are available when States fail to comply with such obligations. Substantive duties refer, instead, to the respect of human rights when States decide on the appropriate level of environmental protection or to the protection that States must provide to their citizens against environmental harm caused by non-State entities.

48 S. ATAPATTU, *supra* note 42, at 71.

human rights obligations, whose activity have resulted in being inconsistent with such duties. It follows that there are several obstacles as to how a jurisprudence that has largely developed around the violation of rights caused by a specific source and usually occurred in one country, may be applied to a global and transnational environmental harm. Unsurprisingly, global warming is often regarded as a question that requires novel legal strategies and approaches to be adequately addressed, particularly so if considering that the first generations of human rights were developed at a moment where the pollution of the environment was not ranging high on the international agenda.

One of the main problems encountered when trying to assess a climate-induced human rights' violation lies in the difficulty of demonstrating the existence of a causal link between a governmental or non-governmental contribution to climate change and the negative impact that the latter will have on human rights. As in the Inuit case, the difficulty of establishing a causal relationship between the GHGs emission rates of individual States and the damages suffered by individuals may weight on the decision of human rights courts to start legal proceedings. This is further hampered by the progressive impact of climate change. While this phenomenon is already producing devastating effects on the human and natural systems, the impacts of global warming are extensive and will be experienced for generations even after a stabilisation of present GHGs emissions. This problem was also noted in the first report on human rights and climate change of the Office of the UN High Commissioner for Human Rights, which alerted that "while climate change has obvious implications for the enjoyment of human rights, it is less obvious whether, and to what extent, such effects can be qualified as human rights violations in a strict legal sense".[49] As previously discussed in the context of climate change litigation, however, it seems today increasingly more possible to trace back causation with the help of attribution studies. The progressive development of such a field will likely help the determination of causation in the future. On the other hand, already traceable are the aggregate contributions of major climate polluters, such as the USA, the EU and China.

While causation mainly refers to a State obligation to respect human rights, the missing link between its contribution to climate change and the infringement of human rights does not prevent to consider if a State has taken adequate steps to protect or fulfil human rights when the harm derived from different sources. As maintained by Knox:

> "Every State has an obligation to protect against the infringement of human rights by the effects of climate change, whether or not the State is directly responsible for the cause of the infringement. This conclusion follows from the nature of their obligations to protect against environmental

49 OHCHR, *Report of the Office of the UN High Commissioner for Human Rights on the relationship between climate change and human rights*, 2009 (UN. Doc. A/HRC/10/61), par. 70.

> harm generally. Human rights bodies have made clear that States should protect against foreseeable environmental impairment of human rights whether or not the States directly cause the harm".[50]

In addition to this causal nexus, there are problems of jurisdiction and related to the transboundary nature of climate change. As previously discussed, the question of whether States' human rights obligations extend beyond their territory is a difficult one to answer. Human rights treaties often include explicit jurisdictional limits, as it is the case of the International Covenant on Civil and Political Rights and the European Convention on Human Rights.[51] On the contrary, no clause has been included in the International Covenant on Economic, Social and Cultural Rights and the Committee on Economic, Social and Cultural Rights has interpreted the International Covenant to give rise to extraterritorial duties. This seems reasonable in light of the rights it aims at securing which, in most cases, require international assistance and cooperation to be effectively fulfilled. The same is often said about climate change that, as a global issue, cannot be effectively addressed but through the cooperation of the international community. Authors such as Viñuales, Knox and Boyle have reflected on the extraterritorial application of human rights obligations in the context of climate change.[52]

As a minimum requirement, even when human rights law is not intended at giving rise to extraterritorial obligations, any State faced with the challenges derived from climate change will be required to ameliorate the effects that global warming may have on the rights of those falling within its jurisdiction. Knox has criticised such an approach for being incomplete when facing an environmental issue of global proportions, and has rather put forward the argument that the principle of international cooperation could provide an answer for applying extraterritorial obligations with regard to climate change.[53]

50 J. H. KNOX, 2019, *supra* note 44, at 13.

51 Such limits are, for instance, found in the ECHR at article 1 or in article 2 of the ICCPR. Boyle has nonetheless reported on how jurisdiction has been interpreted in broad terms in several cases concerning military operations abroad or the occupation of foreign territories. See, A. BOYLE, 2015, *supra* note 29, at 231. In any case, and since the focus of this research is on public participation, it seems important to note that in the case of the Aarhus Convention, no distinction is made between the public living within one State or beyond its borders, since the provisions of the treaties generally apply to the "concerned public". Moreover, article 3 of the Convention expressively recognise the duty of States to apply treaty provisions in a non-discriminatory fashion, *without discrimination as to citizenship, nationality or domicile and, in the case of a legal person, without discrimination as to where it has its registered seat or an effective centre of its activities.* If, as sustained by different authors, the Conventions may be considered as a human rights treaty, it follows the possibility to apply procedural human rights obligations extraterritorially in this context.

52 See, e.g., J. E. VIÑUALES, *supra* note 9; J. H. KNOX, "Diagonal Environmental Rights", in M. GIBNEY and S. SKOGLY (eds.) *Universal Human Rights and Extraterritorial Obligations*. Philadelphia: University of Pennsylvania Press, 2010, pp. 148–178.

53 J. H. KNOX, 2016, *supra* note 15.

Under the UN Charter, States have committed to cooperate in addressing global challenges to human rights. In light of this duty of cooperation, States could negotiate and implement international climate agreements that are able to meet a minimum core of human rights. While Boyle has pointed to the inconsistency of human rights case law on this question, he has nonetheless recognised that the application of a non-discrimination principle has emerged when considering the reach and scope of States' human rights obligations in cases of transnational pollution. In simple words, it would be inconsistent to allow a State to violate its human rights obligations on the territory of another State when, on the contrary, it would not be allowed to do so in its own territory. It follows that, as maintained by the author, "[A] state which fails to control harmful activities within its own territory which cause or risk causing foreseeable environmental harm extraterritorially does owe certain human rights obligations to those affected, because they are within its jurisdiction and control, even if they are not within its territory".[54] Of course, in this case too, the possibility to identify the exact causal link between States' action or inaction and the violation of rights is essential. As challenging as it may be, the possibility to apply human rights obligations extraterritorially may be done by resorting to different principles and core values that inspire international law. Particularly the principle of cooperation, solidarity, non-discrimination and equal treatment hold great value in this sense. While more research may be necessary on this point in order to clarify and reach consensus on this question, more prominent is the need to improve the knowledge on historical contributions and attribution studies as to be able to establish clearer links of causation and thus apply human rights law to climate change more forcefully. In conclusion, while problems remain in determining climate change impacts as a violation of human rights, it seems nonetheless worth exploring the relevance of a human rights-based approach for the reasons that will be explored in the following section.

6.5.1 A Human rights-based approach to climate change: main opportunities

Similar to how the jurisprudence on environmental human rights has differently developed internationally and regionally, there are at least two ways in which a human rights-based approach to climate change could be constructed. The first, an arguably more complex and still-emerging road, would require the establishment of an internationally recognised right to a healthy environment. Alternatively, existing and well-established human rights provisions could be re-interpreted in the context of climate change. As it will be discussed at a later stage, both options hold some value for the improvement of public participation in the context of international climate change law-making.

54 A. BOYLE, 2015, *supra* note 29, at 235.

While different commentators have for some time contended that the human right to a healthy environment is emerging in international law,[55] largely due to the jurisprudence of regional human rights systems on this issue, in recent years this idea has been resumed and more forcefully promoted by the former UN Special Rapporteur on human rights and the environment and by the United Nations General Assembly.

After the Stockholm Declaration and the failed attempt of the UN Sub-Commission on Prevention of Discrimination and Protection of Minorities to recognise a human right to environment, the Special Rapporteur Ksentini invoked its establishment as early as in 1994, issuing the Draft Principles on Human Rights and Environment in her final report to the Human Rights Committee. While this possibility encountered resistance over the following years and was eventually dismissed, it has been resumed with the appointment of John Knox as Special Rapporteur in 2012, whose mandate was renewed in 2015 as Special Rapporteur on human rights obligations related to the enjoyment of a safe, clean, healthy and sustainable environment.[56]

Regardless of the difficulties involved in agreeing on the content, scope and justiciability of a human right to a healthy environment,[57] in a recent report that the now former Special Rapporteur Knox presented to the Human Rights Council in March 2018, he once again underlined the interdependence between human rights and the environment.[58] Furthermore, in a joint statement with UN Environment, the former Rapporteur expressively required the recognition of a human right to a healthy environment and underlined:

> "Recognising the human right to a healthy and sustainable environment would not solve all environmental problems. But it would make clear that a healthy environment is on the same level of importance as other human

55 See, e.g., D. HUNTER, J. SALZMAN and D. ZAELKE, *International Environmental Law and Policy*. St. Paul MN: Foundation Press, 2015.

56 The Human Rights Council established the mandate for the Independent Expert on human rights and the environment in 2012, by UNGA Resolution A/HRC/RES/19/10. The mandate was extended in 2015 with the adoption of the UNGA Resolution A/HRC/RES/28/11.

57 At the moment of writing, there is no unified and qualitative definition of such a right. For instance, to which level the environment should be protected? Should one advocate for a clean, safe, decent, healthy or satisfactory environment? Problems of scope and justiciability have also been discussed in the literature. Nonetheless, different authors have diminished the relevance of such questions, reminding that several of the now protected human rights have also encountered such hurdles in their early articulation. See, e.g., S. AMINZADEH, "A Moral Imperative: The Human Rights Implications of Climate Change", *Hastings International & Comparative Law Review*, Vol. 30, No. 2, 2007, pp. 231–265.

58 That a healthy environment is necessary for the enjoyment of different human rights and, at the same time, the exercise of the latter, including the right to participation, is fundamental for the protection of the environment. See, Human Rights Council, *Report of the Special Rapporteur on the issue of human rights obligations relating to the enjoyment of a safe, clean, healthy and sustainable environment* of 24 January 2018 (UN Doc. A/HRC/37/59).

> rights and that, like other rights, it must be fulfilled in order for all people to enjoy lives of dignity, equality and freedom".[59]

In relation to the latter, an important development has taken place with the adoption of Resolution 72/277 by the UN General Assembly, which has established an *ad hoc* open-ended working group that works on the adoption of a Global Pact for the Environment, a draft text reflecting the principles of environmental law found in the majority of constitutions, international environmental agreements and Declarations. Presented by the former President of the COP21, Mr Laurent Fabius, and by the French *Club des Juristes*, the text has been conceived as a human rights instrument, which aims at codifying and establishing a third generation of fundamental rights, associated with the protection of the environment. Composed of 26 Articles that recall all general principles of international environmental law, the Pact also proposes the codification of a right to an ecologically sound environment in its article 1.[60] The latter is intended as a two-source principle, in which a right to a healthy environment and a duty to take care of the environment are interrelated. In 2019, the first round of negotiations for the Pact took place in Nairobi, Kenya, and have been resumed in July 2020 with the decision to adopt a political declaration by 2022.[61]

Pending such developments, the recognition of a right to a healthy environment holds value for several reasons and could be conceived at the international level with, at least, a dual purpose. On the one hand, and as a culmination of the process launched in 2008 following the Inuit petition, it would provide a stronger framework for the implementation and justiciability of existing obligations under human rights instruments. Particularly so in the context of climate change, given that the Paris Agreement now expressively requires States to respect, promote and consider their human rights' obligations when taking action on climate change. As said, while the right to environment is recognised in a few regional human rights instruments and in over 100 national constitutions, its unequivocal affirmation at the international level would provide for more homogeneity among different human rights systems and thus enhance legal certainty for different human rights holders. On the other hand, the right to a healthy environment could contribute to the development of more abstract human rights that, for example in the case of the rights of future generations, are not yet contemplated in current human rights law. This would lay the foundation for considering intergenerational responsibility as a legal issue and not

59 The full text of the joint statement is available at: https://www.ohchr.org/EN/NewsEvents/Pages/DisplayNews.aspx?NewsID=23162&LangID=E (Last access, 21 September 2020).

60 The first draft of Article 1 of the Global Pact for the Environment reads as follows: "Every person has the right to live in an ecologically sound environment adequate for their health, well-being, dignity, culture and fulfilment". A paper copy of the preliminary draft of the group of experts has been retrieved by the author during the Conference "Towards a Global Pact for the Environment" held at the European Parliament on the 6th of February 2019.

61 See, for reference: https://environmentassembly.unenvironment.org/follow-up-on-ga-res-73-333 (Last access, 02 October 2020).

exclusively as a largely unanswered ethical question.[62] However, whether the work carried out by Knox will be followed by the newly appointed Special Rapporteur David Boyd[63] and whether the ongoing negotiations will bring on the adoption of a meaningful Pact for the environment cannot be concluded at this point. It is the author's view to consider that the debate developed around the relationship between climate change and the enjoyment of human rights has created new momentum for the establishment of higher standards of protection for the environment, in UN bodies as well as at the level of nation states. Particularly at a time in which a great deal of attention and mobilisation has been raised in international public opinion by the climate change question, it will be difficult for States and UN bodies to delay the recognition and codification of existing third generation rights.

A more traditional re-interpretation of human rights in the light of climate change would instead underline the already recognised environmental component of existing and well-established human rights, such as the right to health or the right to life. While this seems to be the most straightforward interpretation of how human rights law may find application in the context of climate change, Cullet has elaborated a more ambitious perspective. Following the author's argument, a human rights-based approach to climate change requires a broader contamination between international environmental law and human rights law, and to put greater emphasis on solidarity rights. The latter are basically third generation rights, whose focus of attention is displaced from the individual to the collectivity, and where the human rights' duties of States are better addressed when they take common action towards the protection and promotion of human rights. In the authors' words:

> "Solidarity therefore provides a model from which to bridge human rights and climate change. It constitutes an appropriate basis to rethink States' rights and obligations in these areas. While States have a duty to cooperate, most of them are unable to fulfil their human rights' commitments linked to climate change alone and most of them should not be expected to shoulder the cost of adaptation for a problem they have contributed little to cause. Solidarity rights can establish the framework within which the global nature of human rights can be considered beyond individual claims in individual countries".[64]

62 For an overreaching discussion on the establishment of a right to a healthy environment, see J. H. KNOX and R. PEJAN (eds.), *The Human Right to a Healthy Environment.* Cambridge: Cambridge University Press, 2018; J. G. MERRILLS, "Environmental Rights", in D. BODANSKY, J. BRUNNÉ and E. HEY (eds.) *The Oxford Handbook of International Environmental Law.* Oxford: Oxford University Press, 2007, pp. 665–675

63 The mandate of the Special Rapporteur on human rights and the environment was further extended by the Human Rights Council in August 2018, with the adoption of the UNGA Resolution A/HRC/RES/37/8.

64 P. CULLET, "Human Rights and Climate Change. Broadening the Rights to Environment", in C. P. CARLARNE, K. R. GRAY and R. TARASOFSKY (eds.) *The Oxford Handbook of International Climate Change Law*, 2016, pp. 495–515, at 513.

Framed in such terms, a human rights-based approach would especially emphasise pending question of climate justice.

Independently from how the human rights-based approach to climate change will be envisioned in the future, there are already evident opportunities to be seized from such a proposition. Moreover, its consideration seems topical after the inclusion of a reference to human rights in the Paris Agreement, suggesting that human rights law will likely become an important viewpoint from which climate change will be looked at in the future.

The most evident and positive contribution that a human rights-based approach to climate change would bear in addressing this environmental harm, is a direct consequence of the pedigree of human rights law as a well-established system of rights and obligations centred on the dignity of human beings, whose institutions are able (although with limitations) to hear complaints, solve disputes and provide redress to victims. As Cullet has made clear:

> "International human rights law goes beyond other areas of international law by providing a framework wherein individuals are the subject of its obligations. As a result, a human rights approach to climate change can contribute to addressing questions that environmental law has failed to address effectively".[65]

In general terms, this approach would add a legal argument and a greater ethical burden to an issue that has been largely addressed for its environmental and economic implications, more than for the impacts that it has on human life and dignity. Being considered exclusively as an environmental problem, climate change regulation has often been subject to the ability to negotiating States to find a political compromise rather than ambitious solutions that take into account the integrity, indivisibility and respect of people's rights. While conceiving global warming as an issue linked to human dignity would allow, for instance, a better conciliation among the different economic, political and environmental interests surrounding this anthropogenic phenomenon, the emphasis on human rights may well substantiate what constitutes an illegal practice as far as the enjoyment of human rights is concerned, irrespective of States adherence to the international climate change regime. This seems increasingly important as major polluters like the USA plan to withdraw from the Paris Agreement in the near future.[66]

65 *Ibid*, at 500.

66 According to what established by article 28 of the Paris Agreement, however, States may withdraw from the Treaty only after three years from the date on which the Agreement has entered into force. Moreover, any withdrawal will take effect upon expiry of one year from the date of receipt of the notification of withdrawal. In any case, therefore, the USA will not be able to depart from the Paris Agreement before 2020.

As the work of the former UN Special Rapporteur on human rights and the environment has assertively affirmed, there is a clear interdependence between the exercise of human rights and the protection of the environment. It follows that any approach that draws on human rights to address climate change is not aimed at diverting attention from other human rights objectives, but rather intended to reinforce their respect. Since a characteristic of human rights is that their protection, respect and fulfilment does not depend on reciprocal relationships, but are obligations that States owe to each individual, another important contribution of human rights law to the making of climate law would be that "the presently dominating inter-state perspective of the climate change regime would have to be reconciled with the normative focus on the individual that comes necessarily with human rights".[67] This includes, as will be considered below, putting greater emphasis on the participatory rights of individual rightsholders. Finally, in addressing climate change litigation, this work has underlined how the international climate change regime built on the UNFCCC is not able to provide effective mechanisms for the resolution of claims, and for sanctioning those countries that are acting in violation of the Framework Convention's provisions. In opposition to this, international and regional human rights systems have established tribunals for hearing complaints, assess human rights violations and eventually provide remedies to victims. As the discussion above has shown, the UN human rights system is well equipped with bodies and appointed Special Rapporteurs able to oversee the status of human rights internationally, as well as to work towards the advancement of international law, as the effective tackling of climate change seems to require.[68]

6.6 Improving the participation of non-state actors in international climate change law-making by framing climate change as a human rights issue

Twenty years ago, following the enunciation of Principle 10 of the Rio Declaration of 1992, the *Aarhus Convention on Access to Information, Public Participation in Decision-Making and Access to Justice in Environmental Matters* was signed by UNECE countries. While Principle 10 has yet to be considered a general principle of international law, the Aarhus Convention was adopted with the specific commitment, under article 3.7, that "each Party shall promote the principles of this Convention in international environmental decision-making

67 A. CARDESA-SALZMANN, "Reflections on the Sustainability of a Human Rights Approach in the Context of the Climate Change Regime", in R. GILES CARNERO (coord.) *Cambio Climático, Energía y Derecho Internacional: Perspectivas de Futuro*. Cizur Menor: Aranzadi, 2012, pp. 169–178, at 175.

68 See, on the role that UN Human Rights bodies may play in the implementation of the Paris Agreement, S. DUYCK and Y. LADOR, "Human Rights into Climate Action After Paris: Opportunities for the UNFCC, the Human Rights Institutions and the G-20", *Human Rights and International Climate Politics Study*, 2016, pp. 3–20.

processes and within the framework of international organizations in matters relating to the environment". Following these twenty years of implementation, several works have traced the development and setbacks occurred in application of the three pillars enshrined in the Convention: access to information, public participation in decision-making and access to justice in environmental matters.[69] Alan Boyle, for example, has qualified procedural rights as the most relevant environmental addition to human rights law since the Rio Declaration of 1992. It is no coincidence that the Preamble of the Aarhus Convention directly recalls Principle 1 of the Stockholm Declaration of 1972 and its main provisions have constituted the basis for the adjudication of human rights violations, at least under the jurisdiction of the ECtHR.[70]

Looking at the international implementation of Principle 10 and of the Aarhus Convention, however, it should not be forgotten that while the first is still largely considered as *lex ferenda,* the Aarhus Convention exclusively applies today to 46 countries and the EU. It follows that the promotion of Principle 10 beyond the UNECE region has thus far been rather limited. Notwithstanding this, in 2018 a positive turn has been marked with the adoption of the Escazú Agreement, a treaty on public participation adopted by Latin American and Caribbean countries. While this is a much-welcomed development, the impact that this new Agreement will have on public participation in international environmental decision-making processes cannot be assessed here, since it has not yet entered into force at the moment of writing. Contextually to the application of Principle 10 and of the second pillar of the Aarhus Convention in international climate change law-making, the third chapter of this research has underlined that the lack of a coherent and systematic approach to public participation in intergovernmental negotiations has at time impaired the right of the public to participate in international climate change law-making. While this has been reported by different authors, Duyck has underlined that: "although the Parties to the UNFCCC have developed rules that describe the ways in which public participation can be exercised in intergovernmental processes, the exclusion of NGOs from crucial phases of the climate negotiations (most recently in Paris) is an issue that must be addressed".[71]

Mindful of the latter, the focus of attention of this work has been the enhancement of public participation in international climate change decision- and law-making. After exposing the emergence of non-governmental entities in international law and in the light of the essential contributions that they provide in the negotiation of environmental agreements, the fourth chapter of this

69 See, e.g., a dedicated monograph recently published in the 9th Volume, No.1, of the 2018 *Catalan Journal of Environmental Law.* The publication is available at: https://revistes.urv.cat/index.php/rcda/issue/view/115 (Last access, 24 September 2020). S. DUYCK, "Promoting the Principles of the Aarhus Convention in International Forums: The Case of the UN Climate Change Regime", *Review of European Community & International Environmental Law,* Vol. 22, No. 4, 2015, pp. 123–137.

70 As, for instance, in the case *Taskin and Others v. Turkey,* judgement of 10 November 2004.

71 S. DUYCK, "The Paris Agreement", 2015, *supra* note 38, at 41.

work has drawn a case study on Arctic IPs, proposing their model of participation in circumpolar affairs as a paradigm for the improvement of NSAs participatory rights in international climate governance. What is particularly relevant of Arctic IPs' practice is that their national and international advocacy and actions have been focused on promoting their rights to participation through human rights-based discourses and claims.[72] While, as seen in the fifth chapter, the appeal to climate change litigation as a strategy of advocacy – which also has Arctic IPs practice as a forerunner – seems to expand transnationally, its efficacy has been (so far) limited at the international level. In this sense, litigation remains a second-best option to the improvement of participatory rights in international intergovernmental processes but nonetheless unveils the disaffection created by a largely State-centred international decision-making system and stands as an argument in support of a more open international climate change decision-making process. Bearing this in mind, this last section wants to assess whether a human rights-based approach to climate change can serve the improvement of public participation in international climate change law-making. In other words, can the participation of non-State actors in international climate change law-making be improved by framing and approaching climate change as a human rights issue?

Hereafter, three main considerations on how a human rights-based approach to climate change could benefit and enhance the participation of non-State actors in international climate change law-making are presented:

(1) Reinterpreting the scope of procedural rights in intergovernmental negotiations.

As exposed above, the inclusion of a human rights language within the Paris Agreement has paved the way for the consideration of States' human rights obligations in the context of international climate change law. While conceiving climate change as a violation of human rights still supposes overcoming different legal questions (primarily the establishment of causation and jurisdiction), nothing precludes the possibility to consider which procedural obligations may bear on States in the context of climate change law-making, in light of existing human rights instruments.

The right to participate in the formulation and implementation of decisions at the international level has been recognised as an aspect of article 25 of the International Covenant on Civil and Political Rights. In its general comment

72 "The ICC's actions demonstrate how to effectively challenge both the basic rules prescribed by the climate change and the structure upheld by international law as a society of states. By raising the human rights petition against the US, the Inuit expanded society's notion of who is entitled to participate in the fight against climate change". See, T. KOIVUROVA, S. DUYCK and L. HEINÄMÄKI, "Climate Change and Human Rights", in E. J. HOLLO, K. KUVOLESI and M. MEHLING (eds.) *Climate Change and the Law*. Dordrecht: Springer, 2013, pp. 287–325, at 323.

on article 25, the Human Rights Committee has interpreted this provision as allowing the participation of the public in the conduct of international affairs and as an obligation that States owe to their citizens.[73] More generally, since all fundamental rights are indivisible and interdependent, the exercise of already established procedural rights in the context of international climate change governance becomes an expression of human rights.

Since the establishment of a relationship between human rights and global warming, States are required to promote, protect and fulfil these rights under the Paris Agreement. This is relevant when considering that public participation has been at time impeded in climate change governance. Provided that article 12 of the Paris Agreement expressively requires its Parties to cooperate in taking measures to enhance public participation, the implementation of the Agreement offers an opportunity for reinterpreting the scope of procedural rights in intergovernmental processes, in the light of States' human rights obligations.

(2) Differentiating among non-State actors and identifying rights-holders.

On the other hand, and largely based on Arctic IPs practice, the affirmation of a human rights-based approach to climate change may also have the effect to empower non-governmental actors and favour their broader representation in international climate change law-making. What sustained here is that it is the condition of individuals as rightsholders under human rights law (as opposed to stakeholders) that justifies and requires their inclusion in this law-making process, being therefore the legal basis on which their entitlement to actively participate in the making of international climate change law builds. As such, the intersection between international climate change law and human rights law as enshrined in the Preamble of the Paris Agreement, may constitute a valid legal argument for the enhancement of the participatory rights of NGOs. In the latter case and resembling the right to self-determination on which Arctic IPs practice have been authorised, the affirmation of a free-standing human right to environment would give greater normative content to this proposal. Pending such development, however, the protection of the environment as a *sine qua non* condition for the enjoyment and exercise of human rights seems already sufficiently established internationally.

This proposal appears particularly appropriate in dealing with climate change, because it might help to strike a balance between different and potentially conflicting interests that the participation of NGOs as observers to the UNFCCC systems aim at upholding. For instance, balancing the interests of the business community with those that work in the promotion of the public good and rights-based claims. Also, to secure the rights of those that will

73 Human Rights Committee, *General Comment No. 25; Article 25 – Participation in Public Affairs and the Right to Vote,* 12 July 1995, par. 5 (UN Doc. CCPR/C/21/Rev. 1/Add.7).

be disproportionally affected by climate change, as it seems to be in the case of indigenous and local communities, women and youth. Whereas a specific arrangement for improving the participation of local communities and indigenous peoples in the context of climate change law-making is now being established, the same could be provided at least for those vulnerable groups that hold specific rights under human rights law, including women and children, or that enjoy a direct democratic legitimisation, as in the case of local authorities.

(3) Ensuring meaningful public participation in international climate change law-making.

Finally, and more broadly, the hierarchical elevation that would follow from approaching climate change as a question of human rights would broaden the spectrum of state obligations on mitigation and adaptation, while placing greater emphasis on the participatory rights of individuals. Thus, according to a publication on human rights and climate change:

> "Human rights can inform processes by placing a focus on participation as a right in itself, including ensuring that those whose rights are affected by climate change have an effective voice in setting national and international mitigation targets and policies, and that affected communities can participate in and have ownership of the design and implementation of adaptation initiatives. International human rights legal standards help establish normative foundations and essential guarantees for active, free and meaningful participation, including the rights to freedom of expression and association and self-determination".[74]

6.7 Concluding remarks

This chapter aimed at exploring the relevance of a human rights-based approach to climate change. The consideration of this approach has allowed a broader reflection on how environmental considerations have been integrated into human rights law over time. While this has primarily been done by "greening" human rights obligations, the potential establishment of a free-standing human right to environment has also been weighted. More importantly, and with regard to climate change law, the introduction of a human rights language in the Paris Agreement offers the opportunity to rethink the scope and application of human rights in all actions aimed at addressing climate change, including international climate change law-making. Whereas obstacles remain as to characterise global warming as a violation of human rights, this body of law provides some useful

74 S. McINERNEY-LANKFORD, M. DARROW and L. RAJAMANI, *Human Rights and Climate Change: A Review of the International Legal Dimensions*. Washington: The International Bank for Reconstruction and Development, 2011, p. 30.

opportunities in addressing this global environmental harm. From the standpoint of public participation, for instance, a human rights-based approach to climate change may help to put emphasis on participation as a right in itself, as well as on the condition of individuals as rightsholders under human rights law. For the latter reason, entitled to participatory rights that should be enhanced – rather than derogated – in the context of international climate change law-making.

Bibliography

Abrisketa, J. and M. Nagore Casas. "Extraterritorial Application of Human Rights Treaties", *Oxford Bibliographies in International Law*, 2016.

Adinolfi, G. "The Right to a Healthy Environment. Delineating the Content (and Contours) of a Slippery Notion", in F F. Zorzi Giustiniani, E. Sommario, F. Casolari And Others (eds.) *Routledge Handbook of Human Rights and Disasters*. New York: Routledge, 2018, pp. 211–227.

Aminzadeh, S. "A Moral Imperative: The Human Rights Implications of Climate Change", *Hastings International & Comparative Law Review*, Vol. 30, No. 2, 2007, pp. 231–265.

Atapattu, S. "The Paris Agreement and Human Rights: Is Sustainable Development the "New Human Right"?, *Journal of Human Rights and the Environment*, Vol. 9, No. 1, 2018, pp. 68–88.

Bodansky, D., Brunnée, J. and L. Rajamani. *International Climate Change Law*. Oxford: Oxford University Press, 2017.

Boyle, A. "Human Rights or Environmental Rights? A Reassessment", *Fordham Environmental Law Review*, Vol. 18, No. 3, 2008, pp. 471–551.

Boyle, A. "Human Rights and the Environment. Where Next?", in B. Boer (ed.) *Environmental Law Dimensions of Human Rights*. Oxford: Oxford University Press, 2015, pp. 201–239.

Cardesa-Salzmann, A. "Reflections on the Sustainability of a Human Rights Approach in the Context of the Climate Change Regime", in R. Giles Carnero (coord.) *Cambio Climático, Energía y Derecho Internacional: Perspectivas de Futuro*. Cizur Menor: Aranzadi, 2012, pp. 169–178.

Clapham, A. "Human Rights Obligations for Non-State-Actors: Where are We Now?", in F. Lafontaine and F. Larocque (eds.) *Doing Peace the Rights Way: Essays in International Law and Relations in Honour of Louise Arbour*. Cambridge: Intersentia, 2018, pp. 1–18.

Coomans, F. "The Ogoni Case Before the African Commission on Human and Peoples' Rights", *International and Comparative Law Quarterly*, Vol. 52, No. 3, 2003, pp. 749–760.

Cullet, P. "Human Rights and Climate Change. Broadening the Rights to Environment", in C. P. Carlarne, K. R. Gray and R. Tarasofsky (eds.) *The Oxford Handbook of International Climate Change Law*. Oxford: Oxford University Press, 2016, pp. 495–515.

Davies, K., Adelman, S., Grear, A. and Others. "The Declaration on Human Rights and Climate Change: A New Legal Tool for Global Policy Change", *Journal of Human Rights and the Environment*, Vol. 8, No. 2, 2017, pp. 217–253.

Duyck, S. "Promoting the Principles of the Aarhus Convention in International Forums: The Case of the UN Climate Change Regime", *Review of European Community & International Environmental Law*, Vol. 22, No. 4, 2015, pp. 123–137.

Duyck, S. "The Paris Agreement and the Protection of Human Rights in a Changing Climate", *Yearbook of International Environmental Law*, Vol. 26, No. 1, 2015, pp. 3–45.

Duyck, S. and Y. Lador. "Human Rights into Climate Action After Paris: Opportunities for the UNFCC, the Human Rights Institutions and the G-20", *Human Rights and International Climate Politics Study*, 2016, Berlin, Germany: Friedrich-Ebert-Stiftung, pp. 3–20.

Ferreira, P. G. "Did the Paris Agreement Fail to Incorporate Human Rights in Operative Provisions? Not if You Consider the 2016 SDGs", *Centre for International Governance Innovation Paper*, No. 113, 2016, pp. 1–11.

Hannum, H. "Reinvigorating Human Rights for the Twenty-First Century", *Human Rights Law Review*, Vol. 16, 2016, pp. 409–451.

Human Rights Council. *Report of the Special Rapporteur on the Issue of Human Rights Obligations Relating to the Enjoyment of a Safe, Clean, Healthy and Sustainable Environment of 24 January 2018* (UN Doc. A/HRC/37/59).

Hunter, D., Salzman, J. and D. Zaelke. *International Environmental Law and Policy*. St. Paul MN: Foundation Press, 2015.

Joseph, S. "Extraterritorial Human Rights Duties", in S. Joseph, *Blame it on the WTO?: A Human Rights Critique*. Oxford: Oxford University Press, 2011, pp. 245–264.

Kirchmeier, F. and Y. Lador. "From Copenhagen to Paris at the UN Human Rights Council. When Climate Change Became a Human Rights Issue", in S. Duyck, S. Jodoin and A. Johl (eds.) *Routledge Handbook of Human Rights and Climate Governance*. New York: Routledge, 2018, pp. 145–164.

Knox, J. H. "Diagonal Environmental Rights", in M. Gibney and S. Skogly (eds.) *Universal Human Rights and Extraterritorial Obligations*. Philadelphia: University of Pennsylvania Press, 2010, pp. 148–178.

Knox, J. H. "Human Rights Principles and Climate Change", in C. P. Carlarne, K. R. Gray and R. Tarasofsky (eds.) *The Oxford Handbook of International Climate Change Law*. Oxford: Oxford University Press, 2016, pp. 214–235.

Knox, J. H. "The Paris Agreement as a Human Rights Treaty", in D. Akande, J. Kuosmanen, H. Mcdermott And Others (eds.) *Human Rights and 21st Century Challenges: Poverty, Conflict, and the Environment*. Oxford: Oxford University Press, 2019, pp. 1–26.

Knox, J. H. and R. Pejan (eds.), *The Human Right to a Healthy Environment*. Cambridge: Cambridge University Press, 2018.

Koivurova, T., Duyck, S. and L. Heinämäki. "Climate Change and Human Rights", in E. J. Hollo, K. Kuvolesi and M. Mehling (eds.) *Climate Change and the Law*. Dordrecht: Springer, 2013, pp. 287–325, at 323.

Loucaides, L. "Environmental Protection Through the Jurisprudence of the European Convention on Human Rights", in L. Loucaides (ed.) *The European Convention on Human Rights. Collected Essays*. Leiden: Brill, 2005, pp. 167–191.

Mcinerney-Lankford, S., Darrow, M. and L. Rajamani. *Human Rights and Climate Change: A Review of the International Legal Dimensions*. Washington: International Bank for Reconstruction and Development, 2011.

Merrills, J. G. "Environmental Rights", in D. Bodansky, J. Brunné and E. Hey, (eds.) *The Oxford Handbook of International Environmental Law*. Oxford: Oxford University Press, 2007, pp. 665–675.

Organisation of African Unity. *African Charter on Human and Peoples' Rights of 27 June 1981* (21 ILM 58).

Organisation of American States. *American Convention on Human Rights of 22 January 1969* (1144 UNTS 123).

Peters, A. "Global Animal Law: What It Is and Why We Need It", *Transnational Environmental Law*, Vo. 5, No. 1, 2016, pp. 9–23.

Savaresi, A. "Climate Change and Human Rights. Fragmentation, Interplay, and Institutional Linkages", in S. Duyck, S. Jodoin and A. Johl (eds.) *Routledge Handbook of Human Rights and Climate Governance*. New York: Routledge, 2018, pp. 31–42.

United Nations General Assembly. *Universal Declaration of Human Rights of 10 December 1948* (217 A (III)).

Viñuales, J. E. "A Human Rights Approach to Extraterritorial Environmental Protection? An Assessment", in N. Bhuta (ed.) *The Frontiers of Human Rights*. Oxford: Oxford University Press, 2016, pp. 177–221.

Wolfe, K. "Greening the International Human Rights Sphere? Environmental Rights and the Draft Declaration Principles on Human Rights and the Environment", *APPEAL: Review of Current Law and Law Reform*, Vol. 9, No. 1, 2003, pp. 45–58.

7 Concluding remarks

Towards a new significance for non-governmental actors in international climate change governance: a proposal for the future

In Chapter 4, this work has discussed why the participation of Arctic indigenous peoples in the Arctic Council is exceptional to the models of participation of the public found in other intergovernmental fora. By virtue of their status as Permanent Participants, Arctic indigenous peoples hold a right to full and effective participation in the decision-making process of the Arctic Council which, despite being a soft-law body, has recently served as the forum for the negotiation of binding treaties. Being participants of a deliberative model in which decisions are made by consensus, Arctic indigenous peoples act in a position that is half way between membership with full voting rights and *observership*. Hereafter, it is considered to which extent this model could be applied to the nine major groups established in Agenda 21, which already acts as observers' constituencies to the UNFCCC system: Business and industry NGOs; Environmental NGOs; Farmers and agricultural NGOs; Indigenous Peoples Organisations; Local Government and municipal authorities; Research and independent NGOs; Trade union NGOs; Women and gender constituency and Youth NGOs.

The expansion of what is here called the "Arctic model of participation" is primarily relevant for other indigenous populations, such as those living in the Pacific Islands or Amazonia, that are already suffering the impacts of global warming. As already proposed by the Inuit Circumpolar Council before and during the celebration of COP21, this expansion could be carried out by promoting the right to full and effective participation in the recently established Local Communities and Indigenous Peoples Platform. In this sense, the expansion of such a model would entail nothing more than the recognition of the status of aboriginal populations as *peoples* under international law. Although the operationalisation of the Platform is still ongoing, it seems important to recall here that no opposition to this prospect has been raised by other UNFCCC observer constituencies.

This model could also be relevant to enhance the normative capacity of those subnational entities that, such as regions, cities, provinces or local governments, already enjoy sufficient legitimisation to intervene in the process of international rule-making on climate change. By virtue of the principle of subsidiarity, which establishes that decisions should be taken as closely as possible to the concerned citizens, greater relevance should be given to those entities that already are the legitimate representatives of subnational instances. This proposal is fully in line with the bottom-up approach to climate change governance promoted by the Paris Agreement, which expressively recognises the importance of local governments and municipal authorities in the achievement of the treaty's objectives. Furthermore, the introduction of such a model would only systemise a reality in which subnational actors – such as networks of cities and majors – have already stepped up their action towards climate change, complementing and sustaining the mitigation and adaptation policies initiated by nation states or acting in lack thereof.

On the other hand, the possible extension of this model to those non-governmental organisations, through which individuals or the civil society participate in climate change governance, certainly requires more efforts, in both theoretical and practical terms.

Theoretically, endorsing such a proposal would imply going beyond the classic and still prevalent approach of international law, which exclusively recognises States and international organiations as legitimate actors in the formulation of internationally binding norms. Undoubtedly, ensuring a more prominent role to NGOs would help to redress the existing conflict between the proliferation of non-governmental entities that already contribute – though largely informally – to the making and implementation of international climate change law and the rather exclusive, central role that is still granted to States. In turn, this would overall reinforce those concepts of sovereignty and international subjectivity weakened by the processes of globalisation and fragmentation of international law. Likewise, a more formal and firm recognition of the role played by civil society organisations in the different processes of elaboration of climate change law, would bring greater transparency to decision-making. For instance, forcing those organisations that work on a hidden agenda or in promotion of particular interests to be accountable for their actions. In this regard, the possibility of building a system of participation based on the "Arctic model of participation" also allows us to draw on Arctic indigenous peoples' advocacy and rights-based discourse.

In an analogy to the right to indigenous self-determination on which Arctic IPs have built their claims of participation, the establishment of a right to a healthy environment would constitute the legal basis for improving the participation of those non-governmental actors that work in the promotion of public good and whose rights are – or will likely be in the future – put at risk by a changing climate. Even though individuals do not yet hold a human right to a healthy environment on which their status as rightsholders could be constructed, the conclusions drawn from the analysis carried out in Chapter 6 allow us to speculate that its codification is incipient. Pending this development, the possibility that a human rights-based approach prevails in future climate change negotiations seems relevant to the demand for a better positioning of non-governmental actors in climate change governance, particularly to enhance the participation of those constituencies' members whose rights, as in the case of women and youth, are directly affected by global warming. In this regard, the adoption of the UN Climate Gender Action Plan which, among other actions, aims to achieve the full, equal and meaningful participation of women in the UNFCCC process, is a promising first step to be followed and institutionalised.

Although, as in the case of the tripartite system of the International Labour Organisation, examples of non-elected NGOs acting on the same level as sovereign States already exist, the possibility for enhancing *tout court* the participatory rights of, for instance, environmental and business NGOs in international climate change law-making, seems difficult to sustain. This would not sufficiently consider the question of legitimacy and democratic representation as embodied by State consent in international law. Therefore, mechanisms for ensuring that the members of different constituencies are real representatives of the interests for which they claim to speak for should also be foreseen, for example by instituting the direct election of constituencies representatives with elections secured by block chain. Alternatively, a mechanism for striking a better balance between constituencies upholding different interests could once again be found in the Arctic model of participation, which confers different degrees of participation to different entities: States with voting rights, Permanent Participants that exercise a *de facto* veto-kind power and, finally Observers. In this sense, a renewed UNFCCC institutional arrangement could be built on a progressive basis. Participation with voting rights could be granted to those States and non-State entities that enjoy democratic legitimisation. Descending a scale of legitimisation then, the status of Permanent Participants could be authorised to those non-governmental actors that, by virtue of their status as rightsholders, should be able to fully and effectively participate in climate change law-making. Finally, the status of Observers would be exercised by non-democratically elected NGOs.

All things considered, because of the efficacy that this paradigm has demonstrated at the regional and international level, the "Arctic model of participation" represents a relevant and potentially innovative precedent for improving the participation of non-governmental actors in international climate change law-making. In spite of its complex realisation, the need to promote a more open international climate change law-making process is manifested in the proliferation of climate change litigation cases before national and international courts, which are symptomatic of a general disaffection of non-governmental entities and individuals with the commitments reached by nation states at the intergovernmental level and, more broadly, of the emergence of a transnational movement that advocates for the respect of their rights, including the right to participate in the making of international climate change norms.

The Parties to the climate change regime have already recognised the need to reconsider the participation of the public in international climate change law-making. The conclusions of this work show that, although further research must be conducted on who is to be considered a legitimate actor in international law-making, a model for improving the participation of individuals and societies in the formation of international climate norms already exists.

Index

AAC *see* Arctic Athabaskan Council (AAC)
Aarhus Convention 1, 26, 40, 71n63, 124, 125; article 3 133n51; article 3.7 10, 42–44, 139–140; article 7.12 11; article 10.2 11, 43; article 11.4 11; article 12 43; article 15 10, 42; Preamble of 140; Principle 10 implementation in international context and 9–12; procedural rights significance and 98; promotion, in climate change regime 42–44; significance of 139; UNFCCC and 42–44
Abad Castelos, M. 14n27, 25
Abate, R.S. 56n14
AC *see* Arctic Council (AC)
Additional Protocol to the American Convention on Human Rights 123; article 11 123
Adelman, A. 127n34
Adinolfi, G. 123
advocacy 17, 18, 45n47, 74, 77, 78, 90, 106
AEPS *see* Arctic Environmental Protection Strategy (AEPS)
African Charter of Human Rights and Peoples' Rights (1981) 123; article 16 123; article 24 123
Agenda 21 7n1, 39, 147
AIA *see* Aleut International Association (AIA)
Alaska 60
Aleut International Association (AIA) 60, 64
Álgu fund 66
Almaty Guidelines on Promoting the Application of the Principles of the Aarhus Convention in International Forums 10, 40
AMAP *see* Arctic Monitoring and Assessment Programme (AMAP)
American Declaration of the Rights and Duties of Man 76
Aminzadeh, S. 135n57
Anaya, J. 57, 64n38
Andersen, P.J. 58n23, 75n77
Annan, K. 20
anthropocentric viewpoint, of climate change 125–126
Aponte Miranda, L. 79
Arab Charter on Human Rights (2004) 122
Arctic actors 75; *see also individual entries*
Arctic Athabaskan Council (AAC) 61, 64
Arctic Caucus 53n1
Arctic Climate Impact Assessment Report (2004) 56, 77
Arctic coastal states 70–71
Arctic Council (AC) 3, 4, 53, 58, 74–75n75; Arctic indigenous peoples in 62–66 (indigenous practice 66–68); Indigenous Peoples' Secretariat 66n49; Observer Manual for Subsidiary Bodies 63n36; regional treaties and 67n51; Rules of Procedure 63n36; significance of 63n35
Arctic Environmental Protection Strategy (AEPS) 62–64, 73, 74
Arctic Five (Arctic 5) (A5) 71
Arctic governance 64, 71n62
Arctic Human Development Report (2014) 54
Arctic indigenous peoples: in Arctic Council 62–66 (indigenous practice 66–68); climate change impact and 56–57; indigenous diplomacy 69–72; international environmental law-making 72–74); and internationalism, against climate change 68–69 (IACHR 74–79; overview of 54–56; significance of 53–54, 147; transnational organisation of 57–62

Arctic Monitoring and Assessment Programme (AMAP) 73, 74; *Assessment Report* 73
Arctic Monitoring Assessment Programme Report 67
Arctic Ocean Conference (2008) 71n61
Arctic Peoples' Conference 61
Asghar Leghani v. Federation of Pakistan 110–111
Association of Peoples of the North of the USSR 60
Association of Southeast Asian Nations (ASEAN) Human Rights Declaration 122–123
Atapattu, S. 130, 131
Athabaskans 55, 61, 78, 94, 98
Australia 94
Averchenkova, A. 87n2

balancing, notion of 121
Barnabas, S.G. 54n6
Berlin Mandate 36
Besson, S. 13n25, 24, 25, 26
Betsill, M. 31
Betzold, C. 17n39, 75n76
Biermann, F. 20–21
biocentric view, of climate change 126
Bodansky, D. 22n53, 37, 93n14, 94n17, 96, 102, 104, 119, 127
Bodle, R. 41, 45
Borgia, F. 72n65
bottom-up approach 148; *see also* climate change litigation
Boyd, D. 137
Boyle, A. 9, 15, 22, 23n57, 124, 125, 133, 134, 140
Brunnée, J. 93n14, 119, 127
Buchanan, A. 22n53

Canada 37, 54n7, 55, 59, 60, 68, 70, 73, 75n77, 78, 98
Cancun Agreement (2010) 129
Cassese, A. 55n12
Castillo Daudí, M. 76n78
causation 132–133; and liability 103
Center for International Environmental Law 127n34
Chan, S. 31
China 23, 30, 37, 132
Chinkin, C. 15, 22, 23n57
Christiano, T. 22n53, 35
CITES *see* Convention on International Trade in Endangered Species of Wild Fauna and Flora (CITES)
civil society organisations 21
Clean Development Mechanism 128
"Climate Change and State Consent" (Christiano) 35
climate change litigation 87–91; cases by country **88–89**; characteristics of 93–95; functions and potentially positive impacts of 105–108; as instrument to uphold procedural rights 111–112; in international environmental law 91–93; legal elements of 95–102; main problems of 102–105; non-US *89*; relevant case law analysis of 108–111
climate change regime: Aarhus Convention promotion in 42–44; international 35–38; public participation in 32–34 (institutional arrangements 38–42; after Paris Agreement adoption 44–47); significance of 30–32
Climate Summit (2014) 16
Colombia 124
Commission on Global Governance 12, 20
Commission on the Limits of the Continental Shelf 70n60
Committee on Economic, Social and Cultural Rights 124, 133
Conde Pérez, E. 70n60
Conference of the Parties (COP) 2n6, 32n14, 36–38, 41, 42, 44–46, 147
Connecticut v. AEP 96
consultative status, to NGOs 14
Convention Concerning the Protection of the World Cultural and Natural Heritage (1972) 94
Convention on Access to Information, Public Participation in Decision-making and Access to Justice in Environmental Matters 9
Convention on Biological Diversity (1993) 72, 75
Convention on International Trade in Endangered Species of Wild Fauna and Flora (CITES) 16
COP *see* Conference of the Parties (COP)
Copenhagen Accord (2009) 23
Coppes, M. 59n25
Corsi, G. 100
Court of Justice of the European Union 110
Cox, R. 109
Cullet, P. 137, 138

Dahl, J. 61
Davies, K. 125, 127n34

decision-making process 3, 11, 26, 91, 106; in Arctic Council 63, 67; civil and political rights and 124; intergovernmental 8, 11, 47; non-state actors (NSAs) and 25; public participation and 18–19; transparency and democracy into 24
Declaration of Principles on Human Rights and the Environment 122
Declaration of the United Nations Conference on the Human Environment 93n14
Declaration on Human Rights and Climate Change 127n34
De la Rosa Jaimes, V. 78n87
democratic deficit 19
democratic legitimacy 25
Denmark 60, 68n54, 70
discovery doctrine 55n12
Doelle, M. 2n6
Doha Amendment 36
Dorough, D.S. 54n6, 69, 72n66
Draft Declaration of Principles on Human Rights and the Environment (1994) 124
Dryzek, J.S. 26n66, 41n40
Duyck, S. 41n41, 42, 43, 65n44, 78, 128n38, 139n68, 140, 141n72

EALLU (Stephen) 55n10
Earth System Governance (Biermann) 21
Ebbesson, J. 9, 10, 43n44
ECHR *see* European Convention on Human Rights (ECHR)
Economic Community of West African States (ECOWAS) 123
ECOSOC *see* UN Economic and Social Council (ECOSOC)
ECOWAS *see* Economic Community of West African States (ECOWAS)
ECtHR *see* European Court of Human Rights (ECtHR)
environmental democracy 1, 7, 9
environmental justice 90–92
environmental protection 12, 34n21, 63n35, 69, 106, 117–118, 131n47
environmental rights 77, 124
epistemic communities 24
Escazú Agreement (2018) 1, 44, 98n27, 140
EU *see* European Union (EU)
EU Directive on Emission Trading System 100
Eurocentric conception of law 126
European Convention on Human Rights (ECHR) 98, 108, 124–125, 133
European Court of Human Rights (ECtHR) 8, 10, 102, 125, 140
European Union (EU) 10, 65, 132
Exner Pirot, H. 67n51
extraterritorial obligations 133; issue of 121

Fabius, L. 136
Falk, R. 20
Fankhauser, S. 87n2
Fenge, T. 73
Fernández Egea 124
Ferrara, S. 63n34
Ferreira, P.G. 129n43
Finland 55, 59, 71
First International Indigenous Conference 61
flexibility mechanisms 36n27
Forster, J. 106n44
Framework Principles on Human Rights and the Environment 126

Gamble, J. 66n47, 70
GAP *see* UN Climate Gender Action Plan (GAP)
GCI *see* Gwich'in Council International (GCI)
Gemenne, F. 92n7
Gerhardt, H. 55n9
Giles Carnero, R. 94n17
global citizenry 20
global constitutionalism 21
globalisation 26, 56, 148; meaning and significance of 12n21
Global Network for the Study of Human Rights and the Environment 127n34
Global Pact for the Environment 136
Global People Assembly 20
global warming 132, 138, 142; Arctic indigenous peoples and 74–75, 78, 80; climate change litigation and 97, 103, 106, 107
Grantham Research Institute on Climate Change 87n2, 90
Grear, A. 127n34
greenhouse gases (GHGs) emissions 25, 30, 31, 77, 100, 105, 127, 132
Greenland 54n7, 55n9, 60, 68, 76
Greenpeace 65
Griffin, P. 103n40
Guerra v Italy 125

Gwich'in Council International (GCI) 61, 64
Gwich'in people 55

Hague Court of Appeal 109
Hague District Court 109
Hannum, H. 119n5
Heinämäki, L. 41n41, 46n51, 53n1, 141n72
Heininen, L. 67n51
Heleniak, T. 54n7
Hickmann, Thomas 33
Hjerpe, M. 39
Huebert, R. 63n34
Huitema, D. 106n44
human rights-based approach 117–118; environment and 121–126; limitations and opportunities and (opportunities 134–139; non-state actors in international climate change law-making and 139–143; significance of 131–134); third generation rights and 118–119 (human rights law application 119–121); United nations role and 126–131
human rights law 75; application of 119–121; climate change litigation and 95, 98, 99, 107; international climate change law-making and 117–118, 122, 127, 130, 131, 133, 134, 136–140, 142–144; international environmental governance and 8, 10, 16, 27
human rights petition 77–78
Hunter, D.B. 106, 112

IACHR *see* Inuit Petition to the Inter-American Commission on Human Rights (IACHR)
IACtHR *see* Inter-American Court of Human Rights (IACtHR)
ICC *see* Inuit Circumpolar Council (ICC)
ICCPR *see* International Covenant on Civil and Political Rights (ICCPR)
Iceland 71
ICESCR *see* International Covenant on Economic, Social and Cultural Rights (ICESCR)
ICJ *see* International Court of Justice (ICJ)
ICRC *see* International Committee of the Red Cross (ICRC)
IGOs *see* intergovernmental organisations (IGOs)
IGOs *see* intergovernmental organisations (IGOs)
IIPFCC *see* International Indigenous Peoples' Forum on Climate Change (IIPFCC)
ILA *see* International Law Association (ILA)
ILC *see* International Law Commission (ILC)
ILO *see* International Labour Organisation (ILO)
Ilulissat Declaration (2008) 71
indigenous diplomacy 69–72
indigenous knowledge 45n50, 57, 67
Indigenous Language Act (2016) (Canada) 59n25
indigenous peoples (IPs) 3–4, 45, 141, 142, 148; non-governmental actors and 53, 54n6, 55–58, 62, 64–69, 71n63, 72n66, 73–75, 80
Indigenous Peoples of the North, Siberia and the Far East 60
indigenous peoples organisations (IPOs) 45, 53n1
input legitimacy 23–24
inside advocacy 17
Inter-American Court of Human Rights (IACtHR) 102, 123–124
intergovernmental decision-making 8, 11, 47
intergovernmental organisations (IGOs) 39
Intergovernmental Panel on Climate Change (IPCC) 24, 36, 56, 102, 127
International Assembly of People and Forum of Civil Society 12n22, 20
International Committee of the Red Cross (ICRC) 16, 23
International Court of Justice (ICJ) 8, 15, 93, 94, 102; article 38 (1) 13
international courts, limited authority of 105
International Covenant on Civil and Political Rights (ICCPR) 8, 16, 64n38, 118n4, 133; article 25 141–142
International Covenant on Economic, Social and Cultural Rights (ICESCR) 16, 118n4, 133
international environmental governance: NGOs and international norm-making and 19–26; non-governmental actors and 12–19; public participation and 7–12
international environmental law 1, 3, 4, 72–74; climate change litigation and 91–93, 100, 106, 107, 112; human rights-based approach and 117, 127n34, 130, 136, 137; non-governmental actors and 9, 12–19, 27
international forum, meaning and significance of 10n17

International Indigenous Peoples' Forum on Climate Change (IIPFCC) 45, 53n1
International Labour Organisation (ILO) 14, 16, 23, 64n38, 149
international law 2, 3, 147, 148, 149; climate change litigation and 87, 90, 93n14, 99–100, 107, 112; human rights-based approach and 120, 126, 130, 134, 135, 139, 140, 141n72; international environmental governance and 8, 12–22, 23n57, 24–27; non-governmental actors and 32, 33n19, 45–47, 54, 55n12, 58, 64, 68, 69, 72n66, 73, 79, 80
International Law Association (ILA) 15n31
International Law Commission (ILC) 9
international relations 13, 71n62
International Tribunal for the Law of the Sea 102
International Work Group for Indigenous Affairs (IWGIA) 58n23, 61
Inuit Circumpolar Council (ICC), 88, 141n72, 147; Arctic indigenous peoples and 53n1, 58, 60–62, 69–71, 78
Inuit Circumpolar Declaration on Sovereignty in the Arctic 71
Inuit-Crown Partnership Committee 59n25
Inuit Declaration on Resources Development Principles in the Arctic 71n61
Inuit people 55n9, 59–61, 70, 71n62, 72, 73, 77, 94, 98, 132
Inuit Petition to the Inter-American Commission on Human Rights (IACHR) 4, 74–79, 94, 105, 106, 117, 127
IPCC *see* Intergovernmental Panel on Climate Change (IPCC)
IPOs *see* indigenous peoples organisations (IPOs)
IPs *see* Indigenous Peoples (IPs)
IWGIA *see* International Work Group for Indigenous Affairs (IWGIA)

Jacobs, M. 16
Japan 37
Jodoin, S. 78
Johannesburg World Summit on Sustainable Development (2002) 8
Johl, A. 78
Jordan, A. 106n44
judicial governance 96, 106
judicial power legitimacy 103–105
Juliana v. United States 101
justiciability 95–97

Keil, K. 56n13
Kenya 136
Keohane, R.O. 33n19, 106
Keul, A. 55n9
Ki-Moon, B. 16, 30n2
Kirchmeier, F. 129
Klabbers, J. 94n17, 98–99n27
Kleivan, H. 61
Knecht, S. 56n13
knowledge 18, 36n26, 45, 55, 66–69, 104, 134; and expertise 24; significance of 19n44
Knox, J. 122, 126, 130, 132, 133, 135, 137
Koivurova, T. 41n41, 58n20, 59n26, 77, 141n72
Konrad, C. 40
Kravchenko, S. 42n43
Kronk Warner, E.A. 56n14
Kyoto Protocol 32, 33, 35, 44, 76n80, 77, 99; effectiveness of 36–37

LAC *see* Latin American and the Caribbean (LAC) States
Lador, Y. 129, 139n68
Lahore High Court 111
Latin American and the Caribbean (LAC) States 11
law-making 2, 3, 73, 149; international environmental governance and 13, 15, 17, 19–22, 23n57, 24–27; *see also* international law
Law of the Sea Convention 63n34, 71n61, 107
Lázaro Touza, L. 34n22
LCIPs *see* Local Communities and Indigenous Peoples (LCIPs)
legal forum, strategic choice of 102
legal framework 27, 65, 71n61, 99
legally binding 10, 11, 30, 93n13, 118
legal rights and obligations, sources of 97; climate science use and 102; European law and 100–101; international law and 99–100; public trust and 101; rights-based claims and 97–99; tort law and 101
legal status 25, 68
legitimacy 3, 112, 143, 147–149; Arctic indigenous peoples and 62, 71; climate change law-making and 41, 46; defining 22–24; international environmental governance and 19–22, 27; of judicial power 103–105; of NGOs 24–26

Lima-Paris Action Agenda (LPAA) 44
Linnér, L.B. 39
Local Communities and Indigenous Peoples (LCIPs) Platform 41, 45, 53, 67, 147
London School of Economics 87n2
Lopez Ostra v. Spain 125
Loukacheva, N. 58n19
LPAA *see* Lima-Paris Action Agenda (LPAA)
Lynge, A. 61

Malé Declaration on the Human Dimension of Global Climate Change 127n35
Manual on Human Rights and the Environment 125
Martí, J.L. 22n52, 24, 25, 26
McCrimmon, D. 78n87
McGolrick, D. 98n25
McLeman, R. 92n7
MEAs *see* multilateral environmental agreements (MEAs)
Meetings of the Parties 10
Mercury in the Arctic report 74
Merrills, J.G. 137n62
Mexico 8n5
Millennium Assembly 20
Minamata Convention on Mercury (2017) 74
Molenaar, E.J. 63n34
Moravcsik, A. 25
Multilateral Agreement on Investment 15
multilateral environmental agreements (MEAs) 2, 4
multiple representation model 25

Nachmany, M. 87n2
Nasiritousi, N. 39
Nationally Determined Contributions (NDCs) 30n5, 36, 37, 92n11, 100, 105
NAZCA *see* Non-State Actor Zone for Climate Action (NAZCA)
NDCs *see* Nationally Determined Contributions (NDCs)
the Netherlands 108–109
New Zealand 37, 100
NGO Millennium Forum 20
Ninth Meeting of the Negotiating Committee of the Regional Agreement on Principle 10 11
non-Arctic states 63–66
non-governmental actors and international environmental law 12–13; NGOs and international norm-making and 13–18; public participation relevance in 18–19
non-governmental organisation(s) (NGOs) 2n4, 4, 140, 142, 147–149; Arctic indigenous peoples and 58n24, 61, 63, 64; climate change law-making and governance and 32–34, 38–48; climate change litigation and 89–90, 97, 98n26, 105, 111, 113; international environmental governance and 10, 12, 13, 27; international norm-making and 13–18 (democratic deficit redressal 19–26); legitimacy of 24–26
non-Parties stakeholders 38, 46, 48
non-state actors (NSAs) 12, 33, 38, 44, 80, 141; in international climate change law-making 139–143; international environmental governance and 14, 22, 24, 25; Paris Agreement and 31, 46
Non-State Actor Zone for Climate Action (NAZCA) 44
Nord, D. 63n34
Nordic Sámi Convention 59
normative legitimacy 24
Norway 55, 59, 68n54, 70, 99, 129
NSAs *see* non-State actors (NSAs)
Nuuk Declaration (1993) 62
Nuuk Rules 65

OAS *see* Organisation of American States (OAS)
Oberthür, S. 40
observers 2, 3, 142, 147, 149; international environmental governance and 14, 15; non-governmental actors and 32, 38–47, 62–66, 63nn35–36, 68, 73, 75n75
Office of the UN High Commissioner for Human Rights (OHCHR) 127, 128, 132
Ogoniland case 123
OHCHR *see* Office of the UN High Commissioner for Human Rights (OHCHR)
Organisation of American States (OAS) 76
Oslo District Court 98n26, 99n30
Osofsky, H.M. 106
Ostrom 33n19
Ottawa Declaration (1996) 59n27, 63, 64n39
Ottawa Traditional Knowledge Principles 67
output legitimacy 23, 24
outside advocacy 17

Pakistan 110
Palau 94
Paris Agreement (2015) 3, 4, 16, 23, 79, 136, 148; article 7.5 45, 46; article 11.2 46; article 12 44–45, 111, 142; article 13 105; article 14 105; article 15 105; article 28 138n66; climate change litigation and 87n2, 92n11, 99, 100, 102; on human rights 129, 130, 138, 141, 142; non-governmental actors and 30–32, 33, 35, 36; Preamble of 46, 92n8, 117, 129–131, 142; public participation after adoption of 44–47; significance of 36n29
Parliamentary Assembly of the Council of Europe (2005) 124
Peel, J. 103n39, 104
Pejan, R. 137n62
People's Climate Case 100
peoples 23, 40, 123, 147; Arctic indigenous 56, 57, 60–62, 64, 66, 72, 79, 80; *see also* indigenous peoples (IPs)
The People v. Arctic Oil 98, 99
Permanent Participants (PPs) 4, 53, 63–66, 68, 69, 71, 73, 74, 79, 147, 149
persistent organic pollutants (POPs) 73, 74
Peters, A. 126n31
PIL *see* public interest litigation (PIL)
Platjouw, F.M. 74
Plaut, S. 61
Plouffe, J. 67n51
Poelzer, G. 68
polities, notion of 70n57
polycentricity 33n19, 106
POPs *see* persistent organic pollutants (POPs)
Powless, B. 45n47, 69, 72n67
PPs *see* Permanent Participants (PPs)
precaution, principles of 100
Prior, T. 46n51
procedural legitimacy 23
procedural obligations 131n47, 141
procedural rights 98, 111–112, 140–142
public interest litigation (PIL) 97
public opinion 16–18, 107, 137
public participation 21, 108, 111–113; in climate change regime 32–34 (institutional arrangements 38–42); human rights-based approach and 133n51, 134, 140–144; in international environmental governance 7–12; after Paris Agreement adoption 44–47; relevance, in international environmental governance and 18–19; right to 1, 3, 7–8, 118; significance of 34
RAIPON *see* Russian Association of the Peoples of the North (RAIPON)
Rajamani, L. 93n14, 119, 127
REDD+ *see* Reduce Emissions from Deforestation and from Forest Degradation (REDD+) programme
Reduce Emissions from Deforestation and from Forest Degradation (REDD+) programme 33
regime complexes 33n19
Regional Agreement on Access to Information, Public Participation and Justice in Environmental Matters in Latin America and the Caribbean 11
Riedel, A. 41, 45
rights-based perspective 3, 4, 10, 72, 79, 80; claims and 97–99
rights-holders 45, 46, 120, 136, 142
Rio+20 Summit (2012) 8, 11
Röben, V. 22n52
Roser, D. 92n8
roster 14
Rottem, S.V. 67n52
Rovaniemi Process 62n32
Roy, S. 109n52
Rubinson Vollmer, A. 98n24
Ruiz, X. 30n1
Rules of Procedure, significance of 38–39
Russia 55, 59, 60, 70, 76
Russian Association of the Peoples of the North (RAIPON) 58n24, 60, 62
Russian Federation 37, 58, 68n54

Sámi Council 53n1, 59–62, 69
Sámi people 55, 59
Savaresi, A. 33n19, 130
SBI *see* Subsidiary Body for Implementation (SBI)
SBSTA *see* Subsidiary Body for Scientific and Technological Advice (SBSTA)
Scandinavia 59
Sconfienza, U. 19n43
Seidel, C. 92n8
self-determination 55n12, 57–58, 69, 71, 80, 142, 143, 148
self-government 55n9, 57, 68
Selin, H. 73n71, 74
separation of powers doctrine 96, 98n25, 110
Shadian, J. 58, 62, 66n47, 70
Siberia 60
Small Island Developing States (SIDS) 78, 92n8, 127
soft law 17, 30, 147

solidarity rights 137
sovereignty 2, 9, 47, 93n14, 104, 121, 148, 149; Arctic indigenous peoples and 55, 58, 69, 70, 71, 72n65
Spain 34
Spiro, P. 24
standing requirements (*locus standi*) 96–97
Steinberg, P. 55n9
Stephen, K. 55n10
Stepien, A. 58n20
Stevenson, H. 26n66, 41n40
stewardship, idea of 126
Stockholm Convention (2001) 73
Stockholm Declaration (1972) 93n14, 135; Principle 1 122, 140
strategic litigation, definition of 90
Strauss, A. 20
subsidiarity principle 34, 147
Subsidiary Body for Implementation (SBI) 41, 43, 46
Subsidiary Body for Scientific and Technological Advice (SBSTA) 41, 45
subsistence 110
substantive duties 131n47
substantive legitimacy 23
sustainability 75, 108–109, 135
sustainable development 1n2, 7; Arctic indigenous peoples and 60, 62, 63n35, 66, 71n62; climate change litigation and 91, 98n27, 100; human rights-based approach and 121, 123, 129, 130
Sweden 55, 59, 71
system legitimacy 23n57

Talanoa tradition 46
Tasch, J. 55n9
Tennberg, M. 58, 64
thick participation 18n43
Thomson v. Minister for Climate Change Issues 100
Torrecuadrada García-Lozano, S. 64n38
TRAFFIC 16n36
Treaty on the Functioning of the European Union (TFUE) 108; article 191.1 100; article 191.2 100
Trudeau administration 59n25
Trump, D. 31, 75n77
Tuvalu (Polynesia) 93, 94

UN Climate Gender Action Plan (GAP) 46, 149
UN Conference on Environment and Development 13, 38
UN Conference on Human Environment (1972) 12
UNDRIP *see* United Nations Declaration on the Rights of Indigenous Peoples (UNDRIP)
UNECE *see* UN Economic Commission for Europe (UNECE)
UN Economic and Social Council (ECOSOC) 13, 60; Resolution 1996/31 14
UN Economic Commission for Europe (UNECE) 9, 11, 44, 139, 140; Convention on Access to Information, Public Participation in Decision-making and Access to Justice in Environmental Matters 1n2
UN Environment Programme 23
UNFCCC *see* United Nation Framework Convention on Climate Change (UNFCCC)
UNGA *see* United Nations General Assembly (UNGA)
UNHRC *see* United Nations Human Rights Council (UNHRC)
United Nation Framework Convention on Climate Change (UNFCCC) 2, 23, 65n44, 75, 149; Aarhus Convention and 42–44; article 4(i) 38; article 6(a) 38; article 6.1 38; article 6.2 38; article 7.1 38; article 7.2 38; article 7.6 38; article 14 93n13; article 17 36; climate change litigation and 93, 99, 112; Constituencies Joint submission on the Local Communities and Indigenous Peoples Platform 45n50; Guidelines for the participation of NGO-representatives 2; human rights-based approach and 130, 139, 140, 142; non-governmental actors and 32, 33, 37–42, 45; objective of 35; participant categories at 39; public participation and 38–41; Rules of Procedure and 38–39; Secretariat 39n33; Subsidiary Body for Implementation 41, 43, 46
United Nations Charter 13, 134; article 55 118
United Nations Declaration on the Rights of Indigenous Peoples (UNDRIP) 54n6, 59n25, 64n38, 68n54, 69, 72n66
United Nations Environmental Programme (UNEP) 21, 31, 87, 106
United Nations General Assembly (UNGA) 20, 118, 122, 135, 136
United Nations Human Rights Committee 8, 124, 142
United Nations Human Rights Council (UNHRC) 78, 117, 118n3, 127, 128, 135nn56, 58; resolutions 128n40

United Nations Permanent Forum on Indigenous Issues (UNPFII) 45, 58, 60, 66, 75
United Nations Rio Declaration on Environment and Development 1n2, 71n63, 140; Principle 10 1, 7–13, 26, 139, 140; Principle 22 62
United Nations Working Group on Indigenous Populations 69
United States of America (USA) 23, 30, 34, 37, 59, 68n54, 70, 73, 75, 76n80, 77, 78, 91, 93, 94, 98, 101, 127, 129, 132, 138
Universal Declaration of Human Rights 118
UNPFII *see* United Nations Permanent Forum on Indigenous Issues (UNPFII)
UN Special Rapporteur 117, 122, 128, 135
UN Sub-Commission on the Prevention of Discrimination and Protection of Minorities 122, 135
Urgenda Foundation v. the State of the Netherlands 34, 96, 98, 101, 108–110
USA *see* United States of America (USA)

Valerieva Yaneva, Z. 70n60
Van Asselt, H. 106n44
van Bekhoven, J. 47
Vanderzwaag, D. 63n34
Vargiu, P. 72n65
veto-kind power 64
Victor, D.G. 33n19, 106
Vienna Convention on the Law of Treaties 30, 130
Viñuales, J.E. 133

Warsaw Conference (2013) 92n11
Watt-Cloutier, S. 76–77
westphalianisation 70
Wheatley, S. 24
Wilson, W.J. 2n6
Woerdman, E. 109n52
Wolfrum, R. 22n52
Working Group of the Parties (WGP) 10, 11, 42n43, 43
World Environment Organisation 21
World Heritage Committee 94
World Trade Organisation Appellative Body 102

For Product Safety Concerns and Information please contact our EU
representative GPSR@taylorandfrancis.com
Taylor & Francis Verlag GmbH, Kaufingerstraße 24, 80331 München, Germany

www.ingramcontent.com/pod-product-compliance
Lightning Source LLC
LaVergne TN
LVHW021129300926
849160LV00010B/938

9780367652005